Federal Laws of
the Reconstruction

ALSO BY FREDERICK E. HOSEN
AND FROM MCFARLAND

The Great Depression and the New Deal: Legislative Acts in Their Entirety (1932–1933) and Statistical Economic Data (1926–1946) (1992)

Unfolding Westward in Treaty and Law: Land Documents in United States History from the Appalachians to the Pacific, 1783–1934 (1988)

Rifle, Blanket and Kettle: Selected Indian Treaties and Laws (1985)

Federal Laws of the Reconstruction

Principal Congressional Acts and Resolutions, Presidential Proclamations, Speeches and Orders, and Other Legislative and Military Documents, 1862–1875

Compiled by
Frederick E. Hosen

McFarland & Company, Inc., Publishers
Jefferson, North Carolina, and London

Library of Congress Cataloguing-in-Publication Data

Federal laws of the reconstruction : principal congressional acts and resolutions, presidential proclamations, speeches and orders, and other legislative and military documents, 1862–1875 / compiled by Frederick E. Hosen.
p. cm.
Includes bibliographical references and index.

ISBN 978-0-7864-4668-1

1. Legislation — United States. I. Hosen, Frederick E., 1938–
KF4945.F43 2010
342.73'057 — dc22 2009046889

British Library cataloguing data are available

On the cover: *from left* Abraham Lincoln, Andrew Johnson, Ulysses S. Grant; *center* Lincoln's inauguration ©2010 Clipart.com

Manufactured in the United States of America

McFarland & Company, Inc., Publishers
Box 611, Jefferson, North Carolina 28640
www.mcfarlandpub.com

Table of Contents

Preface

The period of Reconstruction (1862–1875) during and following the American Civil War (1861–1865) was a time of great social and economic readjustments. Federal laws had to be passed and enforced, at a time of military intervention, to assure that the transition from war to peace would be accomplished.

The approach taken by this work is to present Reconstruction documents (mainly statutes and presidential proclamations) as an integral part of Reconstruction history — i.e., law as history as well as law focused on a single topic. To do this, laws and other documents have been selected that should provide an overall view of the concerns of the federal government, recognizing that the state and local governments were also busily passing laws — often with the goal of circumventing federal mandates.

Thirty-seven Acts of Congress, forty-four Presidential Proclamations, eight Congressional Resolutions, one inaugural speech, one military field order, one presidential order, and two war department circulars are presented in this compilation. For the benefit of the reader, brief quotes from or descriptions of the items are included in the Table of Contents when the document title provides no context.

Reconstruction was primarily a joint effort of the administrative and the legislative branches of the federal government. Generally, while Reconstruction lasted from 1862 to 1875, it might be argued that it is an ongoing process.

The source documents that have been utilized do not use the term African American, but typically "colored" and "Negro." In the interest of accuracy, there has been no adjustment of terminology.

In being true to the source documents there are some inconsistencies in format, spelling, capitalization, and punctuation, primarily due to source documents being prepared by different people over many years.

Whenever brackets [ ] appear in this work they originated from the source document.

The laws from before 1862 that appear in the Appendices provide background and starting points for legislation of later years. Acts of February 12, 1793, and September 18, 1850, set forth the legal basis for some aspects of slavery and the rights of slaves prior to Reconstruction law. Acts of February 28, 1795, and July 29, 1861, provide a basis for the Union to respond to the insurrection with several proclamations in 1861. Blockade proclamations in 1861 were followed by proclamations in 1865 that reopened certain ports.

Finally, the March 2, 1867, law regarding the practice of peonage appears in Appendix G since, conceivably, peonage could be used as a substitute for slavery.

Table I

POPULATION OF REGIONS BY RACE FOR THE YEARS 1860, 1870, 1880 (IN THOUSANDS)

Region and Year		Race		
	TOTAL	White	Negro	Other
Northeast				
1860	10,594	10,438	156	z
1870	12,299	12,117	180	2
1880	14,507	14,274	229	4
North Central				
1860	9,097	8,900	184	13
1870	12,981	12,699	273	10
1880	17,364	16,961	386	17
South				
1860	11,133	7,034	4,097	2
1870	12,288	7,863	4,421	4
1880	16,517	10,555	5,954	7
West				
1860	619	551	4	64
1870	991	910	6	74
1880	1,768	1,612	12	144
TOTAL				
1860	31,443	26,923	4,441	79
1870	38,559	33,589	4,880	90
1880	50,155	43,402	6,581	172

z = less than 500

Source: *Historical Statistics of the United States, Colonial Times to 1970*, U.S. Department of Commerce, Bureau of the Census, p. 22.

Table II

Population of Southern States by Race for the Years 1860, 1870, 1880 (in Thousands)

State	1860				1870				1880			
		Race				Race				Race		
	Total	White	Negro	Other	Total	White	Negro	Other	Total	White	Negro	Other
Alabama	964	526	438	z	997	521	476	z	1,263	662	600	z
Arkansas	435	324	111	z	484	362	122	z	803	592	211	z
Florida	140	78	63	z	188	96	92	z	269	143	127	z
Georgia	1,057	592	466	z	1,184	639	545	z	1,542	817	725	z
Louisiana	708	357	350	z	727	362	364	1	940	455	484	1
Mississippi	791	354	437	z	828	383	444	1	1,132	479	650	2
North Carolina	993	630	362	1	1,071	678	392	1	1,400	867	531	1
South Carolina	704	291	412	z	706	290	416	z	996	391	604	z
Tennessee	1,110	827	283	z	1,259	936	322	z	1,542	1,139	403	z
Texas	604	421	183	z	819	565	253	z	1,592	1,197	393	1
Virginia*	1,597	1,047	549	z	1,225	712	513	z	1,513	881	632	z

z = less than 500

*1860 includes West Virginia. West Virginia became a state June 20, 1863.

Note: Indians living on reservations were not included in population census data until the 1890 census.

Source: *Historical Statistics of the United States, Colonial Times to 1970*, U.S. Department of Commerce, Bureau of the Census, pp. 24–37.

Core Documents

A Proclamation by the President of the United States of America. No. 16. September 22, 1862

I, Abraham Lincoln, President of the United States of America, and commander-in-chief of the army and navy thereof, do hereby proclaim and declare that hereafter, as heretofore, the war will be prosecuted for the object of practically restoring the constitutional relation between the United States and each of the states and the people thereof, in which states the relation is or may be suspended or disturbed.

That it is my purpose, upon the next meeting of Congress, to again recommend the adoption of a practical measure tendering pecuniary aid to the free acceptance or rejection of all slave states, so called, the people whereof may not then be in rebellion against the United States, and which states may then have voluntarily adopted, or thereafter may voluntarily adopt, immediate or gradual abolishment of slavery within their respective limits; and that the effort to colonize persons of African descent with their consent upon this continent or elsewhere, with the previously obtained consent of the governments existing there, will be continued.

That on the first day of January, in the year of our Lord one thousand eight hundred and sixty-three, all persons held as slaves within any state or designated part of a state, the people whereof shall then be in rebellion against the United States, shall be then, thenceforward, and forever free; and the Executive Government of the United States, including the military and naval authority thereof, will recognize and maintain the freedom of such persons, and will do no act or acts to repress such persons, or any of them, in any efforts they may make for their actual freedom.

That the Executive will, on the first day of January aforesaid, by proclamation, designate the states and parts of states, if any, in which the people thereof, respectively, shall then be in rebellion against the United States; and the fact that any State, or the people thereof, shall on that day be, in good faith, represented in the Congress of the United States by members chosen thereto at elections wherein a majority of the qualified voters of such state shall have participated, shall, in absence of strong countervailing testimony, be deemed conclusive evidence that such state, and the people thereof, are not then in rebellion against the United States.

That attention is hereby called to an act of Congress entitled "An Act to make an additional article of war," approved March 13, 1862 which act is in the words and figure following:

"Be it enacted by the Senate and House of Representatives of the United

States of America in Congress assembled, That hereafter the following shall be promulgated as an additional article of war, for the government of the army of the United States, and shall be obeyed and observed as such:

"Article—All officers or persons in the military or naval service of the United States are prohibited from employing any of the forces under their respective commands for the purpose of returning fugitives from service or labor who may have escaped from any persons to whom such services or labor is claimed to be due, and any officer who shall be found guilty by a court-martial of violating this article shall be dismissed from the service.

"Sec. 2 And be it further enacted, That this act shall take effect from and after its passage.'

Also to the ninth and tenth sections of an act entitled "An act to suppress insurrection to punish treason and rebellion, to seize and confiscate property of rebels, and for other purposes," approved July 17, 1862, and which sections are in the words and figures following:

"Sec. 9. And be it further enacted, That all slaves of persons who shall hereafter be engaged in rebellion against the Government of the United States, or who shall in any way give aid or comfort thereto, escaping from such persons and taking refuge within the lines of the army; and all slaves captured from such persons or deserted by them, and coming under the control of the Government of the United States; and all slaves of such persons found on [or] being within any place occupied by rebel forces and afterwards occupied by forces of the United States, shall be deemed captives of war, and shall be forever free of their servitude, and not again held as slaves.

Sec. 10. And be it further enacted, That no slaves escaping into any state, territory, or the District of Columbia, from any other state, shall be delivered up, or in any way impeded or hindered of his liberty, except for crime, or some offence against the laws, unless the person claiming said fugitive shall first make oath that the person whom the labor or service of such fugitive is alleged to be due is his lawful owner, and has not borne arms against the United States in the present rebellion, nor in any way given aid and comfort thereto; and no person engaged in the military or naval service of the United States shall, under any pretence whatever, assume to decide on the validity of the claim of any person to the service or labor of any person, or surrender up any person to the claimant, on pain of being dismissed from the service."

And I do hereby enjoin upon and order all persons engaged in the military and naval service of the United States to observe, obey, and enforce, within their respective spheres of service, the act and sections above recited.

And the Executive will in due time recommend that all citizens of the

United States who shall have remained loyal thereto throughout the rebellion shall (upon the restoration of the constitutional relation between the United States and their respective states and people, if that relation shall have been suspended or disturbed) be compensated for all losses by acts of the United States, including the loss of slaves.

In witness whereof, I have hereunto set my hand, and caused the seal of the United States be affixed.

Done at the city of Washington this twenty-second [L.S.} day of September, in the year of our Lord one thousand eight hundred and sixty-two, and of the Independence of the United States the eighty-seventh.

ABRAHAM LINCOLN.

By the President:

William H. Seward, Secretary of State.

A Proclamation by the President of the United States of America. No. 17. January 1, 1863

Whereas, on the twenty-second day of September, in the year of our Lord one thousand eight hundred and sixty-two, a proclamation was issued by the President of the United States, containing, among other things, the following, to wit:

"That on the first day of January, in the year of our Lord one thousand eight hundred and sixty-three, all persons held as slaves within any state or designated part of a state, the people whereof shall then be in rebellion against the United States, shall be then, thenceforward, and forever, free; and the Executive Government of the United States, including the military and naval authority thereof, will recognize and maintain the freedom of such persons, and will do no act or acts to repress such persons, or any of them, in any effort they may make for actual freedom.

"That the Executive will, on the first day of January aforesaid, by proclamation, designate the states and parts of states, if any, in which the people thereof, respectively, shall then be in rebellion against the United States; and the fact that any state, or people thereof, shall on that day be in good faith represented in the Congress of the United States, by members chosen thereto at elections wherein a majority of the qualified voters of such states shall have participated, shall, in the absence of strong countervailing testimony, be deemed conclusive evidence that such state, and the people thereof, are not then in rebellion against the United States."

Now, therefore, I, Abraham Lincoln, President of the United States, by virtue of the power in me vested as commander-in-chief of the army and navy of the United States, in time of actual armed rebellion against the authority and Government of the United States, and as a fit and necessary war measure for suppressing said rebellion, do, on this first day of January, in the year of our Lord one thousand eight hundred and sixty-three, and in accordance with my purpose so to do, publicly proclaim for the full period of one hundred days from the day first above mentioned, order and designate as the states and parts of states wherein the people thereof, respectively, are this day in rebellion against the United States, the following, to wit:

Arkansas, Texas, Louisiana, (except the parishes of St. Bernard, Plaquemines, Jefferson, St. John, St. Charles, St. James, Ascension, Assumption, Terre Bonne, Lafourche, St. Mary, St. Martin, Orleans, including the city of New Orleans,) Mississippi, Alabama, Florida, Georgia, South Carolina, North Carolina, and Virginia, (except the forty-eight counties designated as West Virginia, and also the counties of Berkeley, Accomac, Northampton, Elizabeth City, York, Princess Ann, and Norfolk, including the cities of Norfolk and Portsmouth,) and which excepted parts are for the present left precisely as if this proclamation were not issued.

And by virtue of the power and for the purpose aforesaid, I do order and declare that all persons held as slaves within said designated states and parts of states are, and henceforward shall be, free; and that the Executive Government of the United States, including the military and naval authorities thereof, will recognize and maintain the freedom of said persons.

And I hereby enjoin upon the people so declared to be free to abstain from all violence, unless in necessary self-defense; and I recommend to them that, in all cases when allowed, they labor faithfully for reasonable wages.

And I further declare and make known that such persons, of suitable condition, will be received into the armed service of the United States to garrison forts, positions, stations, and other places, and to man vessels of all sorts in said service.

And upon this act, sincerely believed to be an act of justice, warranted by the Constitution upon military necessity, I invoke the considerate judgment of mankind and the gracious favor of Almighty God.

In witness whereof, I have hereunto set my hand and caused the seal of the United States to be affixed.

Done at the city of Washington this first day of January, in the year of our Lord one thousand eight hundred [L.S.] and sixty-three, and of the Independence of the United States of America the eighty-seventh.

ABRAHAM LINCOLN.

By the President:

William H. Seward, Secretary of State.

A Proclamation by the President of the United States of America. No. 11. December 8, 1863

Whereas, in and by the Constitution of the United States, it is provided that the President "shall have power to grant reprieves and pardons for offences against the United States, except in cases of impeachment;" and

Whereas, a rebellion now exists whereby the loyal state governments of several states have for a long time been subverted, and many persons have committed, and are now guilty of, treason against the United States; and

Whereas, with reference to said rebellion and treason, laws have been enacted by congress, declaring forfeitures and confiscation of property and liberation of slaves, all upon terms and conditions therein stated, and also declaring that the President was thereby authorized at any time thereafter, by proclamation, to extend to persons who may have participated in the existing rebellion, in any state or part thereof, pardon and amnesty, with such exceptions and at such times and on such conditions as he may deem expedient for the public welfare; and

Whereas, the congressional declaration for limited and conditional pardon accords with well-established judicial exposition of the pardoning power; and

Whereas, with reference to said rebellion, the President of the United States has issued several proclamations, with provisions in regard to the liberation of slaves; and

Whereas, it is now desired by some persons heretofore engaged in said rebellion to resume their allegiance to the United States, and to re-inaugurate loyal state governments within and for their respective states: Therefore —

I, Abraham Lincoln, President of the United States, do proclaim, declare, and make known to all persons who have, directly or by implication, participated in the existing rebellion, except as hereinafter excepted, that a full pardon is hereby granted to them and each of them, with restoration of all rights of property, except as to slaves, and in property cases where rights of third parties shall have intervened, and upon the condition that every such person shall take and subscribe an oath, and thenceforward keep and maintain said oath inviolate; and which oath shall be registered for permanent preservation, and shall be of the tenor and effect following, to wit:—

"I, _____ _____, do solemnly swear, in presence of Almighty God, that I will henceforth faithfully support, protect, and defend the Constitution of the United States and the Union of the States thereunder; and that I will, in like manner, abide by and faithfully support all acts of congress passed during the existing rebellion with reference to slaves, so long and so far as not repealed, modified, or held void by congress, or by decision of the supreme court; and that I will, in like manner, abide by and faithfully support all proclamations of the President made during the existing rebellion having reference to slaves, so long and so far as not modified or declared void by decision of the supreme court. So help me God."

The persons excepted from the benefits of the foregoing provisions are all who are, or shall have been, civil or diplomatic officers or agents of the so-called Confederate government; all who have left judicial stations under the United States to aid the rebellion; all who are, or shall have been, military or naval officers of said so-called Confederate government above the rank of colonel in the army or of lieutenant in the navy; all who left seats in the United States congress to aid the rebellion; all who resigned commissions in the army or navy of the United States and afterwards aided the rebellion; and all who have engaged in any way in treating colored persons, or white persons in charge of such, otherwise than lawfully as prisoners of war, and which persons may have been found in the United States service as soldiers, seamen, or in any other capacity.

And I do further proclaim, declare, and make known that whenever, in any of the States of Arkansas, Texas, Louisiana, Mississippi, Tennessee, Alabama, Georgia, Florida, South Carolina, and North Carolina, a number of persons, not less than one tenth in number of the votes cast in such state at the presidential election of the year of our Lord one thousand eight hundred and sixty, each having taken the oath aforesaid, and not having since violated it, and being a qualified voter by the election law of the state existing immediately before the so-called act of secession, and excluding all others, shall reestablish a state government which shall be republican, and in nowise contravening said oath, such shall be recognized as the true government of the state, and the state shall receive thereunder the benefits of the constitutional provision which declares that "the United States shall guaranty to every state in this Union a republican form of government, and shall protect each of them against invasion; and on application of the legislature, or the executive, (when the legislature cannot be convened,) against domestic violence."

And I do further proclaim, declare, and make known that any provision which may be adopted by such state government in relation to the freed people of such state, which shall recognize and declare their permanent freedom, provide for their education, and which may yet be consistent as a temporary arrangement with their present condition as a laboring, landless, and homeless class, will not be objected to by the National Executive.

And it is suggested as not improper that, in constructing a loyal state government in any state, the name of the state, the boundary, the subdivisions, the constitution, and the general code of laws, as before the rebellion, be maintained, subject only to the modifications made necessary by the conditions hereinbefore stated, and such others, if any, not contravening said conditions, and which may be deemed expedient by those framing the new state government.

To avoid misunderstanding, it may be proper to say that this proclamation, so far as it relates to state governments, has no reference to states wherein loyal state governments have all the while been maintained. And, for the same reason, it may be proper to further say, that whether members sent to congress from any state shall be admitted to seats constitutionally rests exclusively with the respective houses, and not to any extent the Executive. And still further, that this proclamation is intended to present the people of the states wherein the national authority has been suspended, and loyal state governments have been subverted, a mode in and by which the national authority and loyal state governments may be reestablished within said states, or in any of them; and, while the mode presented is the best the Executive can suggest, with his present impressions, it must not be understood that no other possible mode would be acceptable.

Given under my hand at the city of Washington the eighth day of December, A.D. one thousand eight hundred and [L.S.] sixty-three, and of the Independence of the United States of America the eighty-eighth.

ABRAHAM LINCOLN.

By the President:

William H. Seward, Secretary of State.

A Proclamation by the President of the United States of America. No. 14. March 26, 1864

Whereas, it has become necessary to define the cases in which insurgent enemies are entitled to the benefits of the proclamation of the President of the United States, which was made on the eighth day of December, 1863, and the manner in which they shall proceed to avail themselves of those benefits;

And whereas the objects of that proclamation were to suppress the insurrection and to restore the authority of the United States; and whereas the amnesty therein proposed by the President was offered with reference to these objects alone:

Now, therefore, I, Abraham Lincoln, President of the United States of America, do hereby proclaim and declare that the said proclamation does not apply to the cases of persons who, at the time when they seek to obtain the benefits thereof by taking the oath thereby prescribed, are in military, naval, or civil confinement or custody, or under bonds, or on parole of the civil, military, or naval authorities, or agents of the United States, as prisoners of war, or persons detained for offences of any kind, either before or after conviction, and that on the contrary, it does apply only to those persons who, being yet at large, and free from any arrest, confinement, or duress, shall voluntarily come forward and take the said oath, with the purpose of restoring peace and establishing the national authority. Prisoners excluded from the amnesty offered in the said proclamation may apply to the President for clemency, like all other offenders, and their application will receive due consideration.

I do further declare and proclaim that the oath prescribed in the aforesaid proclamation of the 8th of December, 1863, may be taken and subscribed before any commissioned officer, civil, military, or naval, in the service of the United States, or any civil or military officer of a state or territory not in insurrection, who, by the laws thereof, may be qualified for administering oaths. All officers who receive such oaths are hereby authorized to give certificates thereon to the persons respectively by who they are made, and such officers are hereby required to transmit the original records of such oaths at as early a day as may be convenient, to the Department of State, where they will be deposited and remain in the archives of the government. The Secretary of State will keep a register thereof, and will, on application, in proper cases, issue certificates of such records in the customary form of official certificates.

In testimony whereof I have hereunto set my hand, and caused the seal of the United States to be affixed.

Done at the city of Washington, the twenty-sixth day [L. S.] of March, in the year of our Lord one thousand eight hundred and sixty-four, and of the Independence of the United States the eighty-eighth.

ABRAHAM LINCOLN.

By the President:

William H. Seward, Secretary of State.

AN ACT TO REPEAL THE FUGITIVE SLAVE ACT OF EIGHTEEN HUNDRED AND FIFTY, AND ALL ACTS AND PARTS OF ACTS FOR THE RENDITION OF FUGITIVE SLAVES. JUNE 28, 1864

Be it enacted by the Senate and House of Representatives of the United States of America in Congress assembled, That sections three and four of an act entitled "An act respecting fugitives from justice and persons escaping from the service of their masters," passed February twelve, seventeen hundred and ninety-three, and an act entitled "An act to amend and supplementary to, the act entitled 'An act respecting fugitives from justice, and persons escaping from the service of their masters,' passed February twelve, seventeen hundred and ninety-three," passed September, eighteen hundred and fifty, be, and the same are hereby, repealed.

APPROVED, June 28, 1864.

A PROCLAMATION BY THE PRESIDENT OF THE UNITED STATES OF AMERICA. NO. 18. JULY 8, 1864

Whereas, at the late session, congress passed a bill to "guarantee to certain states, whose governments have been usurped or overthrown, a republican form of government," a copy of which is hereunto annexed;

And whereas the said bill was presented to the President of the United States for his approval less than one hour before the sine die adjournment of said session, and was not signed by him;

And whereas the said bill contains, among other things, a plan for restoring the states in rebellion to their proper relation in the Union, which plan expresses the sense of congress upon the subject, and which plan it is now thought fit to lay before the people for their consideration:

Now, therefore, I, Abraham Lincoln, President of the United States, do proclaim, declare, and make known, that, while I am (as I was in December last, when by proclamation I propounded a plan for restoration) unprepared by a formal approval of this bill, to be inflexibly committed to any single plan of restoration; and, while I am also unprepared to declare that the free state constitutions and governments already adopted and installed in Arkansas and Louisiana shall be set aside and held for nought, thereby repelling and discouraging the loyal citizens who have set up the same as to further effort, or to declare a constitutional competency in congress to abolish slavery in states, but am at the same time sincerely hoping and expecting that a constitutional amendment abolishing slavery throughout the nation may be adopted, nevertheless I am fully satisfied with the system for restoration contained in the bill as one very proper plan for the loyal people of any state choosing to adopt it, and that I am, and at all times shall be, prepared to give the executive aid and assistance to any such people, so soon as the military resistance to the United States shall have been suppressed in any such state, and the people thereof shall have sufficiently returned to their obedience to the constitution and the laws of the United States, in which cases military governors will be appointed, with directions to proceed according to the bill.

In testimony whereof, I have hereunto set my hand, and caused the seal of the Unite States to be affixed.

Done at the city of Washington this eighth day of [L. S.] July, in the year of our Lord one thousand eight hundred and sixty-four, and of the Independence of the United States the eighty-ninth.

ABRAHAM LINCOLN.

By the President:

William H. Seward, Secretary of State.

A Bill to guarantee to certain States whose Governments have been usurped or overthrown a Republican Form of Government.

Be it enacted by the Senate and House of Representatives of the United States of America in Congress assembled, That in the states declared in rebellion against the United States, the President shall, by and with the advice and consent of the Senate, appoint for each a provisional governor, whose pay and emoluments shall not exceed that of a brigadier-general of volunteers, who shall be charged with the civil administration of such state until a state government therein shall be recognized as hereinafter provided.

Sec. 2. And be it further enacted, That so soon as the military resistance to the United States shall have been suppressed in any such state, and the people thereof shall have sufficiently returned to their obedience to the constitution and the laws of the United States, the provisional governor shall direct the marshal of the United States, as speedily as may be, to name a sufficient number of deputies, and to enroll all white male citizens of the United States, resident in the state in their respective counties, and to request each one to take the oath to support the constitution of the United States, and in his enrolment to designate those who take and those who refuse to take that oath, which rolls shall be forthwith returned to the provisional governor; and if the persons taking that oath shall amount to a majority of the persons enrolled in the state, he shall, by proclamation, invite the loyal people of the state to elect delegates to a convention charged to declare the will of the people of the state relative to the reestablishment of a state government subject to, and in conformity with, the constitution of the United States.

Sec. 3. And be it further enacted, That the convention shall consist of as many members of both houses of the last constitutional state legislature, apportioned by the provisional governor among the counties, parishes, or districts of the state, in proportion to the white population, returned as electors, by the marshal, in compliance with the provisions of this act. The provisional governor shall, by proclamation, declare the number of delegates to be elected by each county, parish, or election district; name a day of election not less than thirty days thereafter; designate the place of voting in each county, parish, or district, conforming as nearly as may be convenient to the places used in the state elections next preceding the rebellion; appoint one or more commissioners to hold the election at each place of voting, and provide an adequate force to keep the peace during the election.

Sec. 4. And be it further enacted, That the delegates shall be elected by the loyal white male citizens of the United States of the age of twenty-one years, and resident at the time in the county, parish, or district in which they shall offer to vote, and enrolled as aforesaid, or absent in the military service of the United States, and who shall take and subscribe the oath of allegiance to the United States in the form contained in the act of congress of July two, eighteen hundred and sixty-two; and all such citizens of the United States who are in the military service of the United States shall vote at the headquarters of their respective commands, under such regulations as may be prescribed by the provisional governor for the taking and return of their votes; but no person who has held or exercised any office, civil or military, state or confederate, under the rebel usurpation, or who has voluntarily borne arms against the United States, shall vote, or be eligible to be elected as delegate, at such election.

Sec. 5. And be it further enacted, That the said commissioners, or either of them, shall hold the election in conformity with this act, and, so far as may be consistent therewith, shall proceed in the manner used in the state prior to the rebellion. The oath of allegiance shall be taken and subscribed on the poll-book by every voter in the form above prescribed, but every person known by, or proved to, the commissioners to have held or exercised any office, civil or military, state or confederate, under the rebel usurpation, or to have voluntarily borne arms against the United States, shall be excluded, though he offer to take the oath; and in case any person who shall have borne arms against the United States shall offer to vote he shall be deemed to have borne arms voluntarily unless he shall prove the contrary by the testimony of a qualified voter. The poll-book, showing the name and oath of each voter, shall be returned to the provisional governor by the commissioners of the election or the one acting, and the provisional governor shall canvass such returns, and declare the person having the highest number of votes elected.

Sec. 6. And be it further enacted, That the provisional governor shall, by proclamation, convene the delegates elected as aforementioned, at the capital of the state, on a day not more than three months after the election, giving at least thirty days' notice of such day. In case the said capital shall in his judgment be unfit, he shall in his proclamation appoint another place. He shall preside over the deliberations of the convention, and administer to each delegate, before taking his seat in the convention, the oath of allegiance to the United States in the form above prescribed.

Sec. 7. And be it further enacted, That the convention shall declare, on behalf of the people of the state, their submission to the constitution and laws of the United States, and shall adopt the following provisions, hereby prescribed by the United States in the execution of the constitutional duty to guarantee a republican form of government to every state, and incorporate them in the constitution of the state, that is to say:

First. No person who has held or exercised any office, civil or military, except offices merely ministerial, and military offices below the grade of colonel, state or confederate, under the usurping power, shall vote for or be a member of the legislature, or governor.

Second. Involuntary servitude is forever prohibited, and the freedom of all persons is guaranteed in said state.

Third. No debt, state or confederate, created by or under the sanction of the usurping power, shall be recognized or paid by the state.

Sec. 8. And be it further enacted, That when the convention shall have adopted those provisions, it shall proceed to reestablish a republican form of government, and ordain a constitution containing those provisions, which, when adopted, the convention shall by ordinance provide for submitting to the people of the state, entitled to vote under this law, at an election to be held in the manner prescribed by the act for the election of delegates; but at a time and place named by the convention, at which election the said electors, and none others, shall vote directly for or against such constitution and form of state government, and the returns of said election shall be made to the provisional governor, who shall canvass the same in the presence of the electors, and if a majority of the votes cast shall be for the constitution and form of government, he shall certify the same, with a copy thereof, to the

President of the United States, who, after obtaining the assent of congress, shall, by proclamation, recognize the government so established, and none other, as the constitutional government of the state, and from the date of such recognition, and not before, Senators and Representatives, and electors for President and Vice-President may be elected in such state, according to the laws of the state and of the United States.

Sec. 9. And be it further enacted, That if the convention shall refuse to reestablish the state government on the conditions aforesaid, the provisional governor shall declare it dissolved; but it shall be the duty of the President, whenever he shall have reason to believe that a sufficient number of the people of the state entitled to vote under this act, in number not less than a majority of those enrolled, as aforesaid, are willing to reestablish a state government on the conditions aforesaid, to direct the provisional governor to order another election of delegates to a convention for the purpose and in the manner prescribed in this act, and to proceed in all respects as hereinbefore provided, either to dissolve the convention, or to certify the state government reestablished by it to the President.

Sec. 10. And be it further enacted, That, until the United States shall have recognized a republican form of state government, the provisional governor in each of said states shall see that this act, and the laws of the United States, and the laws of the state in force when the state government was overthrown by the rebellion, are faithfully executed within the state; but no law or usage whereby any person was heretofore held in involuntary servitude shall be recognized or enforced by any court or officer in such state, and the laws for the trial and punishment of white persons shall extend to all persons, and jurors shall have the qualification of voters under this law for delegates to the convention. The President shall appoint such officers provided for by the laws of the state when its government was overthrown as he may find necessary to the civil administration of the state, all which officers shall be entitled to receive the fees and emoluments provided by the state laws for such officers.

Sec. 11. And be it further enacted, That until the recognition of a state government as aforesaid, the provisional governor shall, under such regulations as he may prescribe, cause to be assessed, levied, and collected, for the year eighteen hundred and sixty-four, and every year thereafter, the taxes provided by the laws of such state to be levied during the fiscal year preceding the overthrow of the state government thereof, in the manner prescribed by the laws of the state, as nearly as may be; and the officers appointed, as aforesaid, are vested with all powers of levying and collecting such taxes, by distress or sale, as were vested in any officers or tribunal of the state government aforesaid for those purposes. The proceeds of such taxes shall be accounted for to the provisional governor, and be by him applied to the expenses of the administration of the laws of such state, subject to the direction of the President, and the surplus shall be deposited in the treasury of the United States to the credit of such state, to be paid to the state upon an appropriation therefore, to be made when a republican form of government shall be recognized therein by the United States.

Sec. 12. And be it further enacted, That all persons held to involuntary servitude or labor in the states aforesaid are hereby emancipated and discharged therefrom, and they and their posterity shall be forever free. And if any such persons or their posterity shall be restrained of liberty, under pretence of any claim to such service or labor, the courts of the United States shall, on habeas corpus, discharge them.

Sec. 13. And be it further enacted, That if any person declared free by this act, or any law of the United States, or any proclamation of the President, be restrained of liberty, with intent to be held in or reduced involuntary servitude or labor, the person convicted before a court of competent jurisdiction of such act shall be punished by fine of not less than fifteen hundred dollars, and be imprisoned not less than five nor more than twenty years.

Sec. 14. And be it further enacted, That every person who shall hereafter hold or exercise any office, civil or military, except offices merely ministerial, and military officers below the grade of colonel, in the rebel service, state or confederate, is hereby declared not to be a citizen of the United States.

A Resolution submitting to the legislatures of the several states a propisition to amend the Constitution of the United States. No. 11. February 1, 1865. (13th Ammendment)

Resolved by the Senate and House of Representatives of the United States of America in Congress assembled, (two thirds of both Houses concurring,) That the following article be proposed to the legislatures of the several states as an amendment to the constitution of the United States, which, when ratified by three fourths of said legislatures, shall be valid, to all intents and purposes, as a part of the said constitution, namely:—

Article XIII.

Section 1. Neither slavery nor involuntary servitude, except as a punishment for crime whereof the party shall have been duly convicted, shall exist within the United States, or any place subject to their jurisdiction.

Section 2. Congress shall have power to enforce this article by appropriate legislation.

APPROVED, February 1, 1865.

An Act to Establish a Bureau for the Relief of Freedmen and Refugees. March 3, 1865

Be it enacted by the Senate and House of Representatives of the United States of America in Congress assembled, That there is hereby established in the War Department, to continue during the present war of rebellion, and for one year thereafter, a bureau of refugees, freedmen, and abandoned lands, to which shall be committed, as hereinafter provided, the supervision and management of all abandoned lands, and the control of all subjects relating to refugees and freedmen from rebel states, or from any district of country within the territory embraced in the operations of the army, under such rules and regulations as may be prescribed by the head of the bureau and approved by the President. The said bureau shall be under the management and control of a commissioner to be appointed by the President, by and with the advice and consent of the Senate, whose compensation shall be three thousand dollars per annum, and such number of clerks as may be assigned to him by the Secretary of War, not exceeding one chief clerk, two of the fourth class, two of the third class, and five of the first class. And the commissioner and all persons appointed under this act, shall, before entering upon their duties, take the oath of office prescribed in an act entitled "An act to prescribe an oath of office, and for other purposes," approved July second, eighteen hundred and sixty-two, and the commissioner and chief clerk shall, before entering upon their duties, give bonds to the treasurer of the United States, the former in the sum of fifty thousand dollars, and the latter in the sum of ten thousand dollars, conditioned for the faithful discharge of their duties respectively, with securities to be approved as sufficient by the Attorney-General, which bonds shall be filed in the office of the first comptroller of the treasury, to be by him put in suit for the benefit of any injured party upon any breach of the conditions thereof.

Sec. 2. And be it further enacted, That the Secretary of War may direct such issues of provisions, clothing, and fuel, as he may deem needful for the immediate and temporary shelter and supply of destitute and suffering refugees and freedmen and their wives and children, under such rules and regulations as he may direct.

Sec. 3. And be it further enacted, That the President may, by and with the advice and consent of the Senate, appoint an assistant commissioner for each of the states declared to be in insurrection, not exceeding ten in number, who shall, under the direction of the commissioner, aid in the execution of the provisions of this act; and he shall give a bond to the Treasurer of the United States, in the sum of twenty thousand dollars, in the form and manner prescribed in the first section of this act. Each of said commissioners shall receive an annual salary of two thousand five hundred dollars in full compensation for all his services. And any military officer may be detailed and assigned to duty under this act without increase of pay or allowances. The commissioner shall, before the commencement of each regular session of congress, make a full report of his proceedings with exhibits of the state of his accounts to the President, who shall communicate the same to congress, and shall also make special reports whenever required to do so by the President or either house of congress; and the assistant commissioners shall make quarterly reports of their proceedings to the commissioner, and also such other special reports as from time to time may be required.

Sec. 4. And be it further enacted, That the commissioner, under the direction of the President, shall have authority to set apart, for the use of loyal refugees and freedmen, such tracts of land within the insurrectionary states as shall have been abandoned, or to which the United States shall have acquired title by confiscation or sale, or otherwise, and to every male citizen, whether refugee or freedman, as aforesaid, there shall be assigned not more than forty acres of such land, and the person to whom it was so assigned shall be protected in the use and enjoyment of the land for the term of three years at an annual rent not exceeding six per centum upon the value of such land, as it was appraised by the state authorities in the year eighteen hundred and sixty, for the purpose of taxation, and in case no such appraisal can be found, then the rental shall be based upon the estimated value of the land in said year, to be ascertained in such manner as the commissioner may by regulation prescribe. At the end of said term, or at any time during said term, the occupants of any parcels so assigned may purchase the land and receive such title thereto as the United States can convey, upon paying therefor the value of the land, as ascertained and fixed for the purpose of determining the annual rent aforesaid.

Sec. 5. And be it further enacted, That all acts and parts of acts inconsistent with the provisions of this act, are hereby repealed.

APPROVED, March 3, 1865.

AN ACT TO INCORPORATE THE FREEDMAN'S SAVINGS AND TRUST COMPANY. MARCH 3, 1865

Be it enacted by the Senate and House of Representatives of the United States of America in Congress assembled, That Peter Cooper, William C. Bryant, A. A. Low, S. B. Chittenden, Charles H. Marshall, William A. Booth, Gerritt Smith, William A. Hall, William Allen, John Jay, Abraham Baldwin, A. S. Barnes, Hiram Barney, Seth B. Hunt, Samuel Holmes, Charles Collins, R. R. Graves, Walter S. Griffith, A. H. Wallis, D. S. Gregory, J. W. Alvord, George Whipple, A. S. Hatch, Walter T. Hatch, E. A. Lambert, W. G. Lambert, Roe Lockwood, R. H. Manning, R. W. Ropes, Abert Woedruff, and Thos. Dewey, of New York; John M. Forbes, Wm. Claflin, S. G. Howe, George L. Stearns, Edward Atkinson, A. A. Lawrence, and John M. S. Williams, of Massachusetts; Edward Harris and Thomas Davis, of Rhode Island; Stephen Colwell, J. Wheaton Smith, Francis E. Cope, Thomas Webster, B. S. Hunt, and Henry Samuel, of Pennsylvania; Edward Harwood, Adam Poe, Levi Coffin, J. M. Waldon, of Ohio, and their successors, are constituted a body corporate, in the city of Washington, in the District of Columbia, by the name of "The Freedman's Savings and Trust Company," and by that name may sue and be sued in any court of the United States.

Sec. 2. And be it further enacted, That the persons named in the first section of this act shall be the first trustees of the corporation, and all vacancies by death, resignation, or otherwise, in the office of trustee, shall be filled by the board by ballot, without unnecessary delay, and at least ten votes shall be necessary for the election of any trustee. The trustees shall hold a regular meeting at least once in each month, to receive reports of their officers on the affairs of the corporation, and to transact such business as may be necessary; and any trustee omitting to attend the regular meetings of the board for six months in succession, may thereupon be considered as having vacated his place, and a successor may be elected to fill the same.

Sec. 3. And be it further enacted, That the business of the corporation shall be managed and directed by the board of trustees, who shall elect from their number a president and two vice-presidents; and may appoint such other officers as they may see fit; nine of the trustees, of whom the president or one of the vice-presidents shall be one, shall form a quorum for the transaction of business at any regular or adjourned meeting of the board of trustees; and the affirmative vote of at least seven members of the board shall be requisite in making any order for, or authorizing the investment of any moneys, or the sale or transfer of any stock or securities belonging to the corporation, or the appointment of any officer receiving any salary therefrom.

Sec. 4. And be it further enacted, That the board of trustees of the corporation shall have power, from time to time, to make and establish such by-laws and regulations as they shall judge proper with regard to the election of officers and their respective functions, and generally for the management of the affairs of the corporation, provided such by-laws and regulations are not repugnant to this act or to the constitution or laws of the United States.

Sec. 5. And be it further enacted, That the general business and object of the corporation hereby created shall be to receive on deposit such sums of money as may be from time to time offered therefore, by, or on behalf of, persons heretofore held in slavery in the United States, or their descendants, and invest the same in the stocks, bonds, treasury notes, or other securities of the United States.

Sec. 6. And be it further enacted, That it shall be the duty of the trustees of the corporation to invest, as soon as practicable, in the securities named in the next preceding section, all sums received by them beyond an available fund, not exceeding one third of the total amount of deposits with the corporation, at the discretion of the trustees, which available funds may be kept by the trustees to meet current payments of the corporation, and may by them be left on deposit at interest or otherwise, or in such available form as the trustees may direct.

Sec. 7. And be it further enacted, That the corporation may, under such regulations as the board of trustees shall from time to time prescribe, receive any deposit hereby authorized to be received, upon such trusts and for such purposes, not contrary to the laws of the United States, as may be indicated in writing by the depositor, such writing to be subscribed by the depositor and acknowledged or proved before any officer in the civil or military service of the United States, the certificate of which acknowledgement or proof shall be indorsed on the writing; and the writing so acknowledged or proved shall accompany such deposit and be filed among the papers of the corporation, and be carefully preserved therein, and may be read in evidence in any court or before any judicial officer of the United States, without further proof; and the certificate of acknowledgement or proof shall be prima facie evidence only of the due execution of such writing.

Sec. 8. And be it further enacted, That all sums received on deposit shall be repaid to such depositor when required, at such time, with such interest, not exceeding seven per centum per annum, and under such regulations as the board of trustees shall, from time to time, prescribe, which regulations shall be posted up in some conspicuous place in the room where the business of the corporation shall be transacted, but shall not be altered so as to affect any deposit previously made.

Sec. 9. And be it further enacted, That all trusts upon which, and all purposes for which any deposit shall be made, and which shall be indicated in writing to accompany such deposit, shall be faithfully performed by the corporation, unless the performing of the same is rendered impossible.

Sec. 10. And be it further enacted, That when any depositor shall die, the funds remaining on deposit with the corporation to his credit, and all accumulations thereof, shall belong and be paid to the personal representatives of such depositor, in case he shall have left a last will and testament; And in default of a last will and testament, or of any person qualifying under a last will and testament competent to act as executor, the corporation shall be entitled, in respect to the funds so remaining on deposit to the credit of any such depositor, to administration thereon in preference to all other persons, and letters of administration shall be granted to the corporation accordingly in the manner prescribed by law in respect to the granting of letters of administration, with the will annexed, and in cases of intestacy.

Sec. 11. And be it further enacted, That in the case of the death of any depositor, whose deposit shall not be held upon any trust created pursuant to the provisions hereinbefore contained, or where it may prove impossible to execute such trust, it shall be the duty of the corporation to make diligent efforts to ascertain and discover whether such deceased depositor has left a husband, wife, or children surviving, and the corporation shall keep a record of the efforts so made, and of the results thereof, and in case no person lawfully entitled thereto shall be discovered, or shall appear, or claim the funds remaining to the credit of such depositor before the expiration of two years from the death of such depositor, it shall be lawful for the corporation to hold and invest such funds as a separate trust-fund, to be applied, with the accumulations thereof, to the education and improvement of persons heretofore held in slavery, or their descendants, being inhabitants of the United States, in such manner and through such agencies as the board of trustees shall deem best calculated to effect that object: Provided, That if any depositor be not heard from within five years from the date of his last deposit, the trustees shall advertise the same in some paper of general circulation in the state where the principal office of the company is established, and also in the state where the depositor was last heard from; and if within two years thereafter such depositor shall not appear, nor a husband, wife, or child of such depositor, to claim his deposits, they shall be used by the board of trustees as hereinbefore provided for in this section.

Sec. 12. And be it further enacted, That no president, vice president, trustee, officer, or servant of the corporation shall, directly or indirectly, borrow funds of the corporation or its deposits, or in any manner use the same, or any part thereof, except to pay necessary expenses, under the direction of the board of trustees. All certificates [or] other evidences of deposit made by the proper officers shall be as binding on the corporation as if they were made under their common seal. It shall be a duty of the trustees to regulate the rate of interest allowed to the depositors, so that they shall receive as nearly as may be a ratable proportion of all the profits of such corporation after deducting all necessary expenses: Provided, however, That the trustees may allow to depositors, to the amount of five hundred dollars or upwards, one per centum less than the amount allowed others: And provided, also, Whenever it shall appear that, after the payment of the usual interest to depositors, there is in the possession of the corporation an excess of profits over the liabilities amounting to ten per centum upon the deposits, such excess shall be invested for the security of the depositors in the corporation; and thereafter, at each annual examination of the affairs of the corporation, any surplus over and above such ten per centum shall, in addition to the usual interest, be divided ratably among the depositors, in such manner as the board of trustees shall direct.

Sec. 13. And be it further enacted, That whenever any deposit shall be made by any minor, the trustees of the corporation may, at their discretion, pay to such depositor such sums as may be due to him, although no guardian shall have been appointed for such minor, or the guardian of such minor shall not have authorized the drawing of the same; and the check, receipt, or acquittance of such minor shall be as valid as if the same were executed by a guardian of such minor, or the minor were of full age, if such deposit was made personally by such minor. And whenever any deposits shall have been made by married women, the trustees may repay the same on their own receipts.

Sec. 14. And be it further enacted, That the trustees shall not, directly or indirectly, receive any payment or emolument for their services as such, except the president and vice-president.

Sec. 15. And be it further enacted, That the president and vice-president, the subordinate officers and agents of the corporation shall respectively give such security for their fidelity and good conduct as the board of trustees may from time to time require, and the board shall fix the salaries of such officers and agents.

Sec. 16. And be it further enacted, That the books of the corporation shall, at all times during the hours of business, be open for inspection and examination to such persons as congress shall designate or appoint.

APPROVED, March 3, 1865.

A Proclamation by the President of the United States of America. No. 37. May 29, 1865

Whereas the President of the United States, on the 8th say of December, A.D. eighteen hundred and sixty-three, and on the 26th day of March, A.D. eighteen hundred and sixty-four, did, with the object to suppress the existing rebellion, to induce all persons to return to their loyalty, and to restore the authority of the United States, issue proclamations offering amnesty and pardon to certain persons who had directly or by implication participated in the said rebellion; and whereas many persons who had so engaged in said rebellion have since the issuance of said proclamations, failed or neglected to take the benefits offered thereby; and whereas many persons who have been justly deprived of all claim to amnesty and pardon thereunder, by reason of their participation, directly or by implication, in said rebellion, and continued hostility to the government of the United States since the date of said proclamations, now desire to apply for and obtain amnesty and pardon:

To the end, therefore, that the authority of the government of the United States may be restored, and that peace, order, and freedom may be established, I, Andrew Johnson, President of the United States, do proclaim and declare that I hereby grant to all persons who have, directly or indirectly, participated in the existing rebellion, except as herinafter excepted, amnesty and pardon, with restoration of all rights of property, except as to slaves, and except in cases where legal proceedings, under the laws of the United States providing for the confiscation of property of persons engaged in rebellion, have been instituted; but upon the condition, nevertheless, that every such person shall take and subscribe the following oath, (or affirmation) and thenceforward keep and maintain said oath inviolate; and which oath shall be registered for permanent preservation, and shall be of the tenor and effect following, to wit:

"I________, do solemnly swear,(or affirm) in the presence of Almighty God, that I will henceforth faithfully support, protect, and defend the Constitution of the United States, and the union of the States thereunder; and that I will, in like manner, abide by, and faithfully support all laws, and proclamations which have been made during the existing rebellion with reference to the emancipation of slaves. So help me God."

The following classes of persons are excepted from the benefits of the Proclamation:—

1st. All who are or shall have been pretended civil or diplomatic officers, or otherwise domestic or foreign agents, of the pretended confederate government;

2d. All who left judicial stations under the United States to aid the rebellion;

3d. All who shall have been military or naval officers of said pretended confederate government above the rank of colonel in the army or lieutenant in the navy;

4th. All who left seats in the Congress of the United States to aid the rebellion;

5th. All who resigned or tendered resignations of their commissions in the army or navy of the United States to evade duty in resisting the rebellion;

6th. All who have engaged in any way in treating otherwise than lawfully as prisoners of war persons found in the United States service, as officers, soldiers, seamen, or in other capacities;

7th. All persons who have been, or are, absentees from the United States for the purpose of aiding the rebellion;

8th. All military and naval officers in the rebel service, who were educated by the government in the Military Academy at West Point or the United States Naval Academy;

9th. All persons who held the pretended offices of governors of states in insurrection against the United States;

10th. All persons who left their homes within the jurisdiction and protection of the United States, and passed beyond the federal military lines into the pretended confederate states for the purpose of aiding the rebellion;

11th. All persons who have been engaged in the destruction of the commerce of the United States upon the high seas, and all persons who had made raids into the United States from Canada, or been engaged in destroying the commerce of the United States upon the lakes and rivers that separate the British Provinces from the United States;

12th. All persons who, at the time when they seek to obtain the benefits hereof by taking the oath herein prescribed, are in military, naval, or civil confinement, or custody, or under bonds of the civil, military, or naval authorities, or agents of the United States as prisoners of war, or persons detained for offences of any kind, either before or after conviction;

13th. All persons who have voluntarily participated in said rebellion, and the estimated value of whose taxable property is over twenty thousand dollars;

14th. All persons who have taken the oath of amnesty as prescribed in the President's Proclamation of December 8th, A.D. 1863, or an oath of allegiance to the government of the United States since the date of said Proclamation, and who have not thenceforward kept and maintained the same inviolate.

Provided, That special application may be made to the President for pardon by any person belonging to the excepted classes; and such clemency will be liberally extended as may be consistent with the facts of the case and the peace and dignity of the United States.

The Secretary of State will establish rules and regulations* for administering and recording the said amnesty oath, so as to insure its benefit to the people, and guard the government against fraud.

In testimony whereof, I have hereunto set my hand, and caused the seal of the United States to be affixed.

Department of State, Washington, May 29, 1865.

Sir: A copy of the President's Amnesty Proclamation of this date is herewith appended. By a clause in the instrument, the Secretary of State is directed to establish rules and regulations for administering and recording the amnesty oath, so as to insure its benefits to the people and guard the government against fraud. Pursuant to this injunction, you are informed that the oath prescribed in the proclamation may be taken and subscribed before any commissioned officer, civil, military, or naval, in the service of the United States, or any civil or military officer of a loyal state or territory, who, by the laws thereof, may be qualified for administering oaths. All officers who receive such oaths are hereby authorized to give certified copies thereof to the persons respectively by whom they were made. And such officers are hereby required to transmit the originals of such oaths, at as early a day as may be convenient, to this department, where they will be deposited, and remain in the archives of the government. A register thereof will be kept in the department, and on application, in proper cases, certificates will be issued of such records in the customary form of official certificates.

I am sir,
Your obedient servant,
WILLIAM H. SEWARD.

Done at the city of Washington, the twenty-ninth [L. S.] day of May, in the year of our Lord one thousand eight hundred and sixty-five, and of the Independence of the United States the eighty-ninth.

ANDREW JOHNSON.

By the President:
William H. Seward, Secretary of State.

*Rules and Regulations established by the Secretary of State.

A Proclamation by the President of the United States of America. No. 1. April 2, 1866

Whereas, by proclamations of the fifteenth and nineteenth of April, one thousand eight hundred and sixty-one, the President of the United States, in virtue of the power vested in him by the Constitution and the laws, declared that the laws of the United States were opposed, and the execution thereof obstructed, in the States of South Carolina, Georgia, Alabama, Florida, Mississippi, Louisiana, and Texas, by combinations too powerful to be suppressed by the ordinary course of judicial proceedings, or by the powers vested in the marshals by law;

And whereas, by another proclamation, made on the sixteenth day of August, in the same year, in pursuance of an act of Congress approved July thirteen, one thousand eight hundred and sixty-one, the inhabitants of the States of Georgia, South Carolina, Virginia, North Carolina, Tennessee, Alabama, Louisiana, Texas, Arkansas, Mississippi, and Florida (except the inhabitants of that part of the State of Virginia lying west of the Allegheny Mountains, and of such other parts of that State and the other States before named, as might maintain a loyal adhesion to the Union and the Constitution, or might be from time to time occupied and controlled by forces of the United States engaged in the dispersion of insurgents) were declared to be in a state of insurrection against the United States;

And whereas, by another proclamation, of the first day of July, one thousand eight hundred and sixty-two, issued in pursuance of an act of Congress approved June seven, in the same year, the insurrection was declared to be still existing in the States aforesaid, with the exception of certain specified counties in the State of Virginia;

And whereas, by another proclamation, made on the second day of April, One thousand eight hundred and sixty-three, in pursuance of the act of Congress of July thirteen, one thousand eight hundred and sixty-one, the exceptions named in the proclamation of August sixteen, one thousand eight hundred and sixty-one were revoked, and the inhabitants of the States of Georgia, South Carolina, North Carolina, Tennessee, Alabama, Louisiana, Texas, Arkansas, Mississippi, Florida, and Virginia (except the forty-eight counties of Virginia designated as West Virginia, and the ports of New Orleans, Key West, Port Royal, and Beaufort, in North Carolina) were declared to be still in a state of insurrection against the United States;

And whereas the House of Representatives, on the twenty-second day of July, one thousand eight hundred and sixty-one, adopted a resolution in the words following, namely:—

"Resolved by the House of Representatives of the Congress of the United States, That the present deplorable civil war has been forced upon the country by the disunionists of the southern States, now in revolt against the Constitutional government, and in arms around the capital; that in this national emergency, Congress, banishing all feelings of mere passion or resentment, will recollect only its duty to the whole country; that this war is not waged upon our part in any spirit of oppression nor for any purpose of conquest or subjugation, nor purpose of overthrowing or interfering with the rights or established institutions of those States, but to defend and maintain the supremacy of the Constitution, and to preserve the Union with all the dignity, equality, and rights of the several States unimpaired; and that as soon as these objects are accomplished the war ought to cease."

And whereas the Senate of the United States, on the twenty-fifth day of July, one thousand eight hundred and sixty-one, adopted a resolution in the words following, to wit:—

"Resolved, That the present deplorable civil war has been forced upon the country by the disunionists of the Southern States now in revolt against the Constitutional government, and in arms around the capital; that in this national emergency, Congress, banishing all feeling of mere passion or resentment, will recollect only its duty to the whole country; that this war is not prosecuted upon our part in any spirit of oppression not for any purpose of conquest or subjugation, nor purpose of overthrowing or interfering with the rights or established institutions of those States, but to defend and maintain the supremacy of the Constitution and all laws made in pursuance thereof, and to preserve the Union with all the dignity, equality, and rights of the several States unimpaired; that as soon as these objects are accomplished the war ought to cease."

And whereas these resolutions, though not joint or concurrent in form, are substantially identical, and as such may be regarded as having expressed the sense of Congress upon the subject to which they relate;

And whereas, by my proclamation of the thirteenth day of June last, the insurrection in the State of Tennessee was declared to have been suppressed, the authority of the United States therein to be undisputed, and such United States officers as had been duly commissioned to be in the undisputed exercise of their official functions;

And whereas there now exists no organized armed resistance of misguided citizens or others to the authority of the United States in the States of Georgia, South Carolina, Virginia, North Carolina, Tennessee, Alabama, Louisiana, Arkansas, Mississippi, and Florida, and the laws can be sustained and enforced therein by the proper civil authority, State or Federal, and the people of said States are well and loyally disposed, and have conformed or will conform in their legislation to the condition of affairs growing out of the amendment to the Constitution of the United States, prohibiting slavery within the limits and jurisdiction of the United States;

And whereas, in view of the before-recited premises, it is the manifest determination of the American people that no State, of its own will, has the right or the power to go out of, or separate itself from, or be separated from the American Union, and that therefore each State ought to remain and constitute an integral part of the United States;

And whereas the people of the several before-mentioned States have, in the manner aforesaid, given satisfactory evidence that they acquiesce in this sovereign and important resolution of national unity;

And whereas it is believed to be a fundamental principle of government that people who have revolted, and who have been overcome and subdued, must either be dealt with so as to induce them voluntarily to become friends, or else they must be held by absolute military power, or devastated, so as to prevent them from ever again doing harm as enemies, which last-named policy is abhorrent to humanity and to freedom;

And whereas the Constitution of the United States provides for constituent communities only as States, and not Territories, dependences, provinces, or protectorates;

And whereas such constituent States must necessarily be, and by the Constitution and laws of the United States are made equals, and placed upon a like footing as to political rights, immunities, dignity, and power with the several States with which they are united;

And whereas the observance of political equality as a principle of right and justice is well calculated to encourage the people of the aforesaid States to be and become more and more constant and persevering in their renewed allegiance;

And whereas standing armies, military occupation, martial law, military tribunals, and the suspension of the privilege of the writ of habeas corpus are, in time of peace, dangerous to public liberty, incompatible with the individual rights of the citizen, contrary to the genius and spirit of our free institutions, and exhaustive of the national resources, and ought not, therefore, to be sanctioned or allowed, except in cases of actual necessity, for repelling invasion or suppressing insurrection or rebellion;

And whereas the policy of the government of the United States, from the beginning of the insurrection to its overthrow and final suppression, has been in conformity with the principles herein set forth and enumerated;

Now, therefore, I, Andrew Johnson, president of the United States, do hereby proclaim and declare that the insurrection which heretofore existed in the States of Georgia, South Carolina, Virginia, North Carolina, Tennessee, Alabama, Louisiana, Arkansas, Mississippi, and Florida is at an end, and is henceforth to be so regarded.

In testimony whereof, I have hereunto set my hand and caused the seal of the United States to be affixed.

Done at the city of Washington, this second day of [Seal] April, in the year of our Lord one thousand eight hundred and sixty-six, and of the Independence of the United States of America the ninetieth.

ANDREW JOHNSON.

By the President:
William H. Seward,
Secretary of State.

An Act to protect all persons in the United States in their civil rights, and furnish the means of their vindication. April 9, 1866

Be it enacted by the Senate and House of Representatives of the United States of America in Congress assembled, That all persons born in the United States and not subject to any foreign power, excluding Indians not taxed, are hereby declared to be citizens of the United States; and such citizens, of every race and color, without regard to any previous condition of slavery or involuntary servitude, except as a punishment for crime whereof the party shall have been duly convicted, shall have the same right, in every State and Territory in the United States, to make and enforce contracts, to sue, be parties, and give evidence, to inherit, purchase, lease, sell, hold, and convey real and personal property, and to full and equal benefit of all laws and proceedings for the security of person and property, as is enjoyed by the white citizens, and shall be subject to like punishment, pains, and penalties, and to none other, any law, statute, ordinance, regulation, or custom, to the contrary notwithstanding.

Sec. 2. And be it further enacted, That any person who, under color of any law, statute, ordinance, regulation, or custom, shall subject, or cause to be subjected, any inhabitant of any State or Territory to the deprivation of any right secured or protected by this act, or to different punishment, pains, or penalties on account of such person having at any time been held in a condition of slavery or involuntary servitude, except as a punishment for crime whereof the party shall have been duly convicted, or by reason of his color or race, than is prescribed for the punishment of white persons, shall be deemed guilty of a misdemeanor, and, on conviction, shall be punished by fine not exceeding one thousand dollars, or imprisonment not exceeding one year, or both, in the discretion of the court.

Sec. 3. And be it further enacted, That the district courts of the United States, within their respective districts, shall have, exclusively of the courts of the several States, cognizance of all crimes and offences committed against the provisions of this act, and also, concurrently with the circuit courts of the United States, of all causes, civil and criminal, affecting persons who are denied or cannot enforce in the courts or judicial tribunals of the State or locality where they may be any of the rights secured to them by the first section of this act; and if any suit or prosecution, civil or criminal, has been or shall be commenced in any State court, against any such person, for any cause whatsoever, or against any officer, civil or military, or other person, for any arrest or imprisonment, trespasses, or wrongs done or committed by virtue or under color of authority derived from this act or the act establishing a Bureau of the relief of Freedmen and Refugees, and all acts amendatory thereof, or for refusing to do any act upon the ground that it would be inconsistent with this act, such defendant shall have the right to remove such cause for trial to the proper district or circuit court in the manner prescribed by the "Act relating to habeas corpus and regulating judicial proceedings in certain cases," approved March three, eighteen hundred and sixty-three, and all acts amendatory thereof. The jurisdiction in civil and criminal matters hereby conferred on the district and circuit courts of the United States shall be exercised and enforced in conformity with the laws of the United States, so far as such laws are suitable to carry the same into effect; but in all cases where such laws are not adapted to the object, or are deficient in the provisions necessary to furnish suitable remedies and punish offences against law, the common law, as modified and changed by the constitution and statutes of the State wherein the court having jurisdiction of the cause, civil or criminal, is held, so far as the same is not inconsistent with the Constitution and laws of the United States, shall be extended to and govern said courts in the trial and disposition of such cause, and, if of a criminal nature, in the infliction of punishment on the party found guilty.

Sec. 4. And be it further enacted, That the district attorneys, marshals, and deputy marshals of the United States, the commissioners appointed by the circuit and territorial courts of the United States, with powers of arresting, imprisoning, or bailing offenders against the laws of the United States, the officers and agents of the Freedmen's Bureau, and every other officer who may be specially empowered by the President of the United States, shall be, and they are hereby, specially authorized and required, at the expense of the United States, to institute proceedings against all and every person who shall violate the provisions of this act, and cause him or them to be arrested and imprisoned, or bailed, as the case may be, for trial before such court of the United States or territorial court as by this act has cognizance of the offence. And with a view to affording reasonable protection to all persons in their constitutional rights of equality before the law, without distinction of race or color, or previous condition of slavery or involuntary servitude, except as a punishment for crime, whereof the party shall have been duly convicted, and to the prompt discharge of the duties of this act, it shall be the duty of the circuit courts of the United States and the superior courts of the Territories of the United States, from time to time, to increase the number of commissioners, so as to afford a speedy and convenient means for the arrest and examination of persons charged with a violation of this act; and such commissioners are hereby authorized and required to exercise and discharge all the powers and duties conferred on them by this act, and the same duties with regard to offences created by this act, as they are authorized by law to exercise with regard to other offences against the laws of the United States.

Sec. 5. And be it further enacted, That it shall be the duty of all marshals and deputy marshals to obey and execute all warrants and precepts issued under the provisions of this act, when to them directed; and should any marshal or deputy marshal refuse to receive such warrant or other process when tendered, or to use all proper means diligently to execute the same, he shall, on conviction thereof, be fined in the sum of one thousand dollars, to the use of the person upon whom the accused is alleged to have committed the offence. And the better to enable the said commissioners to execute their duties faithfully and efficiently, in conformity with the Constitution of the United States and the requirements of this act, they are hereby authorized and empowered, within their counties respectively, to appoint, in writing, under their hands, any one or more suitable persons, from time to time, to execute all such warrants and other process as may be issued by them in the lawful performance of their respective duties; and the persons so appointed to execute any warrant or process as aforesaid shall have authority to summon and call to their aid the bystanders or posse comitatus of the proper county, or such portion of the land or naval forces of the United States, or of the militia, as may be necessary to the performance of the duty with which they are charged, and to insure a faithful observance of the clause of the Constitution which prohibits slavery, in conformity with the provisions of this act; and said warrants shall run and be executed by said officers anywhere in the State or Territory within which they are issued.

Sec. 6. And be it further enacted, That any person who shall knowingly and willfully obstruct, hinder, or prevent any officer, or other person charged with the execution of any warrant or process issued under the provisions of this act, or any person or persons lawfully assisting him or them, from arresting any person for whose apprehension such warrant or process may have been issued, or shall rescue or attempt to rescue such person from the custody of the officer, other person or persons, or those lawfully assisting as aforesaid, when so arrested pursuant to the authority herein given and declared, or shall aid, abet, or assist any person so arrested as aforesaid, directly or indirectly, to escape from the custody of the officer or other person legally authorized as aforesaid, or shall harbor or conceal any person for whose arrest a warrant or process shall have been issued as aforesaid, so as to prevent his discovery and arrest after notice or knowledge of the fact that a warrant has been issued for the apprehension of such person, shall, for either of said offences, be subject to a fine not exceeding one thousand dollars, and imprisonment not exceeding six months, by indictment and conviction before the district court of the United States for the district in which said offence may have been committed, or before the proper court of criminal jurisdiction, if committed within any one of the organized Territories of the United States.

Sec. 7. And be it further enacted, That the district attorneys, the marshals, their deputies, and the clerks of the said district and territorial courts shall be paid for their services the like fees as may be allowed to them for similar services in other cases; and in all cases where the proceedings are before a commissioner, he shall be entitled to a fee of ten dollars in full for his services in each case, inclusive of all services incident to such arrest and examination. The person or persons authorized to execute the process to be issued by such commissioners for the arrest of offenders against the provisions of this act shall be entitled to a fee of five dollars for each person he or they may arrest and take before any such commissioner as aforesaid, with such other fee as may be deemed reasonable by such commissioner for such other additional services as may be necessarily performed by him or them, such as attending at the examination, keeping the prisoner in custody, and providing him with food and lodging during his detention, and until the final determination of such commissioner, and in general for performing such other duties as may be required in the premises; such fees to be made up in conformity with the fees usually charged by the officers of the courts of justice within the proper district or county, as near as may be practicable, and paid out of the Treasury of the United States on the certificate of the judge of the district within which the arrest is made, and to be recoverable from the defendant as part of the judgment in case of conviction.

Sec. 8. And be it further enacted, That whenever the President of the United States shall have reason to believe that offences have been and are likely to be committed against the provisions of this act within any judicial district, it shall be lawful for him, in his discretion, to direct the judge, marshal, and district attorney of such district to attend at such place within the district, and for such time as he may designate, for the purpose of the more speedy arrest and trial of persons charged with a violation of this act; and it shall be the duty of every judge or other officer, when any such requisition shall be received by him, to attend at the place and for the time therein designated.

Sec. 9. And be it further enacted, That it shall be lawful for the President of the United States, or such person as he may empower for that purpose, to employ such part of the land or naval forces of the United States, or of the militia, as shall be necessary to prevent the violation and enforce the due execution of this act.

Sec. 10. And be it further enacted, That upon all questions of law arising in any cause under the provisions of this act a final appeal may be taken to the Supreme Court of the United States.

SCHUYLER COLFAX,
Speaker of the House of Representatives.
LA FAYETTE S. FOSTER,
President of the Senate, pro tempore.

In the Senate of the United States, April 6, 1866.

The President of the United States having returned to the Senate, in which it originated, the bill entitled "An act to protect all persons in the United States in their civil rights, and furnish the means of their vindication," with his objections thereto, the Senate proceeded, in pursuance of the Constitution, to reconsider the same; and,

Resolved, That the said bill do pass, two-thirds of the Senate agreeing to pass the same.

Attest: J. W. Forney,
Secretary of the Senate.

In the House of Representatives U.S. April 9th, 1866.

The House of Representatives having proceeded, in pursuance of the Constitution, to reconsider the bill entitled "An act to protect all persons in the United States in their civil rights, and furnish the means of their vindication," returned to the Senate by the President of the United States, with his objections, and sent by the Senate to the House of Representatives, with the message of the President returning the bill:

Resolved, That the bill do pass, two-thirds of the House of Representatives agreeing to pass the same.

Attest: Edward McPherson, Clerk,
by Clinton Lloyd, Chief Clerk.

A Joint Resolution proposing an amendment to the Constitution of the United States. No 48. June 16, 1866 (14th Amendment)

Be it resolved by the Senate and House of Representatives of the United States of America in Congress assembled, (two thirds of both Houses concurring.) That the following article be proposed to the legislatures of the several States as an amendment to the Constitution of the United States, which, when ratified by three fourths of said legislatures, shall be valid as part of the Constitution, namely:—

Article XIV.

Sec. 1. All persons born or naturalized in the United States, and subject to the jurisdiction thereof, are citizens of the United States and of the State wherein they reside. No State shall make or enforce any law which shall abridge the privileges or immunities of citizens of the United States; nor shall any State deprive any person of life, liberty, or property, without due process of law, nor deny to any person within its jurisdiction the equal protection of the laws.

Sec. 2. Representatives shall be apportioned among the several States according to their respective numbers, counting the whole number of persons in each State, excluding Indians not taxed. But when the right to vote at any election for the choice of electors for President and Vice-President of the United States, representatives in Congress, the executive and judicial officers of a State, or the members of the legislature thereof, is denied to any of the male inhabitants of such State, being twenty-one years of age, and citizens of the United States, or in any way abridged, except for participation in rebellion or other crimes, the basis of representation therein shall be reduced in the proportion which the number of such male citizens shall bear to the whole number of male citizens twenty-one years of age in such State.

Sec. 3. No person shall be a senator, or representative in Congress, or elector of President and Vice-President, or hold office, civil or military, under the United States, or under any State, who having previously taken an oath, as a member of Congress, or as an officer of the United States, or as a member of any State legislature, or as an executive or judicial officer of any State, to support the Constitution of the United States, shall have engaged in insurrection or rebellion against the same, or given aid or comfort to the enemies thereof. But Congress may by a vote of two thirds of each house remove such disability.

Sec. 4. The validity of the public debt of the United States, authorized by law, including debts incurred for payment of pensions and bounties for services in suppressing insurrection or rebellion, shall not be questioned. But neither the United States nor any State shall assume or pay any debt or obligation incurred in aid of insurrection or rebellion against the United States, or any claim for the loss or emancipation of any slave; but all such debts, obligations, and claims shall be held illegal and void.

Sec. 5. The Congress shall have power to enforce, by appropriate legislation, the provisions of this article.

SCHUYLER COLFAX,
Speaker of the House of Representatives.
LA FAYETTE S. FOSTER,
President of the Senate pro tempore.

Attest: Edw. McPherson,
Clerk of the House of Representatives.
J. W. Forney,
Secretary of the Senate.

Received at Department of State June 16, 1866.

An Act to continue in force and to amend "An Act to establish a Bureau for the Relief of Freedmen and Refugees," and for other purposes. July 16, 1866.

Be it enacted by the Senate and House of Representatives of the United States of America in Congress assembled, That the act to establish a bureau for the relief of freedmen and refugees, approved March third, eighteen hundred and sixty-five, shall continue in force for the term of two years from and after the passage of this act.

Sec. 2. And be it further enacted, That the supervision and care of said bureau shall extend to all loyal refugees and freedmen, so far as the same shall be necessary to enable them as speedily as practicable to become self-supporting citizens of the United States, and to aid them in making the freedom conferred by proclamation of the commander-in-chief, by emancipation under the laws of States, and by constitutional amendment, available to them and beneficial to the republic.

Sec. 3. And be it further enacted, That the President shall, by and with the advice and consent of the Senate, appoint two assistant commissioners, in addition to those authorized by the act to which this is an amendment, who shall give like bonds and receive the same annual salaries provided in said act, and each of the assistant commissioners of the bureau shall have charge of one district containing such refugees or freedmen, to be assigned him by the commissioner with the approval of the President. And the commissioner shall, under the direction of the President, and so far as the same shall be, in his judgment, necessary for the efficient and economical administration of the affairs of the bureau, appoint such agents, clerks, and assistants as may be required for the proper conduct of the bureau. Military officers and enlisted men may be detailed for service and assigned to duty under this act; and the President may, if in his judgment safe and judicious so to do, detail from the army all the officers and agents of this bureau; but no officer so assigned shall have increase of pay or allowances. Each agent or clerk, not heretofore authorized by law, not being a military officer, shall have an annual salary of not less than five hundred dollars, nor more than twelve hundred dollars, according to the service required of him. And it shall be the duty of the commissioner, when it can be done consistently with public interest, to appoint, as assistant commissioners, agents, and clerks, such men as have proved their loyalty by faithful service in the armies of the Union during the rebellion. And all persons appointed to service under this act and the act to which this is an amendment, shall be so far deemed in the military service of the United States as to be under the military jurisdiction, and entitled to the military protection of the government while in discharge of the duties of their office.

Sec. 4. And be it further enacted, That officers of the veteran reserve corps or of the volunteer service, now on duty in the Freedmen's Bureau as assistant commissioners, agents, medical officers, or in other capacities, whose regiments or corps have been or may hereafter be mustered out of service, may be retained upon such duty as officers of said bureau, with the same compensation as is now provided by law for their respective grades; and the Secretary of War shall have power to fill vacancies until other officers can be detailed in their places without detriment to the public service.

Sec. 5. And be it further enacted, That the second section of the act to which this is an amendment shall be deemed to authorize the Secretary of War to issue such medical stores or other supplies and transportation, and afford such medical or other aid as here may be needful for the purposes named in said section: Provided, That no person shall be deemed "destitute," "suffering," or "dependent upon the government for support," within the meaning of this act, who is able to find employment, and could, by proper industry or exertion, avoid such destitution, suffering, or dependence.

Sec. 6. Whereas, by the provisions of an act approved February sixth, eighteen hundred and sixty-three, entitled "An act to amend an act entitled 'An act for the collection of direct taxes in insurrectionary districts within the United States, and for other purposes,' approved June seventh, eighteen hundred and sixty-two," certain lands in the parishes of St. Helena and Saint Luke, South Carolina, were bid in by the United States at public tax sales, and by the limitation of said act the time of redemption of said lands has expired; and whereas, in accordance with instructions issued by President Lincoln on the sixteenth day of September, eighteen hundred and sixty-three, to the United States direct tax commissioners for South Carolina, certain lands bid in by the United States in the parish of Saint Helena, in said State, were in part sold by the said tax commissioners to "heads of families of the African race," in parcels of not more than twenty acres to each purchaser; and whereas, under said instructions, the said tax commissioners did also set apart as "school farms" certain parcels of land in said parish, numbered on their plats from one to thirty-three, inclusive, making an aggregate of six thousand acres, more or less: Therefore, be it further enacted, That the sales made to "heads of families of the African race," under the instructions of President Lincoln to the United States direct tax commissioners for South Carolina, of date of September sixteenth, eighteen hundred and sixty-three, are hereby confirmed and established; and all leases which have been made to such "heads of families," by said direct tax commissioners, shall be changed into certificates of sale in all cases wherein the lease provides for such substitution; and all the lands now remaining unsold, which come within the same designation, being eight thousand acres, more or less, shall be disposed of according to said instructions.

Sec. 7. And be it further enacted, That all other lands bid in by the United States at tax sales, being thirty-eight thousand acres more or less, and now in the hands of the said tax commissioners as the property of the United States, in the parishes of Saint Helena and Saint Luke, excepting the "school farms," as specified in the preceding section, and so much as may be necessary for military and naval purposes at Hilton Head, Bay Point, and Land's End, and excepting also the city of Port Royal, on Saint Helena Island, and the town of Beaufort, shall be disposed of in parcels of twenty acres, at one dollar and fifty cents per acre, to such persons and to such only as have acquired and are now occupying lands under and agreeable to the provisions of General Sherman's special field order, dated at Savannah, Georgia, January sixteenth, eighteen hundred and sixty-five; and the remaining lands, if any, shall be disposed of in like manner to such persons as had acquired land agreeably to the said order of General Sherman, but who have been dispossessed by the restoration of the same to former owners: Provided, That the lands sold in compliance with the provisions of this and the preceding section shall not be alienated by the purchasers within six years from and after the passage of this act.

Sec. 8. And be it further enacted, That the "school farms" in the parish of Saint Helena, South Carolina, shall be sold, subject to any leases of the same, by the said tax commissioners, at public auction, on or before the first day of January, eighteen hundred and sixty-seven, at not less than ten dollars per acre; and the lots in the city of Port Royal, as laid down by the said tax commissioners, and the lots and houses in the town of Beaufort, which are still held in like manner, shall be sold at public auction; and the proceeds of said sales, after paying expenses of the surveys and sales, shall be invested in United States bonds, the interest of which shall be appropriated, under the direction of the commissioner, to the support of schools, without distinction of color or race, on the islands in the parishes of Saint Helena and Saint Luke.

Sec. 9. And be it further enacted, That the assistant commissioners for South Carolina and Georgia are hereby authorized to examine all claims to lands in their respective States which are claimed under the provisions of General Sherman's special field order, and to give each person having a valid claim a warrant upon the direct tax commissioners for South Carolina for twenty acres of land; and the said direct tax commissioners shall issue to every person, or to his or her heirs, but in no case to any assigns, presenting such warrant, a lease of twenty acres of land, as provided for in section seven, for the term of six years; but at any time thereafter, upon the payment of a sum not exceeding one dollar and fifty cents per acre, the person holding such lease shall be entitled to a certificate of sale of said tract of twenty acres from the direct tax commissioner or such officer as may be authorized to issue the same; but no warrant shall be held valid longer than two years after the issue of the same.

Sec. 10. And be it further enacted, That the direct tax commissioners for South Carolina are hereby authorized at the earliest day practicable to survey the lands designated in section seven into lots of twenty acres each, with proper metes and bounds distinctly marked, so that the several tracts shall be convenient in form, and as near as practicable have an average of fertility and woodland; and the expense of such surveys shall be paid from the proceeds of sales of said lands, or, if sooner required, out of moneys received for other lands on these islands, sold by the United States for taxes, and now in the hands of the direct tax commissioners.

Sec. 11. And be it further enacted, That restoration of lands occupied by freedmen under General Sherman's field order dated at Savannah, Georgia, January sixteenth, eighteen hundred and sixty-five, shall not be made until after the crops of the present year shall have been gathered by the occupants of said lands, nor until a fair compensation shall have been made to them by the former owners of such lands, or their legal representatives, for all improvements or betterments erected or constructed thereon, and after due notice of the same being done shall have been given by the assistant commissioner.

Sec. 12. And be it further enacted, That the commissioners shall have power to seize, hold, use, lease, or sell all buildings and tenements, and any lands appertaining to the same, or otherwise, formerly held under color of title by the late so-called confederate states, and not heretofore disposed of by the United States, and any buildings or lands held in trust for the same by any person or persons, and to use the same or appropriate the proceeds derived therefrom to the education of the freed people; and whenever the bureau shall cease to exist, such of said so-called confederate states as shall have made provision for the education of their citizens without distinction of color shall receive the sum remaining unexpended of such sales or rentals, which shall be distributed among said states for educational purposes in proportion to their population.

Sec. 13. And be it further enacted, That the commissioner of this bureau shall at all times co-operate with private benevolent associations of citizens in aid of freedmen, and with agents and teachers, duly accredited and appointed by them, and shall hire or provide by lease buildings for purposes of education whenever such associations shall, without cost to the government, provide suitable teachers and means of instruction; and he shall furnish such protection as may be required for the safe conduct of schools.

Sec. 14. And be it further enacted, That in every State or district where the ordinary course of judicial proceedings has been interrupted by the rebellion, and until the same shall be fully restored, and in every State or district whose constitutional relations to the government have been practically discontinued by the rebellion, and until such State shall have been restored in such relations, and shall be duly represented in the Congress of the United States, the right to make and enforce contracts, to sue, be parties, and give evidence, to inherit, purchase, lease, sell, hold, and convey real and personal property, and to have full and equal benefit of all laws and proceedings concerning personal liberty, personal security, and acquisition, enjoyment, and disposition of estate, real and personal, including the constitutional right to bear arms, shall be secured to and enjoyed by all citizens of such State or district without respect to race or color, or previous condition of slavery. And whenever in either of said States or districts the ordinary course of judicial proceedings has been interrupted by the rebellion, and until the same shall be fully restored, and until such State shall have been restored in its constitutional relations to the government, and shall be duly represented in the Congress of the United States, the President shall, through the commissioners and the officers of the bureau, and under such rules and regulations as the President, through the Secretary of War, shall prescribe, extend military protection and have military jurisdiction over all cases and questions concerning the free enjoyment of such immunities and rights, and no penalty or punishment for any violation of law shall be imposed or permitted because of race or color, or previous condition of slavery, other or greater than the penalty or punishment to which white persons may be liable by law for the like offence. But the jurisdiction conferred by this section upon the officers of the bureau shall not exist in any State where the ordinary course of judicial proceedings has not been interrupted by the rebellion, and shall cease in every State when the courts of the State and the United States are not disturbed in the peaceable course of justice, and after such State shall be fully restored in its constitutional relations to the government, and shall be duly represented in the Congress of the United States.

Sec. 15. And be it further enacted, That all officers, agents, and employees of this bureau, before entering upon the duties of their office shall take the oath prescribed in the first section of the act to which this is an amendment; and all acts or parts of acts inconsistent with the provisions of this act are hereby repealed.

SCHUYLER COLFAX,
Speaker of the House of Representatives.
LA FAYETTE S. FOSTER,
President of the Senate pro tempore.

In the House of Representatives, U.S.,
July 16, 1866.

The President of the United States having returned to the House of Representatives, in which it originated, the bill entitled "An act to continue in force and to amend 'An act to establish a bureau for the relief of freedmen and refugees,' and for other purposes," with his objections thereto, the House of Representatives proceeded, in pursuance of the Constitution, to reconsider the same; and

Resolved, That the said bill pass, two thirds of the House of Representatives agreeing to pass the same.

Attest: EDW. McPHERSON,
Clerk H. Reps, U.S.

In the Senate of the United States,
July 16, 1866.

The Senate having proceeded, in pursuance of the Constitution, to reconsider the bill entitled "An act to continue in force and to amend 'An act to establish a bureau for the relief of freedmen and refugees,' and for other purposes," returned to the House of Representatives by the President of the United States, with his objections, and sent by the House of Representatives to the Senate with the message of the President returning the bill;

Resolved, That the bill do pass, two thirds of the Senate agreeing to pass the same.

Attest: J. W. FORNEY,
Secretary of the Senate, U.S.

A Proclamation by the President of the United States of America. No. 4. August 20, 1866

Whereas, by proclamation of the fifteenth and nineteenth of April, eighteen hundred and sixty-one, the President of the United States, in virtue of the power vested in him by the Constitution and the Laws, declared that the laws of the United States were opposed, and the execution thereof obstructed, in the States of South Carolina, Georgia, Alabama, Florida, Mississippi, Louisiana, and Texas, by combinations too powerful to be suppressed by the ordinary course of judicial proceedings, or by the powers vested in the marshals by law;

And whereas, by another proclamation, made on the sixteenth day of August, in the same year, in pursuance of an act of Congress approved July thirteen, one thousand eight hundred and sixty-one, the inhabitants of the States of Georgia, South Carolina, Virginia, North Carolina, Tennessee, Alabama, Louisiana, Texas, Arkansas, Mississippi, and Florida, (except the inhabitants of that part of the State of Virginia lying west of the Allegheny Mountains, and except also the inhabitants of such other parts of the States, and the other States before named, as might maintain a loyal adhesion to the Union and the Constitution, or might be from time to time occupied and controlled by forces of the United States engaged in the dispersion of insurgents,) were declared to be in a state of insurrection against the United States;

And whereas, by another proclamation, of the first day of July, one thousand eight hundred and sixty-two, issued in pursuance of an act of Congress, approved June seventh, in the same year, the insurrection was declared to be still existing in the States aforesaid, with the exception of certain specified counties in the State of Virginia;

And whereas, by another proclamation, made on the second day of April, one thousand eight hundred and sixty-three, in pursuance of the act of Congress of July thirteen, one thousand eight hundred and sixty-one, the exceptions named in the proclamation of August sixteen, one thousand eight hundred and sixty-one, were revoked, and the inhabitants of the States of Georgia, South Carolina, North Carolina, Tennessee, Alabama, Louisiana, Texas, Arkansas, Mississippi, Florida, and Virginia (except the forty-eight counties of Virginia designated as West Virginia, and the ports of New Orleans, Key West, Port Royal, and Beaufort, in North Carolina) were declared to be still in a state of insurrection against the United States;

And whereas, by another proclamation of the fifteenth day of September, one thousand eight hundred and sixty-three, made in pursuance of the act of Congress approved March third, one thousand eight hundred and sixty-three, the rebellion was declared to be still existing, and the privilege of the writ of habeas corpus was in certain specified cases suspended throughout the United States — said suspension to continue throughout the duration of the rebellion, or until said proclamation should, by a subsequent one to be issued by the President of the United States, be modified or revoked;

And whereas the House of Representatives, on the twenty-second day of July, one thousand eight hundred and sixty-one, adopted a resolution in the words following, namely: —

"Resolved by the House of Representatives of the Congress of the United States, That the present deplorable civil war has been forced upon the country by the disunionists of the southern States, now in revolt against the Constitutional government, and in arms around the capital; that in this national emergency, Congress, banishing all feelings of mere passion or resentment, will recollect only its duty to the whole country; that this war is not waged upon our part in any spirit of oppression nor for any purpose of conquest or subjugation, nor purpose of overthrowing or interfering with the rights or established institutions of those States, but to defend and maintain the supremacy of the Constitution, and to preserve the Union with all the dignity, equality, and rights of the several States unimpaired; and that as soon as these objects are accomplished the war ought to cease."

And whereas, the Senate of the United States, on the twenty-fifth day of July, one thousand eight hundred and sixty-one, adopted a resolution in the words following, to wit:—

"Resolved, That the present deplorable civil war has been forced upon the country by the disunionists of the southern States, now in revolt against the Constitutional government, and in arms around the capital; that in this national emergency, Congress, banishing all feeling of mere passion or resentment, will recollect only its duty to the whole country; that this war is not prosecuted upon our part in any spirit of oppression, nor for any purpose of conquest or subjugation, nor purpose of overthrowing or interfering with the rights or established institutions of those States, but to defend and maintain the supremacy of the Constitution and all laws made in pursuance thereof, and to preserve the Union with all the dignity, equality, and rights of the several States unimpaired; that as soon as these objects are accomplished the war ought to cease."

And whereas these resolutions, and as such have hitherto been and yet are regarded as having expressed the sense of Congress upon the subject to which they relate;

And whereas, the President of the United States by proclamation of the thirteenth of June, eighteen hundred and sixty-five, declared that the insurrection in the State of Tennessee had been suppressed, and that the authority of the United States therein was undisputed, and that such United States officers as had been duly commissioned were in the undisturbed exercise of their official functions;

And whereas, the President of the United States, by further proclamation issued on the second day of April, one thousand eight hundred and sixty-six, did promulgate and declare, that there no longer existed any armed resistance of misguided citizens, or others, to the authority of the United States in any, or in all the States before mentioned, excepting only the State of Texas, and did further promulgate and declare that the laws could be sustained and enforced in the several States before mentioned, except Texas, by the proper civil authorities, State, or Federal, and that the people of the said States, except Texas, are well and loyally disposed, and have conformed or will conform in their legislation to the condition of affairs growing out of the amendment to the Constitution of the United States, prohibiting slavery within the limits and jurisdiction of the United States;

And did further declare in the same proclamation that it is the manifest determination of the American people that no State, of its own will, has a right or power to go out of or separate itself from, or be separated from the American Union; and that, therefore, each State ought to remain and constitute an integral part of the United States;

And did further declare in the same last-mentioned proclamation, that the several aforementioned States, excepting Texas, had, in the manner aforesaid, given satisfactory evidence that they acquiesce in this sovereign and important resolution of national unity;

And whereas, the President of the United States in the same proclamation did further declare that it is believed to be a fundamental principle of government that the people who have revolted, and who have been overcome and subdued, must either be dealt with so as to induce them voluntarily to become friends, or else they must be held by absolute military power, or devastated, so as to prevent them from ever again doing harm as enemies, which last-named policy is abhorrent to humanity and to freedom;

And whereas, the President did in the same proclamation further declare, that the Constitution of the United States provides for constituent communities only as States, and not as Territories, dependencies, provinces or protectorates;

And further, that such constituent States must necessarily be, and by the Constitution and laws of the United States are made equals, and placed upon a like footing as to political rights, immunities, dignity and power with the several States with which they are united;

And did further declare, that the observance of political equality as a principle of right and justice is well calculated to encourage the people of the beforenamed States, except Texas, to be, and to become more and more constant and persevering in their renewed allegiance;

And whereas, the President did further declare that standing armies, military occupation, martial law, military tribunals, and the suspension of the writ of habeas corpus are, in time of peace, dangerous to public liberty, incompatible with individual rights of the citizen, contrary to the genius and spirit of our free institutions, and exhaustive of the national resources, and ought not, therefore, to be sanctioned, or allowed, except in cases of actual necessity, for repelling invasion or suppressing insurrection or rebellion;

And the President did further in the same proclamation declare that the policy of the government of the United States from the beginning of the insurrection to its overthrow and final suppression, had been conducted in conformity with the principles in the last-named proclamation recited;

And whereas, the President in the said proclamation of the thirteenth of June, one thousand eight hundred and sixty-five, upon the grounds therein stated and hereinbefore recited, did then and thereby proclaim and declare that the insurrection which heretofore existed in the several States before named, except in Texas, was at an end, and was henceforth to be so regarded;

And whereas, subsequently to the said second day of April, one thousand eight hundred and sixty-six, the insurrection in the State of Texas has been completely and everywhere suppressed and ended, and the authority of the United States has been successfully and completely established in the said State of Texas, and now remains therein un-resisted and undisputed, and such of the proper United States officers as have been duly commissioned within the limits of the said State, are now in the undisturbed exercise of their official functions;

And whereas, the laws can now be sustained and enforced in the said State of Texas, by the proper civil authority, State or Federal, and the people of the said State of Texas, like the people of the other States before named, are well and loyally disposed, and have conformed or will conform in their legislation to the condition of affairs growing out of the amendment of the Constitution of the United States, prohibiting slavery within the limits and jurisdiction of the United States;

And whereas all the reasons and conclusions set forth in regard to the several States therein specially named now apply equally and in all respects to the State of Texas, as well as to the other States which has been involved in insurrection;

And whereas, adequate provision has been made by military orders, to enforce the execution of the acts of Congress, aid the civil authorities, and secure obedience to the Constitution and laws of the United States within the State of Texas, if a resort to military force for such purpose should at any time become necessary;

Now, therefore, I, Andrew Johnson, President of the United States, do hereby proclaim and declare that the insurrection which heretofore existed in the State of Texas is at an end, and is to be henceforth so regarded in that State, as in the other States before named, in which the said insurrection was proclaimed to be at an end, by the aforesaid proclamation of the second say of April, one thousand eight hundred and sixty-six.

And I do further proclaim that the said insurrection is at an end, and that peace, order, tranquility and civil authority now exist in and throughout the whole of the United States of America.

In testimony whereof, I have hereunto set my hand and caused the seal of the United States to be affixed.

Done at the city of Washington this twentieth day of [SEAL.] August, in the year of our Lord one thousand eight hundred and sixty-six, and of the Independence of the United States of America the ninety-first.

ANDREW JOHNSON.

By the President:
William H. Seward,
Secretary of State.

A Joint Resolution authorizing the employment of a public vessel for the transportation of provisions to the people of the Southern States. No. 23. February 22, 1867

Be it resolved by the Senate and House of Representatives of the United States of America in Congress assembled, That the Secretary of the Navy be, and is hereby, authorized and directed, upon the application of the contributors, to assign a public vessel for the transportation to Charleston, Savannah, and Mobile, of any supplies of food and clothing that may be contributed by the people of the United States, for the use of any portion of the people of the Southern States, who may be suffering from the failure of crops or other causes, under such regulations as may, by the Secretary of the Navy, be prescribed.

Approved, February 22, 1867

An Act to provide for the more efficient government of the Rebel States. March 2, 1867

Whereas no legal State government or adequate protection for life or property now exists in the rebel States of Virginia, North Carolina, South Carolina, Georgia, Mississippi, Alabama, Louisiana, Florida, Texas, and Arkansas; and whereas it is necessary that peace and good order should be enforced in said States until loyal and republican State governments can be legally established: Therefore,

Be it enacted by the Senate and House of Representatives of the United States of America in Congress assembled, That said rebel States shall be divided into military districts and made subject to the military authority of the United States as hereinafter prescribed, and for that purpose Virginia shall constitute the first district; North Carolina and South Carolina the second district; Georgia, Alabama, and Florida the third district; Mississippi and Arkansas the fourth district; and Louisiana and Texas the fifth district.

Sec. 2. And be it further enacted, That it shall be the duty of the President to assign to the command of each of said districts an officer of the army, not below the rank of brigadier-general, and to detail a sufficient military force to enable such officer to perform his duties and enforce his authority within the district to which he is assigned.

Sec. 3. And be it further enacted, That it shall be the duty of each officer assigned as aforesaid, to protect all persons in their rights of person and property, to suppress insurrection, disorder, and violence, and to punish, or cause to be punished, all disturbers of the public peace and criminals; and to this end he may allow local civil tribunals to take jurisdiction of and to try offenders, or, when in his judgment it may be necessary for the trial of offenders, he shall have power to organize military commissions or tribunals for that purpose, and all interference under color of State authority with the exercise of military authority under this act, shall be null and void.

Sec. 4. And be it further enacted, That all persons put under military arrest by virtue of this act shall be tried without unnecessary delay, and no cruel or unusual punishment shall be inflicted, and no sentences of any military commission or tribunal hereby authorized, affecting the life or liberty of any person, shall be executed until it is approved by the officer in command of the district, and the laws and regulations for the government of the army shall not be affected by this act, except in so far as they conflict with its provisions: Provided, That no sentence of death under the provisions of this act shall be carried into effect without the approval of the President.

Sec. 5. And be it further enacted, That when the people of any one of said rebel States shall have formed a constitution of government in conformity with the Constitution of the United States in all respects, framed by a convention of delegates elected by the male citizens of said State, twenty-one years and upward, of whatever race, color or previous condition, who have been resident in said State for one year previous to the day of such election, except such as may be disfranchised for participation in the rebellion or for felony at common law, and when such constitution shall provide that the elective franchise shall be enjoyed by all such persons as have the qualifications herein stated for electors of delegates, and when such constitution shall be ratified by a majority of the persons voting on the question of ratification who are qualified as electors for delegates, and when such constitution shall have been submitted to Congress for examination and approval, and Congress shall have approved the same, and when said State, by a vote of its legislature elected under said constitution, shall have adopted the amendment to the Constitution of the United States, proposed by the Thirty-ninth Congress, and known as article fourteen, and when said article shall have become a part of the Constitution of the United States, said State shall be declared entitled to representation in Congress, and senators and representatives shall be admitted therefrom on their taking the oath prescribed by law, and then and thereafter the preceding sections of this act shall be inoperative in said State: Provided, That no person excluded from the privilege of holding office by said proposed amendment to the Constitution of the United States, shall be eligible to election as a member of the convention to frame a constitution for any of said rebel States, nor shall any such person vote for members of such convention.

Sec. 6. And be it further enacted, That, until the people of said rebel States shall be by law admitted to representation in the Congress of the United States, any civil governments which may exist therein shall be deemed provisional only, and in all respects subject to the paramount authority of the United States at any time to abolish, modify, control, or supersede the same; and in all elections to any office under such provisional governments all persons shall be entitled to vote, and none others, who are entitled to vote, under the provisions of the fifth section of this act; and no person shall be eligible to any office under any such provisional governments who would be disqualified from holding office under the provisions of the third article of said constitutional amendment.

SCHUYLER COLFAX,
Speaker of the House of Representatives.
LA FAYETTE S. FOSTER,
President of the Senate, pro tempore.

In the House of Representatives}
March 2, 1867. }

The President of the United States having returned to the House of Representatives, in which it originated, the bill entitled "An act to provide for the more efficient government of the rebel States," with his objections thereto, the House of Representatives proceeded, in pursuance of the Constitution, to reconsider the same; and

Resolved, That the said bill do pass, two thirds of the House of Representatives agreeing to pass the same.

Attest: EDWD. McPHERSON,
Clerk of H.R.U.S.

In Senate of the United States,}
March 2, 1867. }

The Senate having proceeded, in pursuance of the Constitution, to reconsider the bill entitled "An act to provide for the more efficient government of the rebel States," returned to the House of Representatives by the President of the United States, with his objections, and sent by the House of

Representatives to the Senate, with the message of the President returning the bill:

Resolved, That the bill do pass, two thirds of the Senate agreeing to pass the same.

Attest: J. W. FORNEY,
Secretary of the Senate.

A Resolution for Relief of Freedmen or Destitute Colored People in the District of Columbia. No 4. March 16, 1867

Resolved by the Senate and House of Representatives of the United States of America in Congress assembled, That fifteen thousand dollars be, and the same is hereby, appropriated, out of any money in the treasury not otherwise appropriated, for the relief of freedmen or destitute colored people in the District of Columbia, the same to be expended under the direction of the commissioner of the bureau of freedmen and refugees.

Approved, March 16, 1867.

An Act supplementary to an Act entitled "An Act to provide for the more efficient Government of the Rebel States," passed March 2, 1867, and to facilitate Restoration. March 23, 1867

Be it enacted by the Senate and House of Representatives of the United States of America in Congress assembled, That before the first day of September, eighteen hundred and sixty-seven, the commanding general in each district defined by an act entitled "An act to provide for the more efficient government of the rebel States," passed March second, eighteen hundred and sixty-seven, shall cause a registration to be made of the male citizens of the United States, twenty-one years of age and upwards, resident in each county or parish in the State or States included in his district, which registration shall include only those persons who are qualified to vote for delegates by the act aforesaid, and who shall have taken and subscribed the following oath or affirmation: "I,________, do solemnly swear (or affirm), in the presence of Almighty God, that I am a citizen of the state of________; that I have resided in said State for _____months next preceding this day, and now reside in the county of ______________, or the parish of ____________, in said State (as the case may be); that I am twenty-one years old; that I have not been disfranchised for participation in any rebellion or civil war against the United States, nor for felony committed against the laws of any State or of the United States; that I have never been a member of any State legislature, nor held any executive or judicial office in any State and afterwards engaged in insurrection or rebellion against the United States, or given aid or comfort to the enemies thereof; that I have never taken an oath as a member of Congress of the United States, or as an officer of the United States, or as a member of any State legislature, or as an executive or judicial officer of any State, to support the Constitution of the United States, and afterwards engaged in insurrection or rebellion against the United States, or given aid or comfort to the enemies thereof; that I will faithfully support the Constitution and obey the laws of the United States, and will, to the best of my ability, encourage others so to do, so help me God"; which oath or affirmation may be administered by any registering officer.

Sec. 2. And be it further enacted, That after the completion of the registration hereby provided for in any State, at such time and places therein as the commanding general shall appoint and direct, of which at least thirty days' public notice shall be given, an election shall be held of delegates to a convention for the purpose of establishing a constitution and civil government for such State loyal to the Union, said convention in each State, except Virginia, to consist of the same number of members as the most numerous branch of the State legislature of such State in the year eighteen hundred and sixty, to be apportioned among the several districts, counties, or parishes of such State by the commanding general, giving to each representative in the ratio of voters registered as aforesaid as nearly as may be. The convention in Virginia shall consist of the same number of members as represented the territory now constituting Virginia in the most numerous branch of the legislature of said State in the year eighteen hundred and sixty, to be apportioned as aforesaid.

Sec. 3. And be it further enacted, That at said election the registered voters of each State shall vote for or against a convention to form a constitution therefore under this act. Those voting in favor of such a convention shall have written or printed on the ballots by which they vote for delegates, as aforesaid, the words "For a convention," and those voting against such a convention shall have written or printed on such ballots the words "Against a convention." The persons appointed to superintend said election, and to make return of the votes given thereat, as herein provided, shall count and make return of the votes given for and against a convention; and the commanding general to who the same shall have been returned shall ascertain and declare the total vote in each State for and against a convention. If a majority of the votes given on that question shall be for a convention, then such convention shall be held as hereinafter provided; but if a majority of said votes shall be against a convention, then no such convention shall be held under this act: Provided, That such convention shall not be held unless a majority of all such registered voters shall have voted on the question of holding such convention.

Sec. 4. And be it further enacted, That the commanding general of each district shall appoint as many boards of registration as may be necessary, consisting of three loyal officers or persons to make and complete the registration, superintend the election, and make return to him of the votes, list of voters, and of the persons elected as delegates by a plurality of the votes cast at said election; and upon receiving said returns he shall open the same, ascertain the persons elected as delegates, according to the returns of the officers who conducted said election, and make proclamation thereof; and if a majority of the votes given on that question shall be for a convention, the commanding general, within sixty days from the date of election, shall notify the delegates to assemble in convention, at a time and place to be mentioned in the notification, and said convention, when organized, shall proceed to frame a constitution and civil government according to the provisions of this act, and the act to which it is supplementary; and when the same shall have been so framed, said constitution shall be submitted by the convention for ratification to the persons registered under the provisions of this act at an election to be conducted by the officers or persons appointed or to be appointed by the commanding general, as hereinbefore provided, and to be held after the expiration of thirty days from the date of notice thereof, to be given by said convention; and the returns thereof shall be made to the commanding general of the district.

Sec. 5. And be it further enacted, That if, according to said returns, the constitution shall be ratified by a majority of the votes of the registered electors qualified as herein specified, cast at said election, at least one half of all registered voters voting upon the question of such ratification, the president of the convention shall transmit a copy of the same, duly certified, to the President of the United States, who shall forthwith transmit the same to Congress, if then in session, and if not in session, then immediately upon its next assembling; and if it shall moreover appear to Congress that the election was one at which all the registered and qualified electors in the State had an opportunity to vote freely and without restraint, fear, or the influence of fraud, and if the Congress shall be satisfied that such constitution meets the approval of the majority of all the qualified electors in the State, and if the said constitution shall be declared by Congress to be in conformity with the provisions of the act to which this is supplementary, and the other provisions of said act shall have been complied with, and the said constitution shall be approved by Congress, the State shall be declared entitled to representation and senators and representatives shall be admitted therefrom as therein provided.

Sec. 6. And be it further enacted, That all elections in the States mentioned in the said "Act to provide for the more efficient government of the rebel States," shall, during the operation of said act, be by ballot; and all officers making the said registration of voters and conducting said elections shall, before entering upon the discharge of their duties, take and subscribe the oath prescribed by the act approved July second, eighteen hundred and sixty-two, entitled "An act to prescribe an oath of office": Provided, That if any person shall knowingly and falsely take and subscribe any oath in this act prescribed, such person so offending and being thereof duly convicted shall be subject to the pains, penalties, and disabilities which by law are provided for the punishment of the crime of willful and corrupt perjury.

Sec. 7. And be it further enacted, That all expenses incurred by the several commanding generals, or by virtue of any orders issued, or appointments made, by them, under or by virtue of this act, shall be paid out of any moneys in the treasury not otherwise appropriated.

Sec. 8. And be it further enacted, That the convention for each State shall prescribe the fees, salary, and compensation to be paid to all delegates and other officers and agents herein authorized or necessary to carry into effect the purposes of this act not herein otherwise provided for, and shall provide for the levy and collection of such taxes on the property in such State as may be necessary to pay the same.

Sec. 9. And be it further enacted, That the word "article," in the sixth section of the act to which this is supplementary, shall be construed to mean "section."

SCHUYLER COLFAX,
Speaker of the House of Representatives.
B. F. WADE,
President of the Senate pro tempore.

In the House of Representatives, U.S.,}
March 23, 1867}

The President of the United States having returned to the House of Representatives, in which it originated, the bill entitled "An act supplementary to an act entitled 'An act to provide for the more efficient government of the rebel States,' passed March second, eighteen hundred and sixty-seven, and to facilitate restoration," with his objections thereto, the House of Representatives proceeded, in pursuance of the Constitution, to reconsider the same; and

Resolved, That the said bill do pass, two thirds of the House of Representatives agreeing to pass the same.

Attest: Edwd. McPherson,
Clerk H.R.U.S.

In the Senate of the United States}
March 23, 1867 }

The Senate having proceeded, in pursuance of the Constitution, to reconsider the bill entitled "An act supplementary to an act entitled 'An act to provide for the more efficient government of the rebel States,' passed March second, eighteen hundred and sixty-seven, and to facilitate restoration," returned to the House of Representatives by the President of the United States with his objections, and sent by the House of Representatives to the Senate, with the message of the President returning the bill:—

Resolved, That the bill do pass, two thirds of the Senate agreeing to pass the same.

Attest: J. W. Forney,
Secretary.

A Joint Resolution to furnish transportation of provisions to the destitute in the South. No. 17, March 29, 1867

Be it resolved by the Senate and House of Representatives of the United States of America in Congress assembled, That the Secretary of the Navy, upon the application of the contributors or of any person on their behalf, be, and he is hereby, authorized and directed to charter a vessel to convey provisions contributed by the people from Baltimore, Maryland, to Wilmington, North Carolina, for gratuitous distribution among the destitute of the South, under the direction of the contributors and such regulations as may, by the Secretary of the Navy, be prescribed.

Approved, March 29, 1867.

A Resolution for the relief of the destitute in the Southern and Southwestern States. No. 28, March 30, 1867

Resolved by the Senate and House of Representatives of the United States of America in Congress assembled, That the Secretary of War be and hereby is empowered and directed to issue supplies of food sufficient to prevent starvation and extreme want to any and all classes of destitute or helpless persons of the people in those southern and southwestern States where a failure of the crops and other causes have occasioned wide-spread destitution; that the issues be made through the freedmen's bureau, under such regulations as the Secretary of War shall prescribe. And to that end the Secretary of War is hereby authorized and directed, through the commissioner of the freedmen's bureau, to apply so much as he may deem necessary for the purposes aforesaid of the unexpended moneys heretofore appropriated to supply freedmen and refugees with provisions or rations: Provided, That the expenditure shall not extend beyond the present appropriations already made for the freedmen's bureau.

Approved, March 30, 1867.

An Act supplementary to an Act entitled "An Act to provide for the more efficient government of the Rebel States," passed on March 2, 1867, and the Act supplementary thereto, passed March 23, 1867. July 19, 1867

Be it enacted by the Senate and House of Representatives of the United States of America in Congress assembled, That it is hereby declared to have been the true intent and meaning of the act of the second day of March, one thousand eight hundred and sixty-seven, entitled "An act to provide for the more efficient government of the rebel States," and of the act supplementary thereto, passed on the twenty-third day of March, in the year one thousand eight hundred and sixty-seven, that the governments then existing in the rebel States of Virginia, North Carolina, South Carolina, Georgia, Mississippi, Alabama, Louisiana, Florida, Texas, and Arkansas were not legal State governments; and that thereafter said governments, if continued, were to be continued subject in all respects to the military commanders of the respective districts, and to the paramount authority of Congress.

Sec. 2. And be it further enacted, That the commander of any district named in said act shall have power, subject to the disapproval of the General of the army of the United States, and to have effect till disapproved, whenever in the opinion of such commander the proper administration of said act shall require it, to suspend or remove from office, or from the performance of official duties and the exercise of official powers, any officer or person holding or exercising, or professing to hold or exercise, any civil or military office or duty in such district under any power, election, appointment or authority derived from, or granted by, or claimed under, any so-called State or government thereof, or any municipal or other division thereof, and upon such suspension or removal such commander, subject to the disapproval of the General as aforesaid, shall have power to provide from time to time for the performance of the said duties of such officer or person so suspended or removed, by the detail of some competent officer or soldier of the army, or by the appointment of some other person, to perform the same, and to fill vacancies occasioned by death, resignation, or otherwise.

Sec. 3. And be it further enacted, That the General of the army of the United States shall be invested with all the powers of suspension, removal, appointment, and detail granted in the preceding section to district commanders.

Sec. 4. And be it further enacted, That the acts of the officers of the army already done in removing in said districts persons exercising the functions of civil officers, and appointing others in their stead, are hereby confirmed: Provided, That any person heretofore or hereafter appointed by any district commander to exercise the functions of any civil office, may be removed either by the military officer in command of the district, or by the General of the army. And it shall be the duty of such commander to remove from office as aforesaid all persons who are disloyal to the government of the United States, or who use their official influence in any manner to hinder, delay, prevent, or obstruct the due and proper administration of this act and the acts to which it is supplementary.

Sec. 5. And be it further enacted, That the boards of registration provided for in the act entitled "An act supplementary to an act entitled 'An act to provide for the more efficient government of the rebel States,' passed March two, eighteen hundred and sixty-seven, and to facilitate restoration," passed March twenty-three, eighteen hundred and sixty-seven, shall have power, and it shall be their duty before allowing the registration of any person, to ascertain, upon such facts or information as they can obtain, whether such person is entitled to be registered under said act, and the oath required by said act shall not be conclusive on such question, and no person shall be registered unless such board shall decide that he is entitled thereto; and such board shall also have power to examine, under oath, (to be administered by any member of such board,) any one touching the qualification of any person claiming registration; but in every case of refusal by the board to register an applicant, and in every case of striking his name from the list as hereinafter provided, the board shall make a note or memorandum, which shall be returned with the registration list to the commanding general of the district, setting forth the grounds of such refusal or such striking from the list: Provided, That no person shall be disqualified as member of any board of registration by reason of race or color.

Sec. 6. And be it further enacted, That the true intent and meaning of the oath prescribed in said supplementary act is (among other things,) that no person who has been a member of the legislature of any State, or who has held any executive or judicial office in any State, whether he has taken an oath to support the Constitution of the United States or not, and whether he was holding such office at the commencement of the rebellion, or had held it before, and who has afterwards engaged in insurrection or rebellion against the United States, or given aid or comfort to the enemies thereof, is entitled to be registered or to vote; and the words "executive or judicial office in any State" in said oath mentioned shall be construed to include all civil offices created by law for the administration of any general law of a State, or for the administration of justice.

Sec. 7. And be it further enacted, That the time for completing the original registration provided for in said act may, in the discretion of the commander of any district be extended to the first day of October, eighteen hundred and sixty-seven; and the boards of registration shall have power, and it shall be their duty, commencing fourteen days prior to any election under said act, and upon reasonable public notice of the time and place thereof, to revise, for a period of five days, the registration lists, and upon being satisfied that any person not entitled thereto has been registered, to strike the name of such person from the list, and such person shall not be allowed to vote. And such board shall also, during the same period, add to such registry the names of all persons who at that time possess the qualifications required by said act who have not been already registered; and no person shall, at any time, be entitled to be registered or to vote by reasons of any executive pardon or amnesty for any act or thing which, without such pardon or amnesty, would disqualify him from registration or voting.

Sec. 8. And be it further enacted, That section four of said last-named act shall be construed to authorize the commanding general named therein, whenever he shall deem it needful, to remove any member of a board of registration and to appoint another in his stead, and to fill any vacancy in such board.

Sec. 9. And be it further enacted, That all members of said boards of registration and all persons hereafter elected or appointed to office in said military districts, under any so-called State or municipal authority, or by detail or appointment of the district commanders, shall be required to take and subscribe the oath of office prescribed by law for officers of the United States.

Sec. 10. And be it further enacted, That no district commander or member of the board of registration, or any of the officers or appointees acting under them, shall be bound in his action by any opinion of any civil officer of the United States.

Sec. 11. And be it further enacted, That all the provisions of this act and of the acts to which this is supplementary shall be construed liberally, to the end that all the intents thereof may be fully and perfectly carried out.

SCHUYLER COLFAX,
Speaker of the House of Representatives.
B. F. WADE,
President of the Senate pro tempore.

In the House of Representatives, U.S.,}
July 19th, 1867. }

The President of the United States, having returned to the House of Representatives, in which it originated, the bill entitled " An act supplementary to an act entitled 'An act to provide for the more efficient government of the rebel States,' passed on the second day of March, eighteen hundred and sixty-seven, and the act supplementary thereto passed on the twenty-third day of March, eighteen hundred and sixty-seven," with his objections thereto, the House of Representatives proceeded, in pursuance of the Constitution, to recognize the same; and

Resolved, That the bill do pass, two-thirds of the House of Representatives agreeing to pass the same.

Attest: EDWD. McPHERSON,
Clerk H.R.U.S.

In the Senate of the United States,}
July 19, 1867. }

The Senate having proceeded, in pursuance of the Constitution, to reconsider the bill entitled "An act supplementary to an act entitled 'An act to provide for the more efficient government of the rebel States,' passed on the second day of March, eighteen hundred and sixty-seven, and the act supplementary thereto, passed on the twenty-third day of March, eighteen hundred and sixty-seven," returned to the House of Representatives by the President of the United States, with his objections, and sent by the House of Representatives to the Senate, with the message of the President returning the bill:

Resolved, That the bill do pass, two-thirds of the Senate agreeing to pass the same.

Attest: J. W. FORNEY,
Secretary,
By W. R. McDONALD,
Chief Clerk.

A Proclamation by the President of the United States of America. No. 3. September 7, 1867.

Whereas, in the month of July, anno Domini one thousand eight hundred and sixty-one, the two Houses of Congress, with extraordinary unanimity, solemnly declared that the war then existing was not waged on the part of the Government in any spirit of oppression, nor for any purpose of conquest or subjugation, nor purpose of overthrowing or interfering with the rights or established institutions of the States, but to defend and maintain the supremacy of the Constitution, and to preserve the Union with all the dignity, equality, and rights, of the several States unimpaired, and that as soon as these objects should be accomplished the war ought to cease;

And whereas the President of the United States, on the eighth day of December, anno Domini one thousand eight hundred and sixty-three, and on the twenty-sixth day of March, anno Domini one thousand eight hundred and sixty-four, did, with the objects of suppressing the then existing rebellion, of inducing all persons to return to their loyalty, and of restoring the authority of the United States, issue proclamations offering amnesty and pardon to all persons who had directly or indirectly participated in the then existing rebellion, except as in those proclamations was specified and reserved;

And whereas the President of the United States did, on the twenty-ninth day of May, anno Domini one thousand eight hundred and sixty-five, issue a further proclamation with the same objects before mentioned, and to the end that the authority of the Government of the United States might be restored, and that peace, order, and freedom might be established, and the

President did, by the said last-mentioned proclamation, proclaim and declare that he thereby granted to all persons who had directly or indirectly participated in the then existing rebellion, except as therein excepted, amnesty and pardon, with the restoration of all rights of property, except as to slaves, and except in certain cases where legal proceedings had been instituted, but upon condition that such persons should take and subscribe an oath therein prescribed, which oath should be registered for permanent preservation;

And whereas, in and by the said last-mentioned proclamation of the twenty-ninth day of May, anno Domini one thousand eight hundred and sixty-five, fourteen extensive classes of persons, therein specially described, were altogether excepted and excluded from the benefits thereof;

And whereas the President of the United States did, on the second day of April, anno Domini one thousand eight hundred and sixty-six, issue a proclamation declaring that the insurrection was at an end, and was thenceforth to be so regarded;

And whereas there now exists no organized armed resistance of misguided citizens or others to the authority of the United States in the States of Georgia, South Carolina, Virginia, North Carolina, Tennessee, Alabama, Louisiana, Arkansas, Mississippi, Florida, and Texas, and the laws can be sustained and enforced therein by the proper civil authority, State or Federal, and the people of said States are well and loyally disposed, and have conformed, or if permitted to do so, will conform in their legislation to the condition of affairs growing out of the amendment to the Constitution of the United States prohibiting slavery within the limits and jurisdiction of the United States;

And whereas there no longer exists any reasonable ground to apprehend, within the States which were involved in the late rebellion, any renewal thereof, or any unlawful resistance by the people of said States to the Constitution and laws of the United States;

And whereas large standing armies, military occupation, martial law, military tribunals, and the suspension of the privilege of the writ of habeas corpus and the right of trial by jury, are, in time of peace, dangerous to public liberty, incompatible with the individual rights of the citizen, contrary to the genius and spirit of our free institutions, and exhaustive of the national resources, and ought not, therefore, to be sanctioned or allowed, except in cases of actual necessity for repelling invasion or suppressing insurrection or rebellion;

And whereas a retaliatory or vindictive policy, attended by unnecessary disqualifications, pains, penalties, confiscations, and disfranchisements, now, as always, could only tend to hinder reconciliation among the people and national restoration, while it must seriously embarrass, obstruct, and repress popular energies and national industry and enterprise;

And whereas, for these reasons, it is now deemed essential to the public welfare, and to the more perfect restoration of constitutional law and order, that the said last-mentioned proclamation, so as aforesaid issued on the twenty-ninth day of May, anno Domini one thousand eight hundred and sixty-five, should be modified, and that the full and beneficent pardon conceded thereby should be opened and further extended to a large number of the persons who, by its aforesaid exceptions, have been hitherto excluded from executive clemency:

Now, therefore, be it known that I, Andrew Johnson, President of the United States, do hereby proclaim and declare that the full pardon described in the said proclamation of the twenty-ninth day of May, anno Domini one thousand eight hundred and sixty-five, shall henceforth be opened [offered] and extend to all persons who, directly or indirectly, participated in the late rebellion, with the restoration of all privileges, immunities, and rights of property, except as to property with regard to slaves, and except in cases of legal proceedings under the laws of the United States; but upon this condition, nevertheless: that every such person who shall seek to avail himself of this proclamation shall take and subscribe the following oath, and shall cause the same to be registered for permanent preservation, in the same manner and with the same effect as with the oath prescribed in the said proclamation of the twenty-ninth day of May, one thousand eight hundred and sixty-five, namely:

"I,_______ _______, do solemnly swear,(or affirm,) in presence of Almighty God, that I will henceforth faithfully support, protect, and defend the Constitution of the United States, and the Union of the States thereunder; and that I will, in like manner, abide by and faithfully support all laws and proclamations which have been made during the late rebellion with reference to the emancipation of slaves: So help me God."

The following persons, and no others, are excluded from the benefits of this proclamation, and of the said proclamation of the twenty-ninth day of May, one thousand eight hundred and sixty-five, namely:

First. The chief or pretended chief executive officers, including the President, the Vice-President, and all Heads of Departments of the pretended Confederate or Rebel Government, and all who were agents thereof in foreign States and countries, and all who held, or pretended to hold, in the service of the said pretended Confederate Government, a military rank or title above the grade of brigadier-general, or naval rank or title above that of captain, and all who were or pretended to be Governors of States, while maintaining, aiding, abetting, or submitting to and acquiescing in the rebellion.

Second. All persons who in any way treated otherwise than as lawful prisoners of war who in any capacity were employed or engaged in the military or naval service of the United States.

Third. All persons who, at the time they may seek to obtain the benefits of this proclamation, are actually in civil, military, naval confinement or custody, or legally held to bail, either before or after conviction, and all persons who are engaged directly or indirectly in the assassination of the late President of the United States, or in any plot or conspiracy in any manner therewith connected.

In testimony whereof, I have signed these presents with my hand, and have caused the seal of the United States to be hereunto affixed.

Done at the city of Washington, the seventh day of [Seal] September, in the year of our Lord one thousand eight hundred and sixty-seven, and of the Independence of the United States of America, the ninety-second.

ANDREW JOHNSON.

By the President:

William H. Seward, Secretary of State.

A Proclamation by the President of the United States of America. No. 4. October 7, 1867.

Whereas, it has been ascertained that in the nineteenth paragraph of the proclamation of the President of the United States, of the twentieth of August, one thousand eight hundred and sixty-six, declaring the insurrection at an end which had therefore existed in the State of Texas, the previous proclamation of the thirteenth of June, one thousand eight hundred and sixty-five, instead of that of the second of April, one thousand eight hundred and sixty-six, was referred to. Now, therefore, be it known that I, ANDREW JOHNSON, President of the United States, do hereby declare and proclaim that the said words, "thirteenth of June, one thousand eight hundred and sixty-five," are to be regarded as erroneous in the paragraph adverted to, and that the words "second day of April, one thousand eight hundred and sixty-six" are to be considered as substituted therefore.

In testimony whereof, I have hereunto set my hand, and caused the seal of the United States to be affixed.

Done at the city of Washington, this seventh day of October, in the year of our Lord one thousand eight hundred and sixty-seven, and of the [L. S.] Independence of the United States of America the ninety-second.

ANDREW JOHNSON.

By the President:

William H. Seward, Secretary of State.

A Joint Resolution for the Relief of destitute persons in the South. No. 7. January 31, 1868

Be it resolved by the Senate and House of Representatives of the United States of America in Congress assembled, That the Secretary of War be hereby authorized to issue, for the relief of any and all classes of destitutes in the South, such desiccated potatoes and desic[c]ated mixed vegetables as have accumulated during the war and are not needed for use in the army; the same to be issued under the direction of the commissioner of the bureau of refugees, freedmen, and abandoned lands.

Approved, January 31, 1868.

An Act to amend the Act passed March 23, 1867, entitled "An Act supplementary to 'An Act to provide for the more efficient government of the Rebel States,' passed March 2, 1867, and to facilitate their restoration." March 11, 1868.

Be it enacted by the Senate and House of Representatives of the United States of America in Congress assembled, That hereafter any election authorized by the act passed March twenty-three, eighteen hundred and sixty-seven, entitled "An act supplementary to 'An act to provide for the more efficient government of the rebel States,' passed March two, [second,] eighteen hundred and sixty-seven, and to facilitate their restoration," shall be decided by a majority of the votes actually cast; and at the election in which the question of the adoption or rejection of any constitution is submitted, any person duly registered in the State may vote in the election district where he offers to vote when he has resided therein for ten days next preceding such election, upon presentation of his certificate of registration, his affidavit, or other satisfactory evidence, under such regulations as the district commanders may prescribe.

Sec. 2. And be it further enacted, That the constitutional convention of any of the States mentioned in the acts to which this is amendatory may provide that at the time of voting upon the ratification of the constitution the registered voters may vote also for members of the House of Representatives of the United States, and for all elective officers provided for by the said constitution; and the same election officers who shall make the return of the votes cast on the ratification or rejection of the constitution, shall enumerate and certify the votes cast for members of Congress.

SCHUYLER COLFAX,
Speaker of the House of Representatives.
B. F. WADE,
President of the Senate pro tempore.

Indorsed by the President: "Received February 28, 1868."

[Note by the Department of State.— The foregoing act having been presented to the President of the United States for his approval, and not having been returned by him to the House of Congress in which it originated within the time prescribed by the Constitution of the United States, has become a law without his approval.]

An Act to admit the States of North Carolina, South Carolina, Louisiana, Georgia, Alabama, and Florida, to representation in Congress. June 25, 1868.

Whereas the people of North Carolina, South Carolina, Louisiana, Georgia, Alabama, and Florida have, in pursuance of the provisions of an act entitled "An act for the more efficient government of the rebel States," passed March second, eighteen hundred and sixty-seven, and the acts supplementary thereto, framed constitutions of State government which are republican, and have adopted said constitutions by large majorities of the votes cast at the elections held for the ratification or rejection of the same: Therefore,

Be it enacted by the Senate and House of Representatives of the United States of America in Congress assembled, That each of the States of North Carolina, South Carolina, Louisiana, Georgia, Alabama, and Florida, shall be entitled and admitted to representation in Congress as a State of the Union when the legislature of such State shall have duly ratified the amendment to the Constitution of the United States proposed by the Thirty-ninth Congress, and known as article fourteen, upon the following fundamental conditions: That the constitutions of neither of said States shall ever be so amended or changed as to deprive any citizen or class of citizens of the United States of the right to vote in said State, who are entitled to vote by the constitution thereof herein recognized, except as a punishment for such crimes as are now felonies at common law, whereof they shall have been duly convicted under laws equally applicable to all the inhabitants of said State: Provided, That any alteration of said constitution may be made with regard to the time and place of residence of voters; and the State of Georgia shall only be entitled and admitted to representation upon this further fundamental condition: that the first and third subdivisions of section seventeen of the fifth article of the constitution of said State, except the proviso to the first subdivision, shall be null and void, and that the general assembly of said State by solemn public act shall declare the assent of the State to the foregoing fundamental condition.

Sec. 2. And be it further enacted, That if the day fixed for the first meeting of the legislature of either of said States by the constitution or ordinance thereof shall have passed or have so nearly arrived before the passage of this act that there shall not be time for the legislature to assemble at the period fixed, such legislature shall convene at the end of twenty days from the time this act takes effect, unless the governor elect shall sooner convene the same.

Sec. 3. And be it further enacted, That the first section of this act shall take effect as to each State, except Georgia, when such State shall by its legislature, duly ratify article fourteen of the amendments to the Constitution of the United States, proposed by the Thirty-ninth Congress, and as to the State of Georgia when it shall in addition give the assent of said State to the fundamental condition hereinbefore imposed upon the same; and thereupon the officers of each State duly elected and qualified under the constitution thereof shall be inaugurated without delay; but no person prohibited from holding office under the United States, or under any State, by section three of the proposed amendment to the Constitution of the United States, known as article fourteen, shall be deemed eligible to any office in either of said States, unless relieved from disability as provided in said amendment; and it is hereby made the duty of the President within ten days after receiving official information of the ratification of said amendment by the legislature of either of said States to issue a proclamation announcing that fact.

SCHUYLER COLFAX,
Speaker of the House of Representatives.
B. F. WADE,
President of the Senate pro tempore.

In the House of Representatives, U.S.,}
June 25, 1868. }

The President of the United States, having returned to the House of Representatives, in which it originated, the bill entitled "An act to admit the States of North Carolina, South Carolina, Louisiana, Georgia, Alabama, and Florida to representation in Congress," with his objections thereto, the House of Representatives proceeded, in pursuance of the Constitution, to reconsider the same; and

Resolved, That the said bill do pass, two thirds of the House of Representatives agreeing to pass the same.

Attest: EDWD. McPHERSON,
Clerk H.R.U.S.

In the Senate of the United States,}
June 25, 1868. }

The Senate having proceeded, in pursuance of the Constitution, to reconsider the bill entitled "An act to admit the States of North Carolina, South Carolina, Louisiana, Georgia, Alabama, and Florida to representation in Congress," returned to the House of Representatives by the President of the United States, with his objections, and sent by the House of Representatives to the Senate, with the message of the President returning the bill:

Resolved, That the bill do pass, two thirds of the Senate agreeing to pass the same.

Attest: GEO. C. GORHAM,
Secretary of the Senate.

A Proclamation by the President of the United States of America. No. 6. July 4, 1868

Whereas in the month of July, anno Domini 1861, in accepting the condition of civil war, which was brought about by insurrection and rebellion in several of the States which constitute the United States, the two Houses of Congress did solemnly declare that that war was not waged on the part of the Government in any spirit of oppression, nor for any purpose of conquest or subjugation, nor for any purpose of overthrowing or interfering with the rights or established institutions of the States, but only to defend and maintain the supremacy of the Constitution of the United States, and to preserve the Union with all the dignity, equality, and rights of the several States unimpaired, and that so soon as those objects should be accomplished, the war on the part of the Government should cease;

And whereas the President of the United States has heretofore, in the spirit of that declaration, and with the view of securing for it ultimate and complete effect, set forth several proclamations, offering amnesty and pardon to persons who had been or were concerned in the aforenamed rebellion, which proclamations, however, were attended with prudential reservations and exceptions, then deemed necessary and proper, and which proclamations were respectively issued on the eighth day of December, one thousand eight hundred and sixty-three, on the twenty-sixth day of March, one thousand eight hundred and sixty-four, on the twenty-ninth day of May, one thousand eight hundred and sixty-five, and on the seventh day of September, one thousand eight hundred and sixty-seven;

And whereas the said lamentable civil war has long since altogether ceased, with an acknowledgement by all the States of the supremacy of the Federal Constitution and of the Government thereunder, and there no longer exists any reasonable ground to apprehend a renewal of the said civil war, or any foreign interference, or any unlawful resistance by any portion of the people of any of the States to the Constitution and laws of the United States;

And whereas it is desirable to reduce the standing army, and to bring to a speedy termination military occupation, martial law, military tribunals, abridgement of the freedom of speech and of the press, and suspension of the privilege of habeas corpus, and of the right of trial by jury,—such encroachments upon our free institutions in time of peace being dangerous to public liberty, incompatible with the individual rights of the citizens, contrary to the genius and spirit of our republican form of Government, and exhaustive of the national resources;

And whereas it is believed that amnesty and pardon will tend to secure a complete and universal establishment and prevalence of municipal law and order, in conformity with the Constitution of the United States, and to remove all appearances or presumptions of a retaliatory or vindictive policy on the part of the Government, attended by unnecessary disqualifications, pains, penalties, confiscations, and disfranchisements, and, on the contrary, to promote and procure complete fraternal reconciliation among the whole people, with due submission to the Constitution and laws:

Now, therefore, be it known that I, Andrew Johnson, President of the United States, do, by virtue of the Constitution and in the name of the people of the United States, hereby proclaim and declare, unconditionally and without reservation, to all and to every person who directly or indirectly participated in the late insurrection or rebellion, excepting such person or persons as may be under presentment or indictment in any court of the United States having competent jurisdiction, upon a charge of treason or other felony, a full pardon and amnesty for the offence of treason against the United States, or of adhering to their enemies during the late civil war, with restoration of all rights of property, except as to slaves, and except also as to any property of which any person may have been legally divested under the laws of the United States.

In testimony whereof I have signed these presents with my hand, and have caused the seal of the United States to be hereunto affixed.

Done at the city of Washington, the fourth day of July, in the year of our Lord one thousand eight hundred [SEAL] and sixty-eight, and of the Independence of the United States of America the ninety-third.

ANDREW JOHNSON.

By the President:

William H. Seward, Secretary of State.

AN ACT TO CONTINUE THE BUREAU FOR THE RELIEF OF FREEDMEN AND REFUGEES, AND FOR OTHER PURPOSES. JULY 6, 1868

Be it enacted by the Senate and House of Representatives of the United States of America in Congress assembled, That the act entitled "An act to establish a bureau for the relief of freemen and refugees," approved March three, eighteen hundred and sixty-five, and the act entitled "An act to continue in force and to amend 'An act to establish a bureau for the relief of freedmen and refugees,' and for other purposes," passed on the sixteenth of July, anno Domini eighteen hundred and sixty-six, shall continue in force for the term of one year from and after the sixteenth of July, in the year one thousand eight hundred and sixty-eight, excepting so far as the same shall be herein modified. And the Secretary of War is hereby directed to re-establish said bureau where the same has been wholly or in part discontinued: Provided, [That] he shall be satisfied that the personal safety of freedmen shall require it.

Sec. 2. And be it further enacted, That it shall be the duty of the Secretary of War to discontinue the operations of the bureau in any State whenever such State shall be fully restored in its constitutional relations with the government of the United States, and shall be duly represented in the Congress of the United States, unless, upon advising with the commissioner of the bureau, and upon full consideration of the condition of freedmen's affairs in such State, the Secretary of War shall be of opinion that the further continuance of the bureau shall be necessary: Provided, however, That the educational division of said bureau shall not be affected, or in any way interfered with, until such State shall have made suitable provision for the education of the children of freedmen within said State.

Sec. 3. And be it further enacted, That unexpected balances in the hands of the commissioner, not required otherwise for the due execution of the law, may be, in the discretion of the commissioner, applied for the education of freedmen and refugees, subject to the provisions of laws applicable thereto.

Sec. 4. And be it further enacted, That officers of the veteran reserve corps or the volunteer service, now on duty in the freedmen's bureau as assistant commissioners, agents, medical officers, or in other capacities, who have been or may be mustered out of service, may be retained by the commissioner, when the same shall be required for the proper execution of the laws, as officers of the bureau, upon such duty and with the same pay, compensation, and all allowances, from the date of their appointment, as now provided by law for their respective grades and duties at the dates of their muster-out and discharge; and such officers so retained shall have, respectively, the same authority and jurisdiction as now conferred upon "officers of the bureau" by act of Congress passed the sixteenth of July, in the year eighteen hundred and sixty-six.

Sec. 5. And be it further enacted, That the commissioner is hereby empowered to sell for cash, or by installments with ample security, school buildings and other buildings constructed for refugees and freedmen by the bureau, to the associations, corporate bodies, or trustees who now use them for purposes of education or relief of want, under suitable guarantees that the purposes for which such buildings were constructed shall be observed: Provided, That all funds derived therefrom shall be returned to the bureau appropriation and accounted for to the treasury of the United States.

SCHUYLER COLFAX,
Speaker of the House of Representatives.
B. F. WADE,
President of the Senate pro tempore.

Indorsed by the President: "Received June 24th, 1868."

[Note by the Department of State.—The foregoing act having been presented to the President of the United States for his approval, and not having been returned by him to the House of Congress in which it originated within the time prescribed by the constitution of the United States, has become a law without his approval.]

An Act relating to the Freedmen's Bureau and providing for its discontinuance. July 25, 1868.

Be it enacted by the Senate and House of Representatives of the United States of America in Congress assembled, That the duties and powers of commissioner of the bureau for the relief of freedmen and refugees shall continue to be discharged by the present commissioner of the bureau, and in case of vacancy in said office occurring by reason of his death or resignation, the same shall be filled by appointment of the President on the nomination of the Secretary of War, and with the advice and consent of the Senate; and no officer of the army shall be detailed for service as commissioner or shall enter upon duties of commissioner unless appointed by and with the advice and consent of the Senate; and all assistant commissioners, agents, clerks, and assistants, shall be appointed by the Secretary of War on the nomination of the commissioner of the bureau. In case of vacancy in the office of the commissioner happening during the recess of the Senate, the duties of commissioner shall be discharged by the acting assistant adjutant-general of the bureau until such vacancy can be filled.

Sec. 2. And be it further enacted, That the commissioner of the bureau shall, on the first day of January next, cause the said bureau to be withdrawn from the several States within which said bureau has acted and its operations shall be discontinued. But the educational department of the said bureau and the collection and payment of moneys due the soldiers, sailors, and marines, or their heirs, shall be continued as now provided by law until otherwise ordered by act of Congress.

SCHUYLER COLFAX,
Speaker of the House of Representatives.
B. F. WADE,
President of the Senate pro tempore.

In Senate of the United States,
July 25, 1868.

The President of the United States having returned to the Senate, in which it originated, the bill entitled "An act relating to the Freedmen's Bureau and providing for its Discontinuance," with his objections thereto, the Senate proceeded, in pursuance of the Constitution, to reconsider the same; and

Resolved, That the said bill do pass, two thirds of the Senate agreeing to pass the same.

Attest: GEO. C. GORHAM,
Secretary of the Senate.

In the House of Representatives, U.S.,
July 25th, 1868.

The House of Representatives having proceeded, in pursuance of the Constitution, to reconsider the bill entitled "An act relating to the Freedmen's Bureau and providing for its Discontinuance," returned to the Senate by the President of the United States, with his objections, and sent by the Senate to the House of Representatives, with the message of the President returning the bill—

Resolved, That the bill do pass, two thirds of the House of Representatives agreeing to pass the same.

EDWD. McPHERSON,
Clerk H.R.U.S.

A Proclamation by the President of the United States of America. No. 15. December 25, 1868.

Whereas the President of the United States has heretofore set forth several proclamations, offering amnesty and pardon to persons who had been or were concerned in the late rebellion against the lawful authority of the government of the United States, which proclamations were severally issued on the eighth day of December, 1863, on the twenty-sixth day of March, 1864, on the twenty ninth day of May, 1865, on the seventh day of September, 1867, and on the fourth day of July, in the present year;

And whereas, the authority of the Federal Government having been reestablished in all States and Territories within the jurisdiction of the United States, it is believed that such prudential reservations and exceptions as at the dates of said several proclamations were deemed necessary and proper may now be wisely and justly relinquished, and that a universal amnesty and pardon for participation in said rebellion extended to all who have borne any part therein will tend to secure permanent peace, order, and prosperity throughout the land, and to renew and fully restore confidence and fraternal feeling among the whole people, and their respect for an attachment to the National Government, designed by its patriotic founders for the general good;

Now, therefore, be it known that I, Andrew Johnson, President of the United States, by virtue of the power and authority in me vested by the Constitution, and in the name of the sovereign people of the United States, do hereby proclaim and declare unconditionally, and without reservation, to all and to every person who directly or indirectly participated in the late insurrection or rebellion, a full pardon and amnesty for the offence of treason against the United States, or of adhering to their enemies during the late civil war, with restoration of all rights, privileges, and immunities under the Constitution and the laws which have been made in pursuance thereof.

In testimony whereof, I have signed these present with my hand, have caused the seal of the United States to be hereunto affixed.

Done at the city of Washington, the twenty-fifth day [Seal] of December, in the year of our Lord one thousand eight hundred and sixty-eight, and of the Independence of the United States of America, the ninety-third.

ANDREW JOHNSON.

By the President:
F. W. Seward,
Acting Secretary of State.

A Resolution proposing an Amendment to the Constitution of the United States. No. 14. February 27, 1869 (15th Amendment).

Resolved by the Senate and House of Representatives of the United States of America in Congress assembled, (two thirds of both houses concurring,) That the following article be proposed to the legislatures of the several States as an amendment to the Constitution of the United States, which, when ratified by three fourths of said legislatures, shall be valid as part of the Constitution, namely:

Article XV.

Section 1. The right of citizens of the United States to vote shall not be denied or abridged by the United States or by any State on account of race, color, or previous condition of servitude.

Sec. 2. The Congress shall have power to enforce this article by appropriate legislation.

SCHUYLER COLFAX,
Speaker of the House of Representatives.
B. F. WADE,
President of the Senate pro tempore.

Attest: Edwd. McPherson,
Clerk of House of Representitives.
Geo. C. Gorham,
Sec'y of Senate U.S.

Received at Department of State February 27, 1869.

An Act to enforce the Right of Citizens of the United States to vote in the several States of this Union, and for other purposes. May 31, 1870.

Be it enacted by the Senate and House of Representatives of the United States of America in Congress assembled, That all citizens of the United States who are or shall be otherwise qualified by law to vote at any election by the people in any State, Territory, district, county, city, parish, township, school district, municipality, or other territorial subdivision, shall be entitled and allowed to vote at all such elections, without distinction of race, color, or previous condition of servitude; any constitution, law, custom, usage, or regulation of any State or Territory, or by or under its authority, to the contrary notwithstanding.

Sec. 2. And be it further enacted, That if by or under the authority of the constitution or laws of any State, or the laws of any Territory, any act is or shall be required to be done as a prerequisite or qualification for voting, and by such constitution or laws persons or officers are or shall be charged with the performance of duties in furnishing to citizens an opportunity to perform such prerequisite, or to become qualified to vote, it shall be the duty of every such person and officer to give all citizens of the United States the same and equal opportunity to perform such prerequisite, and to become qualified to vote without distinction of race, color, or previous condition of servitude; and if any such person or officer shall refuse or knowingly omit to give full effect to this section, he shall, for every offence, forfeit and pay the sum of five hundred dollars to the person aggrieved thereby, to be recovered by an action on the case, with full costs, and such allowance for counsel fees as the court shall deem just, and shall also, for every such offence, be deemed guilty of a misdemeanor, and shall, on conviction thereof, be fined not less than five hundred dollars, or be imprisoned not less than one month and not more than one year, or both, at the discretion of the court.

Sec. 3. And be it further enacted, That whenever, by or under the authority of the constitution or laws of any State, or the laws of any Territory, any act is or shall be required to [be] done by any citizen as a prerequisite to qualify or entitle him to vote, the offer of any such citizen to perform the act required to be done as aforesaid shall, if it fail to be carried into execution by reason of the wrongful act or omission aforesaid of the person or officer charged with the duty of receiving or permitting such performance or offer to perform, or acting thereon, be deemed and held as a performance in law of such act; and the person so offering and failing as aforesaid, and being otherwise qualified, shall be entitled to vote in the same manner and to the same extent as if he had in fact performed such act; and any judge, inspector, or other officer of election whose duty it is or shall be to receive, count, certify, register, report, or give effect to the vote of any such citizen who shall wrongfully refuse or omit to receive, count, certify, register, report, or give effect to the vote of such citizen upon the presentation by him of his affidavit stating such offer and the time and place thereof, and the name of the officer or person whose duty it was to act thereon, and that he was wrongfully prevented by such person or officer from performing such act, shall for every such offence forfeit and pay the sum of five hundred dollars to the person aggrieved thereby, to be recovered by an action on the case, with full costs, and such allowance for counsel fees as the court shall deem just, and shall also for every such offence be guilty of a misdemeanor, and shall, on conviction thereof, be fined not less than five hundred dollars, or be imprisoned not less than one month and not more than one year, or both, at the discretion of the court.

Sec. 4. And be it further enacted, That if any person, by force, bribery, threats, intimidation, or other unlawful means, shall hinder, delay, prevent, or obstruct, or shall combine and confederate with others to hinder, delay, prevent, or obstruct, any citizen from doing any act required to be done to qualify him to vote or from voting at any election as aforesaid, such person shall for every such offence forfeit and pay the sum of five hundred dollars to the person aggrieved thereby, to be recovered by an action on the case, with full costs, and such allowance for counsel fees as the court shall deem just, and shall also for every such offence be guilty of a misdemeanor, and shall, on conviction thereof, be fined not less than five hundred dollars, or be imprisoned not less than one month and not more than one year, or both, at the discretion of the court.

Sec. 5. And be it further enacted, That if any person shall prevent, hinder, control, or intimidate, or shall attempt to prevent, hinder, control, or intimidate, any person from exercising or in exercising the right of suffrage, to whom the right of suffrage is secured or guaranteed by the fifteenth amendment to the Constitution of the United States, by means of bribery, threats, or threats of depriving such person of employment or occupation, or of ejecting such person from rented house, lands, or other property, or by threats of refusing to renew leases or contracts for labor, or by threats of violence to himself or family, such person so offending shall be deemed guilty of a misdemeanor, and shall, on conviction thereof, be fined not less than five hundred dollars, or be imprisoned not less than one month and not more than one year, or both, at the discretion of the court.

Sec. 6. And be it further enacted, That if two or more persons shall band or conspire together, or go in disguise upon the public highway, or upon the premises of another, with intent to violate any provision of this act, or to injure, oppress, threaten, or intimidate any citizen with intent to present or hinder his free exercise and enjoyment of any right or privilege granted or secured to him by the Constitution or laws of the United States, or because of his having exercised the same, such persons shall be held guilty of felony, and, on conviction thereof, shall be fined or imprisoned, or both, at the discretion of the court,—the fine not to exceed five thousand dollars, and the imprisonment not to exceed ten years,—and shall, moreover, be thereafter ineligible to, and disabled from holding, any office or place of honor, profit, or trust created by the Constitution or laws of the United States.

Sec. 7. And be it further enacted, That if the act of violating any provision in either of the two preceding sections, any other felony, crime, or misdemeanor shall be committed, the offender, on conviction of such violation of said sections, shall be punished for the same with such punishments as are attached to the said felonies, crimes, and misdemeanors by the laws of the State in which the offence may be committed.

Sec. 8. And be it further enacted, That the district courts of the United States within their respective districts, shall have, exclusively of the courts of the several States, cognizance of all crimes and offences committed against the provisions of this act, and also, concurrently with the circuit courts of the United States, of all causes, civil and criminal, arising under this act, except as herein otherwise provided, and the jurisdiction hereby conferred shall be exercised in conformity with the laws and practice governing United States courts; and all crimes and offences committed against the provisions of this act may be prosecuted by the indictment of a grand jury, or, in cases of crimes and offences not infamous, the prosecution may be either by indictment or information filed by the district attorney in a court having jurisdiction.

Sec. 9. And be it further enacted, That the district attorneys, marshals, and deputy marshals of the United States, the commissioners appointed by the circuit and territorial courts of the United States, with powers of arresting, imprisoning, or bailing offenders against the laws of the United States, and every other officer who may be specially empowered by the President of the United States, shall be, and they are hereby, specially authorized and required, at the expense of the United States, to institute proceedings against all and every person who shall violate the provisions of this act, and cause him or them to be arrested and imprisoned, or bailed, as the case may be, for trial before such court of the United States or territorial court as has cognizance of the offense. And with a view to afford reasonable protection to all persons in their constitutional right to vote without distinction of race, color, or previous condition of servitude, and to the prompt discharge of the duties of this act, it shall be the duty of the circuit courts of the United States, and the superior courts of the Territories of the United States, from time to time, to increase the number of commissioners, so as to afford a speedy and convenient means for the arrest and examination of persons charged with a violation of this act; and such commissioners and hereby authorized and required to exercise and discharge all the powers and duties conferred on them by this act, and the same duties with regard to offences created by this act as they are authorized by law to exercise with regard to other offences against the laws of the United States.

Sec. 10. And be it further enacted, That it shall be the duty of all marshals and deputy marshals to obey and execute all warrants and precepts issued under the provisions of this act, when to them directed; and should any marshal or deputy marshal refuse to receive such warrant or other process when tendered, or to use all proper means diligently to execute the same, he shall, on conviction thereof, be fined in the sum of one thousand dollars, to the use of the person deprived of the rights conferred by this act. And the better to enable the said commissioners to execute their duties faithfully and efficiently, in conformity with the Constitution of the United States and the requirements of this act, they are hereby authorized and empowered, within their districts respectively, to appoint, in writing, under their hands, any one or more suitable persons, from time to time, to execute all such warrants and other process as may be issued by them in the lawful performance of their respective duties, and the persons so appointed to execute any warrant or process as aforesaid shall have authority to summon and call to their aid the bystanders or posse comitatus of the proper county, or such portion of the land or naval forces of the United States, or of the militia, as may be necessary to the performance of the duty with which they are charged, and to insure a faithful observance of the fifteenth amendment to the Constitution of the United States; and such warrants shall run and be executed by said officers anywhere in the State or Territory within which they are issued.

Sec. 11. And be it further enacted, That any person who shall knowingly and willfully obstruct, hinder, or prevent any officer or other person charged with the execution of any warrant or process issued under the provisions of this act, or any person or persons lawfully assisting him or them from arresting any person for whose apprehension such warrant or process may have been issued, or shall rescue or attempt to rescue such person from the custody of the officer or other person or persons, or those lawfully assisting as aforesaid, when so arrested pursuant to the authority herein given and declared, or shall aid, abet, or assist any person so arrested as aforesaid, directly or indirectly, to escape from the custody of the officer or other person legally authorized as aforesaid, or shall harbor or conceal any person for whose arrest a warrant or process shall have been issued as aforesaid, so as to prevent his discovery and arrest after notice or knowledge of the fact that a warrant has been issued for the apprehension of such person, shall, for either of said offences, be subject to a fine not exceeding one thousand dollars, or imprisonment not exceeding six months, or both, at the discretion of the court, or conviction before the district or circuit court of the United States for the district or circuit in which said offence may have been committed, or before the proper court of criminal jurisdiction, if committed within any one of the organized Territories of the United States.

Sec. 12. And be it further enacted, That the commissioners, district attorneys, the marshals, their deputies, and the clerks of the said district, circuit, and territorial courts shall be paid for their services the like fees as may be allowed to them for similar services in other cases. The person or persons authorized to execute the process to be issued by such commissioners for the arrest of offenders against the provisions of this act shall be entitled to the usual fees allowed to the marshal for an arrest of each person he or they may arrest and take before any such commissioner as aforesaid, with such other fees as may be deemed reasonable by such commissioner for such other additional services as may be necessarily performed by him or them, such as attending at the examination, keeping the prisoner in custody, and providing him with food and lodging during and until the final determination of such commissioner, and in general for performing such other duties as may be required in the premises; such fees to be made up in conformity with the fees usually charged by the officers of the courts of justice within the proper district or county as near as may be practicable, and paid out of the treasury of the United States on the certificate of the judge of the district within which the arrest is made, and to be recoverable from the defendant as part of the judgment in case of conviction.

Sec. 13. And be it further enacted, That it shall be lawful for the President of the United States to employ such part of the land or naval forces of the United States, or of the militia, as shall be necessary to aid in the execution of judicial process issued under this act.

Sec. 14. And be it further enacted, That whenever any person shall hold office, except as a member of Congress or of some State legislature, contrary to the provisions of the third section of the fourteenth article of amendment of the Constitution of the United States, it shall be the duty of the district attorney of the United States for the district in which such person shall hold office, as aforesaid, to proceed against such person, by writ of quo warranto, returnable to the circuit or district court of the United States in such district, and to prosecute the same to the removal of such person from office; and any writ of quo warranto so brought, as aforesaid, shall take precedence of all other cases on the docket of the court to which it is made returnable, and shall not be continued unless for cause provided to the satisfaction of the court.

Sec. 15. And be it further enacted, That any person who shall hereafter knowingly accept or hold any office under the United States, or any State to which he is ineligible under the third section of the fourteenth article of amendment of the Constitution of the United States, or who shall attempt to hold or exercise the duties of any such office, shall be deemed guilty of a misdemeanor against the United States, and upon conviction thereof before the circuit or district court of the United States, shall be imprisoned not more than one year, or fined not exceeding one thousand dollars, or both, at the discretion of the court.

Sec. 16. And be it further enacted, That all persons within the jurisdiction of the United States shall have the same right in every State and Territory in the United States to make and enforce contracts, to sue, be parties, give evidence, and to the full and equal benefit of all laws and proceedings for the security of person and property as is enjoyed by white citizens, and shall be subject to like punishment, pains, penalties, taxes, licenses, and exactions of every kind, and none other, any law, statute, ordinance, regulation, or custom to the contrary notwithstanding. No tax or charge shall be imposed or enforced by any State upon any person immigrating thereto from a foreign country which is not equally imposed and enforced upon every person immigrating to such State from any other foreign country; and any law of any State in conflict with this provision is hereby declared null and void.

Sec. 17. And be it further enacted, That any person who, under color of any law, statute, ordinance, regulation, or custom, shall subject, or cause to be subjected, any inhabitant of any State or Territory to the deprivation of any right secured or protected by the last preceding section of this act, or to different punishment, pains, or penalties on account of such person being an alien, or by reason of his color or race, than is prescribed for the punishment of citizens, shall be deemed guilty of a misdemeanor, and, on conviction, shall be punished by fine not exceeding one thousand dollars, or imprisonment not exceeding one year, or both, in the discretion of the court.

Sec. 18. And be it further enacted, That the act to protect all persons in the United States in their civil rights, and furnish the means of their vindication, passed April nine, eighteen hundred and sixty-six, is hereby re-enacted; and sections sixteen and seventeen hereof shall be enforced according to the provisions of said act.

Sec. 19. And be it further enacted, That if at any election for representative or delegate in the Congress of the United States any person shall knowingly personate and vote, or attempt to vote, in the name of any other person, whether living, dead, or fictitious; or vote more than once at the same election for any candidate for the same office; or vote at a place where he may not be lawfully entitled to vote; or vote without having a lawful right to vote; or do any unlawful act to secure a right or an opportunity to vote for himself or any other person; or by force, threat, menace, intimidation, bribery, reward, or offer, or promise thereof, or otherwise unlawfully prevent any qualified voter of any State of the United States of America, or of any Territory thereof, from freely exercising the right of suffrage, or by any such means induce any voter to refuse to exercise such right; or compel or induce by any such means, or otherwise, any officer of an election in any such State or Territory to receive a vote from a person not legally qualified or entitled to vote; or interfere in any manner with any officer of said elections in the discharge of his duties; or by any of such means, or other unlawful means, induce any officer of an election, or officer whose duty it is to ascertain, announce, or declare the result of any such election, or give or make any certificate, document, or evidence in relation thereto, to violate or refuse to comply with his duty, or any law regulating the same; or knowingly and willfully receive the vote of any person not entitled to vote, or refuse to receive the vote of any person entitled to vote; or aid, counsel, procure, or advise any such voter, person, or officer to do any act hereby made a crime, or to omit to do any duty the omission of which is hereby made a crime, or attempt to do so, every such person shall be deemed guilty of a crime, and shall for such crime be liable to prosecution in any court of the United States of competent jurisdiction, and, on conviction thereof, shall be punished by a fine not exceeding five hundred dollars, or by imprisonment for a term not exceeding three years, or both, in the discretion of the court, and shall pay the costs of prosecution.

Sec. 20. And be it further enacted, That if, at any registration of voters for election for representative or delegate in the Congress of the United States, any person shall knowingly personate and register, or attempt to register, in the name of any other person, whether living, dead, or fictitious, or fraudulently register, or fraudulently attempt to register, not having a lawful right so to do; or do any unlawful act to secure registration for himself or any other person; or by force, threat, menace, intimidation, bribery, reward, or offer, or promise thereof, or other unlawful means, prevent or hinder any person having a lawful right to register from duly exercising such right; or compel or induce, by any of such means, or other lawful means, any officer of registration to admit to registration any person not legally entitled thereto, or interfere in any manner with any officer of registration in the discharge of his duties, or by any such means, or other unlawful means, induce any officer of registration to violate or refuse to comply with his duty, or any law regulating the same; or knowingly and willfully receive the vote of any person not entitled to vote, or refuse to receive the vote of any person entitled to vote, or aid, counsel, procure, or advise any such voter, person, or officer to do any act hereby made a crime, or to omit any act, the omission of which is hereby made a crime, every such person shall be deemed guilty of a crime, and shall be liable to prosecution and punishment therefore, as provided in section nineteen of this act for persons guilty of any of the crimes therein specified: Provided, That every registration made under the laws of any State or Territory, for any State or other election at which such representative or delegate in Congress shall be chosen, shall be deemed to be a registration within the meaning of this act, notwithstanding the same shall also be made for the purposes of any State, territorial, or municipal election.

Sec. 21. And be it further enacted, That whenever, by the laws of any State or Territory, the name of any candidate or person to be voted for as representative or delegate in Congress shall be required to be printed, written, or contained in any ticket or ballot with other candidates or persons to be voted for at the same election for State, territorial, municipal, or local officers, it shall be sufficient prima facie evidence, either for the purpose of indicating or convicting any person charged with voting, or attempting or offering to vote, unlawfully under the provisions of the preceding sections, or for committing either of the offenses thereby created, to prove that the person so charged or indicted, voted, or attempted or offered to vote, such ballot or ticket, or committed either of the offenses named in the preceding sections of this act with reference to such ballot. And the proof and establishment of such facts shall be taken, held, and deemed to be presumptive evidence that such person voted, or attempted or offered to vote, for such representative or delegate, as the case may be, or that such offense was committed with reference to the election of such representative or delegate, and shall be sufficient to warrant his conviction, unless it shall be shown that any such ballot, when cast, or attempted or offered to be cast, by him, did not contain the name of any candidate for the office of representative or delegate in the Congress of the United States, or that such offense was not committed with reference to the election of such representative or delegate.

Sec. 22. And be it further enacted, That any officer of any election at which any representative or delegate in the Congress of the United States shall be voted for, whether such officer of election be appointed or created by or under any law or authority of the United States, or by or under any State, territorial, district, or municipal law or authority, who shall neglect or refuse to perform any duty in regard to such election required of him by any law of the United States, or of any State or Territory thereof; or violate any duty so imposed, or knowingly do any act thereby unauthorized, with intent to affect any such election, or the result thereof; or fraudulently make any false certificate of the result of such election in regard to such representative or delegate; or withhold, conceal, or destroy any certificate of record so required by law respecting, concerning, or pertaining to the election of any such representative or delegate; or neglect or refuse to make and return the same as so required by law; or aid, counsel, procure, or advise any voter, person, or officer to do any act by this or any of the preceding sections made a crime; or to omit to do any duty the omission of which is by this or any of said sections made a crime, or attempt to do so, shall be deemed guilty of a crime and shall be liable to prosecution and punishment therefore, as provided in the nineteenth section of this act for persons guilty of any of the crimes therein specified.

Sec. 23. And be it further enacted, That whenever any person shall be defeated or deprived of his election to any office, except elector of President or Vice-President, representative or delegate in Congress, or member of a State legislature, by reason of the denial to any citizen or citizens who shall offer to vote, of the right to vote, on account of race, color, or previous condition of servitude, his right to hold and enjoy such office, and the emoluments thereof, shall not be impaired by such denial; and such person may bring any appropriate suit or proceeding to recover possession of such office, and in cases where it shall appear that the sole question touching the title to such office arises out of the denial of the right to vote to citizens who so offered to vote, on account of race, color, or previous condition of servitude, such suit or proceeding may be instituted in the circuit or district court of the United States of the circuit or district in which such person resides. And said circuit or district court shall have, concurrently with the State courts, jurisdiction thereof so far as to determine the rights of the parties to such office by reason of the denial of the right guaranteed by the fifteenth article of amendment to the Constitution of the United States, and secured by this act.

Approved, May 31, 1870.

An Act to amend an Act approved May 31, 1870, entitled "An Act to enforce the Rights of Citizens of the United States to vote in the several States of this Union, and for other purposes." February 28, 1871.

Be it enacted by the Senate and House of Representatives of the United States of America in Congress assembled, That section twenty of the "Act to enforce the rights of citizens of the United States to vote in the several States of this Union, and for other purposes," approved May thirty-one, eighteen hundred and seventy, shall be, and hereby is, amended so as to read as follows: —

Sec. 20. And be it further enacted, That if, [at] any registration of voters for an election for representative or delegate in the Congress of the United States, any person shall knowingly personate and register, or attempt to register, in the name of any other person, whether living, dead, or fictitious, or fraudulently register, fraudulently attempt to register, not having a lawful right so to do; or do any unlawful act to secure registration for himself or any other person; or by force, threat, menace, intimidation, bribery, reward, or offer, or promise thereof, or other unlawful means, prevent or hinder any person having a lawful right to register from duly exercising such right; or compel or induce, by any of such means, or other unlawful means, any officer of registration to admit to registration any person not legally entitled thereto, or interfere in any manner with any officer of registration in the discharge of his duties, or by any such means, or other unlawful means, induce any officer of registration to violate or refuse to comply with his duty or any law regulating the same; or if any such officer shall knowingly and willfully register as a voter any person not entitled to be registered, or refuse to so register any person entitled to be registered; or if any such officer or other person whose duty it is to perform any duty in relation to such registration or election, or to ascertain, announce, or declare the result thereof, or give or make any certificate, document, or evidence in relation thereto, shall knowingly neglect or refuse to perform any duty required by law, or violate any duty imposed by law, or do any act unauthorized by law relating to or affecting such registration or election, or the result thereof, or any certificate, document, or evidence in relation thereto, or if any person shall aid, counsel, procure, or advise any such voter, person, or officer to do any act hereby made a crime, or to omit any act the omission of which is hereby made a crime, every such person shall be deemed guilty of a crime, and shall be liable to prosecution and punishment therefore as provided in section nineteen of said act of May thirty-one, eighteen hundred and seventy, for persons guilty of any of the crimes therein specified: Provided, That every registration made under the laws of any State or Territory for any State or other election at which such representative or delegate in Congress shall be chosen, shall be deemed to be a registration within the meaning of this act, notwithstanding the same shall also be made for the purposes of any State, territorial, or municipal election."

Sec. 2. And be it further enacted, That whenever in any city or town having upward of twenty thousand inhabitants, there shall be two citizens thereof who, prior to any registration of voters for an election for representative or delegate in the Congress of the United States, or prior to any election at which a representative or delegate in Congress is to be voted for, shall make known, in writing, to the judge of the circuit court of the United States for the circuit wherein such city or town shall be, their desire to have said registration, or said election, or both, guarded and scrutinized, it shall be the duty of the said judge of the circuit court, within not less than ten days prior to said registration, if one there be, or, if no registration be required, within not less than ten days prior to said election, to open the said circuit court at the most convenient point in said circuit. And the said court, when so opened by said judge, shall proceed to appoint and commission, from day to day and from time to time, and under the hand of the said circuit court judge, and under the seal of said court, for each election district or voting precinct in each and every such city or town as shall, in the manner herein prescribed, have applied therefor, and to revoke, change, or renew said appointment from time to time, two citizens, residents of said city or town, who shall be of different political parties, and able to read and write the English language, and who shall be known and designated as supervisors of election. And the said circuit court, when opened by the said circuit judge as required herein, shall therefrom and thereafter, and up to and including the day following the day of election, be always open for the transaction of business under this act, and the powers and jurisdiction hereby granted and conferred shall be exercised as well in vacation as in term time; and a judge sitting at chambers shall have the same powers and jurisdiction, including the power of keeping order and of punishing any contempt of his authority, as when sitting in court.

Sec. 3. And be it further enacted, That whenever, from sickness, injury, or otherwise, the judge of the circuit court of the United States in any judicial circuit shall be unable to perform and discharge the duties by this act imposed, it shall be his duty, and he is hereby required, to select and to direct and assign to the performance thereof, in his place and stead, such one of the judges of the district courts of the United States within his circuit as he shall deem best; and upon such selection and assignment being made, it shall be lawful for, and shall be the duty of, the district judge so designated to perform and discharge, in the place and stead of the said circuit judge, all the duties, powers, and obligations imposed and conferred upon the said circuit judge by the provisions of this act.

Sec. 4. And be it further enacted, That it shall be the duty of the supervisors of election, appointed under this act, and they and each of them are hereby authorized and required, to attend at all times and places fixed for the registration of voters, who, being registered, would be entitled to vote for a representative or delegate in Congress, and to challenge any person offering to register; to attend at all times and places when the names of registered voters may be marked for challenge, and to cause such names registered as they shall deem proper to be so marked; to make, when required, the lists, or either of them, provided for in section thirteen of this act, and verify the same; and upon any occasion, and at any time when in attendance under the provisions of this act, to personally inspect and scrutinize such registry, and for purposes of identification to affix their or his signature to each and every page of the original list, and of each and every copy of any such list of registered voters, at such times, upon each day when any name may or shall be received, entered, or registered, and in such manner as will, in their or his judgment, detect and expose the improper or wrongful removal therefrom, or addition thereto, in any way, of any name or names.

Sec. 5. And be it further enacted, That it shall also be the duty of the said supervisors of election, and they, and each of them, are hereby authorized and required, to attend at all times and places for holding elections of representatives or delegates in Congress, and for counting the votes cast at said elections; to challenge any vote offered by any person whose legal qualifications the supervisors, or either of them, shall doubt; to be and remain where the ballot-boxes are kept at all times after the polls are open until each and every vote cast at said time and place shall be counted, the canvass of all votes polled be wholly completed, and the proper and requisite certificates or returns made, whether said certificates or returns be required under any law of the United States, or any State, territorial, or municipal law, and to personally inspect and scrutinize, from time to time, and at all times, on the day of election, the manner in which the voting is done, and the way and method in which the poll-books, registry-lists, and tallies or check books, whether the same are required by any law of the United States, or any State, territorial, or municipal law, are kept; and to the end that each candidate for the office of representative or delegate in Congress shall obtain the benefit of every vote for him cast, the said supervisors of election are, and each of them is, hereby required, in their or his respective election districts or voting precincts, to personally scrutinize, count, and canvass each and every ballot in their or his election district or voting precinct cast, whatever may be the indorsement on said ballot, or in whatever box it may have been placed or be found; to make and forward to the officer who, in accordance with the provisions of section thirteen of this act, shall have been designated as the chief supervisor of the judicial district in which the city or town wherein they or he shall serve shall be, such certificates and returns of all such ballots as said officer may direct and require, and to attach to the registry list, and any and all copies thereof, and to any certificate, statement, or return, whether the same, or any part or portion thereof, be required by any law of the United States, or of any state, territorial, or municipal law, any statement touching the truth or accuracy of the registry, or the truth or fairness of the election and canvass, which the said supervisors of election, or either of them, may desire to make or attach, or which should properly and honestly be made or attached, in order that the facts may become known, any law of any State or Territory to the contrary notwithstanding.

Sec. 6. And be it further enacted, That the better to enable the said supervisors of election to discharge their duties, they are, and each of them is, hereby authorized and directed, in their or his respective election districts or voting precincts, on the day or days of registration, on the day or days when registered voters may be marked to be challenged, and on the day or days of election, to take, occupy, and remain in such position or positions, from time to time, whether before or behind the ballot-boxes, as will, in their judgment, best enable them or him to see each person offering himself for registration or offering to vote, and as will best conduce to their or his scrutinizing the manner in which the registration or voting is being conducted; and at the closing of the polls for the reception of votes, they are, and each of them is, hereby required to place themselves or himself in such position in relation to the ballot-boxes for the purpose of engaging in the work of canvassing the ballots in said boxes contained as will enable them or him to fully perform the duties in respect to such canvass provided in this act, and shall there remain until every duty in respect to such canvass, certificates, returns, and statements shall have been wholly completed, any law of any State or Territory to the contrary notwithstanding.

Sec. 7. And be it further enacted, That if any election district or voting precinct in any city, town, or village, for which there shall have been appointed supervisors of election for any election at which a representative or delegate in Congress shall be voted for, the said supervisors of election, or either of them, shall not be allowed to exercise and discharge, fully and freely, and without bribery, solicitation, interference, hindrance, molestation, violence, or threats thereof, on the part of or from any person or persons, each and every of the duties, obligations, and powers conferred upon them by this act and the act hereby amended, it shall be the duty of the supervisors of election, and each of them, to make prompt report, under oath, within ten days after the day of election, to the officer who, in accordance with the provisions of section thirteen of this act, shall have been designated as the chief supervisor of the judicial district in which the city or town wherein they or he served shall be, of the manner and means by which they were, or he was, not so allowed to fully and freely exercise and discharge the duties and obligations required and imposed by this act. And upon receiving any such report, it shall be the duty of the said chief supervisor, acting both in such capacity and officially as a commissioner of the circuit court, to forthwith examine into all the facts thereof; to subpoena and compel the attendance before him of any witnesses; administer oaths and take testimony in respect to the charges made; and prior to the assembling of the Congress for which any such representative or delegate was voted for, to have filed with the clerk of the House of Representatives of the Congress of the United States all evidence by him taken, all information by him obtained, and all reports to him made.

Sec. 8. And be it further enacted, That whenever an election at which representatives or delegates in Congress are to be chosen shall be held in any city or town of twenty thousand inhabitants or upward, the marshal of the United States for the district in which said city or town is situated shall have power, and it shall be his duty, on the application, in writing, of a least two citizens residing in any such city or town, to appoint special deputy marshals, whose duty it shall be, when required as provided in this act, to aid and assist the supervisors of election in the verification of any list of persons made under the provisions of this act, who may have registered, or voted, or either; to attend in each election district or voting precinct at the times and places fixed for the registration of voters, and at times and places when and where said registration may by law be scrutinized, and the names of registered voters be marked for challenge; and also to attend, at all times for holding such elections, the polls of the election in such district or precinct. And the marshal and his general deputies, and such special deputies, shall have power, and it shall be the duty of such special deputies, to keep the peace, and support and protect the supervisors of elections in the discharge of their duties, preserve order at such places of registration and at such polls, prevent fraudulent registration and fraudulent voting thereat, or fraudulent conduct on the part of any officer of election, and immediately, either at said place of registration or polling-place, or elsewhere, and either before or after registering or voting, to arrest and take into custody, with or without process, any person who shall commit, or attempt or offer to commit, any of the acts or offences prohibited by this act, or the act hereby amended, or who shall commit any offence against the laws of the United States: Provided, That no person shall be arrested without process for any offence not committed in the presence of the marshal or his general or special deputies, or either of them, or of the supervisors of election, or either of them, and, for the purposes of arrest or the preservation of the peace, the supervisors of election, and each of them, shall, in the absence of the marshal's deputies, or if required to assist said deputies, have the same duties and powers as deputy marshals: And provided further, That no person shall, on the day or days of any such election, be arrested without process for any offence committed on the day or days of registration.

Sec. 9. And be it further enacted, That whenever any arrest is made under any provision of this act, the person so arrested shall forthwith be brought before a commissioner, judge, or court of the United States for examination of the offences alleged against him; and such commissioner, judge, or court shall proceed in respect thereto as authorized by law in case of crimes against the United States.

Sec. 10. And be it further enacted, That whoever, with or without any authority, power, or process, or pretended authority, power, or process, of any State, territorial, or municipal authority, shall obstruct, hinder, assault, or by bribery, solicitation, or otherwise, interfere with or prevent the supervisors of election, or either of them, or the marshal or his general or special deputies, or either of them, in the performance of any duty required of them, or either of them, or which he or they, or either of them, may be authorized to perform by any law of the United States, whether in the execution of process or otherwise, or shall by any of the means before mentioned hinder or prevent the free attendance and presence at such places of registration or at such polls of election, or full and free access and egress to and from any such place of registration or poll of election, or in going to and from such place of registration or poll of election, or to and from any room where any such registration or election or canvass of votes, or of making any returns or certificates thereof, may be had, or shall molest, interfere with, remove, or eject from any such place of registration or poll of election, or of canvassing votes cast thereat, or of making returns or certificates thereof, any supervisor of election, the marshal, or his general or special deputies, or either of them, or shall threaten, or attempt, or offer so to do, or shall refuse or neglect to aid and assist any supervisor of election, or the marshal or his general or special deputies, or either of them, in the performance of his or their duties when required by him or them, or either of them, to give such aid and assistance, he shall be guilty of a misdemeanor, and liable to instant arrest without process, and on conviction thereof shall be punished by imprisonment not more than two years, or by fine not more than three thousand dollars, or by both such fine and imprisonment, and shall pay the costs of the prosecution. Whoever shall, during the progress of any verification of any list of the persons who may have registered or voted, and which shall be had or made under any of the provisions of this act, refuse to answer, or refrain from answering, or answering shall knowingly give false information in respect to any inquiry lawfully made, such person shall be liable to arrest and imprisonment as for a misdemeanor, and on conviction thereof shall be punished by imprisonment not to exceed thirty days, or by fine not to exceed one hundred dollars, or by both such fine and imprisonment, and shall pay the costs of the prosecution.

Sec. 11. And be it further enacted, That whoever shall be appointed a supervisor of election or a special deputy marshal under the provisions of this act, and shall take the oath of office as such supervisor of election or such special deputy marshal, who shall thereafter neglect or refuse, without good and lawful excuse, to perform and discharge fully the duties, obligations, and requirements of such office until the expiration of the term for which he was appointed, shall not only be subject to removal from office with loss of all pay or emoluments, but shall be guilty of a misdemeanor, and on conviction shall be punished by imprisonment for not less than six months nor more than one year, or by fine not less than two hundred dollars and not exceeding five hundred dollars, or by both fine and imprisonment, and shall pay the costs of prosecution.

Sec. 12. And be it further enacted, That the marshal, or his general deputies, or such special deputies as shall be thereto specially empowered by him, in writing, and under his hand and seal, whenever he or his said general deputies or his special deputies, or either or any of them, shall be forcibly resisted in executing their duties under this act, or the act hereby amended, or shall, by violence, threats, or menaces, be prevented from executing such duties, or from arresting any person or persons who shall commit any offence for which said marshal or his general or his special deputies are authorized to make such arrest, are, and each of them is hereby, empowered to summon and call to his or their aid the bystanders or posse comitatus of his district.

Sec. 13. And be it further enacted, That it shall be the duty of each of the circuit courts of the United States in and for each judicial circuit, upon the recommendation in writing of the judge thereof, to name and appoint, on or before the first day of May, in the year eighteen hundred and seventy-one, and thereafter as vacancies may from any cause arise, from among the circuit court commissioners in and for each judicial district in each of said judicial circuits, one of such officers, who shall be known for the duties required of him under this act as the chief supervisor of elections of the judicial district in and for which he shall be a commissioner, and shall, so long as faithful and capable, discharge the duties of this act imposed, and whose duty it shall be to prepare and furnish all necessary books, forms, blanks, and instructions for the use and direction of the supervisors of election in the several cities and towns in their respective districts; to receive the applications of all parties for appointment to such positions; and upon the opening, as contemplated in this act, of the circuit court for the judicial circuit in which the commissioner so designated shall act, to present such application to the judge thereof, and furnish information to said judge in respect to the appointment by the said court of such supervisors of election; to require of the supervisors of election, where necessary, lists of the persons who may register and vote, or either, in their respective election districts or voting precincts, and to cause the names of those upon any such list whose right to register or vote shall be honestly doubted to be verified by proper inquiry and examination at the respective places by them assigned as their residences; and to receive, preserve, and file all oaths of office of said supervisors of election, and of all special deputy marshals appointed under the provisions of this act, and all certificates, returns, reports, and records of every kind and nature contemplated or made requisite under and by the provisions of this act, save where otherwise herein specially directed. And it is hereby made the duty of all United States marshals and commissioners who shall in any judicial district perform any duties under the provisions of this act, or the act hereby amended, relating to, concerning, or affecting the election of representatives or delegates in the Congress of the United States, to, from time to time, and with all due diligence, forward to the chief supervisor in and for their judicial district all complaints, examinations, and records pertaining thereto, and all oaths of office by them administered to any supervisor of election or special deputy marshal, in order that the same may be properly preserved and filed.

Sec. 14. And be it further enacted, That there shall be allowed and paid to each chief supervisor, for his services as such officer, the following compensation, apart from and in excess of all fees allowed by law for the performance of any duty as circuit court commissioner: For filing and caring for every return, report, record, document, or other paper required to be filed by him under any of the provisions of this act, ten cents; for affixing a seal to any paper, record, report, or instrument, twenty cents; for entering and indexing the records of his office, fifteen cents per folio; and for arranging and transmitting to Congress, as provided for in section seven of this act, any report, statement, record, return, or examination, for each folio, fifteen cents; and for any copy thereof, or of any paper on file, a like sum. And there shall be allowed and paid to each and every supervisor of election, and each and every special deputy marshal who shall be appointed and shall perform his duty under the provisions of this act, compensation at the rate of five dollars per day for each and every day he shall have actually been on duty, not exceeding ten days. And the fees of the said chief supervisors shall be paid at the treasury of the United States, such accounts to be made out, verified, examined, and certified as in the case of accounts of commissioners, save that the examination or certificate may be made by either the circuit or district judge.

Sec. 15. And be it further enacted, That the jurisdiction of the circuit court of the United States shall extend to all cases in law or equity arising under the provisions of this act or the act hereby amended; and if any person shall receive any injury to his person or property for or on account of any act by him done under any of the provisions of this act or the act hereby amended, he shall be entitled to maintain suit for damages therefor in the circuit court of the United States in the district wherein the party doing the injury may reside or shall be found.

Sec. 16. And be it further enacted, That in any case where suit or prosecution, civil or criminal, shall be commenced in a court of any State against any officer of the United States, or other person, for or on account of any act done under the provisions of this act, or under color thereof, or for or on account of any right, authority, or title set up or claimed by such officer or other person under any of said provisions, it shall be lawful for the defendant in such suit or prosecution, at any time before trial, upon a petition to the circuit court of the United States in and for the district in which the defendant shall have been served with process, setting forth the nature of said suit or prosecution, and verifying the said petition by affidavit, together with a certificate signed by an attorney or counselor at law of some court of record of the State in which such suit shall have been commenced, or of the United States, setting forth that as counsel for the petition[er] he has examined the proceedings against him, and has carefully inquired into all the matters set forth in the petition, and that he believes the same to be true, which petition, affidavit, and certificate shall be presented to the said circuit court, if in session, and, if not, to the clerk thereof at his office, and shall be filed in said office, and the cause shall thereupon be entered on the docket of said court, and shall be thereafter proceeded in as a cause originally commenced in that court; and it shall be the duty of the clerk of said court, if the suit was commenced in the court below by summons, to issue a writ of certiorari to the State court, requiring said court to send to the said circuit court the record and proceedings in said cause; or if it was commenced by capias, he shall issue a writ of habeas corpus cum causa, a duplicate of which said writ shall be delivered to the clerk of the State court, or left at his office by the marshal of the district, or his deputy, or some person duly authorized thereto; and thereupon it shall be the duty of the said State court to stay all further proceedings in such cause, and the said suit or prosecution, upon delivery of such process, or leaving the same as aforesaid, shall be deemed and taken to be moved to the said circuit court, and any further proceedings, trial, or judgment therein in the State court shall be wholly null and void; and any person, whether an attorney or officer of any State court, or otherwise, who shall thereafter take any steps, or in any manner proceed in the State court in any action so removed, shall be guilty of a misdemeanor, and liable to trial and punishment in the court to which the action shall have been removed, and upon conviction thereof shall be punished by imprisonment for not more or less than six months nor more than one year, or by fine not less than five hundred nor more than one thousand dollars, or by both such fine and imprisonment, and shall in addition thereto be amenable to the said court to which said action shall have been removed as for a contempt; and if the defendant in any such suit be in actual custody on mesne process therein, it shall be the duty of the marshal, by virtue of the writ of habeas corpus cum causa, to take the body of the defendant into custody, to be dealt with in the said cause according to the rules of law and the order of the circuit court, or of any judge thereof in vacation. And all attachments made and all bail or other security given upon such suit or prosecution shall be and continue in like force and effect as if the same suit or prosecution had proceeded to final judgment and execution in the State court. And if upon the removal of any such suit or prosecution it shall be made to appear to the said circuit court that no copy of the record and proceedings therein in the State court can be obtained, it shall be lawful for said circuit court to allow and require the plaintiff to proceed de novo, and to file a declaration of his cause of action, and the parties may thereupon proceed as in actions originally brought in said circuit court; and on failure of so proceeding judgment of non prosequitur may be rendered against the plaintiff, with costs for the defendant.

Sec. 17. And be it further enacted, That in any case in which any party is or may be by law entitled to copies of the record and proceedings in any suit or prosecution in any State court to be used in any court of the United States, if the clerk of said State court, upon demand and payment or tender of the legal fees, refuse or neglect to deliver to such party certified copies of such record and proceedings, the court of the United States in which such record and proceedings may be needed, on proof by affidavit that the clerk of such State court has refused or neglected to deliver copies thereof on demand as aforesaid, may direct and allow such record to be supplied by affidavit or otherwise, as the circumstances of the case may require and allow; and thereupon such proceeding, trial, and judgment may be had in the said court of the United States, and all such processes awarded, as if certified copies of such records and proceedings had been regularly before the said court; and hereafter in all civil actions in the courts of the United States either party thereto may notice the same for trial.

Sec. 18. And be it further enacted, That sections five and six of the act of the Congress of the United States approved July fourteen, eighteen hundred and seventy, and entitled "An act to amend the naturalization laws, and to punish crimes against the same," be, and the same are hereby, repealed; but this repeal shall not affect any proceeding or prosecution now pending for any offence under said sections, or either of them, or any question which may arise therein respecting the appointment of the persons in said sections, or either of them, provided for, or the powers, duties, or obligations of such persons.

Sec. 19. And be it further enacted, That all votes for representatives in Congress shall hereafter be by written or printed ballot, any law of any State to the contrary notwithstanding; and all votes received or recorded contrary to the provisions of this section shall be of none effect.

Approved, February 28, 1871.

A Proclamation by the President of the United States of America. No. 17. March 24, 1871.

Whereas it is provided in the Constitution of the United States that the United States shall protect every State in this Union, on application of the legislature, or of the executive, (when the legislature cannot be convened,) against domestic violence;

And whereas it is provided in the laws of the United States that, in all cases of insurrection in any State, or of obstruction to the laws thereof, it shall be lawful for the President of the United States, on application of the legislature of such State, or of the executive, (when the legislature cannot be convened) to call forth the militia of any other State or States, or to employ such part of the land and naval force as shall be judged necessary for the purpose of suppressing such insurrection, or of causing the laws to be duly executed;

And whereas I have received information that combinations of armed men, unauthorized by law, are now disturbing the peace and safety of the citizens of the State of South Carolina, and committing acts of violence in said State of a character and to an extent which render the power of the State and its officers unequal to the task of protecting life and property, and securing public order therein;

An whereas the legislature of said State is not now in session and cannot be convened in time to meet the present emergency, and the executive of said State has therefore made application to me for such part of the military force of the United States as may be necessary and adequate to protect said State and the citizens thereof against the domestic violence hereinbefore mentioned, and to enforce the due execution of the laws;

And whereas the laws of the United States require that, whenever it may be necessary, in the judgment of the President, to use the military force for the purpose aforesaid, he shall forthwith, by proclamation, command such insurgents to disperse and retire peaceably to their respective abodes within a limited time:

Now, therefore, I, Ulysses S. Grant, President of the United States, do hereby command the persons composing the unlawful combinations aforesaid to disperse and retire peaceably to their respective abodes within twenty days from this date.

In witness whereof, I have hereunto set my hand and caused the seal of the United States to be affixed.

Done at the city of Washington, this twenty-fourth day [L. S.] of March, in the year of our Lord eighteen hundred and seventy-one, and of the Independence of the United States the ninety-fifth.

U.S. GRANT.

By the President:
Hamilton Fish, Secretary of State.

An Act to enforce the provisions of the Fourteenth Amendment to the Constitution of the United States, and for other purposes. April 20, 1871

Be it enacted by the Senate and House of Representatives of the United States of America in Congress assembled, That any person who, under color of any law, statute, ordinance, regulation, custom, or usage of any State, shall subject, or cause to be subjected, any person within the jurisdiction of the United States to the deprivation of any rights, privileges, or immunities secured by the Constitution of the United States, shall, any such law, statute, ordinance, regulation, custom, or usage of the State to the contrary notwithstanding, be liable to the party injured in, any action at law, suit in equity, or other proper proceeding for redress; such proceeding to be prosecuted in the several district or circuit courts of the United States, with and subject to the same rights of appeal, review upon error, and other remedies provided in like cases in such courts, under the provisions of the act of the ninth of April, eighteen hundred and sixty-six, entitled "An act to protect all persons in the United States in their civil rights, and to furnish the means of their vindication"; and the other remedial laws of the United States which are in their nature applicable in such cases.

Sec. 2. That if two or more persons within any State or Territory of the United States shall conspire together to overthrow, or to put down, or to destroy by force the government of the United States, or to levy war against the United States, or to oppose by force the authority of the government of the United States, or by force, intimidation, or threat to prevent, hinder, or delay the execution of any law of the United States, or by force to seize, take, or possess any property of the United States contrary to the authority thereof, or by force, intimidation, or threat to prevent any person from accepting or holding any office or trust or place of confidence under the United States, or from discharging the duties thereof, or by force, intimidation, or threat to induce any officer of the United States to leave any State, district, or place where his duties as such officer might lawfully be performed, or to injure him in his person or property on account of his lawful discharge of the duties of his office, or to injure his person while engaged in the lawful discharge of the duties of his office, or to injure his property so as to molest, interrupt, hinder, or impede him in the discharge of his official duty, or by force, intimidation, or threat to deter any party or witness in any court of the United States from attending such court, or from testifying in any matter pending in such court fully, freely, and truthfully, or to injure any such party or witness in his person or property on account of his having so attended or testified, or by force, intimidation, or threat to influence the verdict, presentment, or indictment, of any juror or grand juror in any court of the United States, or to injure such juror in his person or property on account of any verdict, presentment, or indictment lawfully assented to by him, or on account of his being or having been such juror, or shall conspire together, or go in disguise upon the public highway or upon the premises of another for the purpose, either directly or indirectly, of depriving any person or any class of persons of the equal protection of the laws, or of equal privileges or immunities under the laws, or for the purpose of preventing or hindering the constituted authorities of any State from giving or securing to all persons within such State the equal protection of the laws, or shall conspire together for the purpose of in any manner impeding, hindering, obstructing, or defeating the due course of justice in any State or Territory, with intent to deny to any citizen of the United States the due and equal protection of the laws, or to injure any person in his person or his property for lawfully enforcing the right of any person or class of persons to the equal protection of the laws, or by force, intimidation, or threat to prevent any citizen of the United States lawfully entitled to vote from giving his support or advocacy in a lawful manner towards or in favor of the election of any lawfully qualified person as an elector of President or Vice-President of the United States, or as member of the Congress of the United States, or to injure any such citizen in his person or property on account of such support or advocacy, each and every person so offending shall be deemed guilty of a high crime, and, upon conviction thereof in any district or circuit court of the United States or district or supreme court of any Territory of the United States having jurisdiction of similar offences, shall be punished by a fine not less than five hundred nor more than five thousand dollars, or by imprisonment, with or without hard labor, as the court may determine, for a period of not less than six months nor more than six years, as the court may determine, or both such fine and imprisonment as the court shall determine. And if any one or more persons engaged in any such conspiracy shall do, or cause to be done, any act in furtherance of the object of such conspiracy, whereby any person shall be injured in his person or property, or deprived of having and exercising any right or privilege of a citizen of the United States, the person so injured or deprived of such rights and privileges may have and maintain an action for the recovery of damages occasioned by such injury or deprived of rights and privileges against any one or more of the persons engaged in such conspiracy, such action to be prosecuted in the proper district or circuit court of the United States, with and subject to the same rights of appeal, review upon error, and other remedies provided in like cases in such courts under the provisions of the act of April ninth, eighteen hundred and sixty-six, entitled "An act to protect all persons in the United States in their civil rights, and to furnish the means of their vindication."

Sec. 3. That in all cases where insurrection, domestic violence, unlawful combinations, or conspiracies in any State shall so obstruct or hinder the execution of the laws thereof, and of the United States, as to deprive any portion or class of the people of such State of any of the rights, privileges, or immunities, or protection, named in the Constitution and secured by this act, and the constituted authorities of such State shall either be unable to protect, or shall, from any cause, fail in or refuse protection of the people in such rights, such facts shall be deemed a denial by such State of the equal protection of the laws to which they are entitled under the Constitution of the United States; and in all such cases, or whenever any such insurrection, violence, unlawful combination, or conspiracy shall oppose or obstruct the laws of the United States or the due execution thereof, or impede or obstruct the due course of justice under the same, it shall be lawful for the President, and it shall be his duty to take such measures, by the employment of the militia or the land and naval forces of the United States, or of either, or by other means, as he may deem necessary for the suppression of such insurrection, domestic violence, or combinations; and any person who shall be arrested under the provisions of this and the preceding section shall be delivered to the marshal of the proper district, to be dealt with according to law.

Sec. 4. That whenever in any State or part of a State the unlawful combinations named in the preceding section of this act shall be organized and armed, and so numerous and powerful as to be able, by violence, to either overthrow or set at defiance the constituted authorities of such State, and of the United States within such State, or when the constituted authorities are in complicity with, or shall connive at the unlawful purposes of, such powerful and armed combinations; and whenever, by reason of either or all of the causes aforesaid, the conviction of such offenders and preservation of the public safety shall become in such district impracticable, in every such case such combinations shall be deemed a rebellion against the government of the United States, and during the continuance of such rebellion, and within the limits of the district which shall be under the sway thereof, such limits to be prescribed by proclamation, it shall be lawful for the President of the United States, when in his judgment the public safety shall require it, to suspend the privileges of the writ of habeas corpus, to the end that such rebellion may be overthrown: Provided, That all the provisions of the second section of an act entitled "An act relating to habeas corpus, and regulating judicial proceedings in certain cases," approved March third, eighteen hundred and sixty-three, which relate to the discharge of prisoners other than prisoners of war, and to the penalty for refusing to obey the order of the court, shall be in full force so far as the same are applicable to the provisions of this section: Provided further, That the President shall first have made proclamation, as now provided by law, commanding such insurgents to disperse: And provided also, That the provisions of this section shall not be in force after the end of the next regular session of Congress.

Sec. 5. That no person shall be a grand or petit juror in any court of the

United States upon any inquiry, hearing, or trial of any suit, proceedings, or prosecution based upon or arising under the provisions of this act who shall, in the judgment of the court, be in complicity with any such combination or conspiracy; and every such juror shall, before entering upon any such inquiry, hearing, or trial, take and subscribe an oath in open court that he has never, directly or indirectly, counseled, advised, or voluntarily aided any such combination or conspiracy; and each and every person who shall take this oath, and shall therein swear falsely, shall be guilty of perjury, and shall be subject to the pains and penalties declared against that crime, and the first section of the act entitled, "An act defining additional causes of challenges and prescribing an additional oath for grand and petit jurors in the United States courts," approved June seventeenth, eighteen hundred and sixty-two, be, and the same is hereby, repealed.

Sec. 6. That any person or persons, having knowledge that any of the wrongs conspired to be done and mentioned in the second section of this act are about to be committed, and having power to prevent or aid in preventing the same, shall neglect, or refuse so to do, and such wrongful act shall be committed, such person or persons shall be liable to the person injured, or his legal representatives, for all damages caused by any such wrongful act which such first-named person or persons by reasonable diligence could have prevented; and such damages may be recovered in an action on the case in the proper circuit court of the United States, and any number of persons guilty of such wrongful neglect or refusal may be joined as defendants in such action: Provided, That such action shall be commenced within one year after such cause of action shall have accrued; and if the death of any person shall be caused by any such wrongful act and neglect, the legal representatives of such deceased person shall have such action therefor, and may recover not exceeding five thousand dollars damages therein, for the benefit of the widow of such deceased person, if any there be, or if there be no widow, for the benefit of the next of kin of such deceased person.

Sec. 7. That nothing herein contained shall be construed to supersede or repeal any former act or law except so far as the same may be repugnant thereto; and any offences heretofore committed against the tenor of any former act shall be prosecuted, and any proceeding already commenced for the prosecution thereof shall be continued and completed, the same as if this act had not been passed, except so far as the provisions of this act may go to sustain and validate such proceedings.

Approved, April 20, 1871.

A Proclamation by the President of the United States of America. No. 2. May 3, 1871.

The act of Congress, entitled "An act to enforce the provisions of the fourteenth amendment to the Constitution of the United States, and for other purposes," approved April 20, A.D. 1871, being a law of extraordinary public importance, I consider it my duty to issue this my proclamation calling the attention of the people of the United States thereto; enjoining upon all good citizens and especially upon all public officers, to be zealous in the enforcement thereof, and warning all persons to abstain from committing any of the acts thereby prohibited.

This law of Congress applies to all parts of the United States, and will be enforced everywhere, to the extent of the powers vested in the Executive. But inasmuch as the necessity therefor is well known to have been caused chiefly by the persistent violations of the rights of citizens of the United States, by combinations of lawless and disaffected persons in certain localities lately the theatre of insurrection and military conflict, I do particularly exhort the people of those parts of the country to suppress all such combinations by their own voluntary efforts through the agency of local laws, and to maintain the rights of all citizens of the United States, and to secure to all such citizens the equal protection of the laws.

Fully sensible of the responsibility imposed upon the Executive by the act of Congress to which public attention is now called, and reluctant to call into exercise any of the extraordinary powers thereby conferred upon me, except in cases of imperative necessity, I do, nevertheless, deem it my duty to make known that I will not hesitate to exhaust the powers thus vested in the Executive, whenever and wherever it shall become necessary to do so for the purpose of securing to all citizens of the United States the peaceful enjoyment of the rights guaranteed to them by the Constitution and laws.

It is my earnest wish that peace and cheerful obedience to law may prevail throughout the land, and that all traces of our late unhappy civil strife may be speedily removed. These ends can be easily reached by acquiescence in the results of the conflict, now written in our Constitution, and by the due and proper enforcement of equal, just, and impartial laws in every part of our country.

The failure of local communities to furnish such means for the attainment of results so earnestly desired imposes upon the National Government the duty of putting forth all its energies for the protection of its citizens of every race and color, and for the restoration of peace and order throughout the entire country.

In testimony whereof, I have hereunto set my hand and caused the seal of the United States to be affixed.

Done at the city of Washington, this third day of May, [Seal.] in the year of our Lord one thousand eight hundred and seventy-one, and of the Independence of the United States the ninety-fifth.

U.S. GRANT.

By the President:

Hamilton Fish, Secretary of State.

A Proclamation by the President of the United States of America. No. 3. October 12, 1871.

Whereas unlawful combinations and conspiracies have long existed and do still exist in the State of South Carolina, for the purpose of depriving certain portions and classes of people of that State of the rights, privileges, immunities, and protection named in the Constitution of the United States, and secured by the act of Congress approved April the twentieth, one thousand eight hundred and seventy-one, entitled "An act to enforce the provisions of the fourteenth amendment to the Constitution of the United States;"

And whereas in certain parts of said State — to wit, in the counties of Spartansburg, York, Marion, Chester, Laurens, Newberry, Fairfield, Lancaster, and Chesterfield — such combinations and conspiracies do so obstruct and hinder the execution of the laws of said State and of the United States as to deprive the people aforesaid of the rights, privileges, immunities, and protection aforesaid, and do oppose and obstruct the laws of the United States and their due execution, and impede and obstruct the due course of justice under the same;

And whereas the constituted authorities of said State are unable to protect the people aforesaid in such rights within the said counties;

And whereas the combinations and conspiracies aforesaid; within the counties aforesaid, are organized and armed, and are so numerous and powerful as to be able to defy the constituted authorities of said State and of the United States within the said State, and by reason of said causes the conviction of such offenders and the preservation of the public peace and safety have become impracticable in said counties;

Now, therefore, I, Ulysses S. Grant, President of the United States of

America, do hereby command all persons composing the unlawful combinations and conspiracies aforesaid to disperse and to retire peaceably to their homes within five days of the date hereof, and to deliver, either to the marshal of the United States for the district of South Carolina, or to any of his deputies, or to any military officer of the United States within said counties, all arms, ammunition, uniforms, disguises, and other means and implements, used, kept, possessed, or controlled by them, for carrying out the unlawful purposes for which the combinations and conspiracies are organized.

In witness whereof I have hereunto set my hand, and caused the seal of the United States to be affixed.

Done at the city of Washington this twelfth day of [Seal.] October, in the year of our Lord one thousand eight hundred and seventy-one, and of the Independence of the United States of America the ninety-sixth.

U.S. GRANT.

By the President:
Hamilton Fish, Secretary of State.

A Proclamation by the President of the United States of America. No. 4. October 17, 1871.

Whereas by an act of Congress, entitled "An act to enforce the provisions of the fourteenth amendment to the Constitution of the United States, and for other purposes," approved the twentieth day of April, anno Domini one thousand eight hundred and seventy-one, power is given to the President of the United States, when, in his judgment, the public safety shall require it, to suspend the privileges of the writ of habeas corpus in any State or part of a State whenever combinations and conspiracies exists in such State or part of a State, for the purpose of depriving any portion or class of the people of such State of the rights, privileges, immunities, and protection named in the Constitution of the United States, and secured by the act of Congress aforesaid; and whenever such combinations and conspiracies do so obstruct and hinder the execution of the laws of any such State, and of the United States, as to deprive the people aforesaid of the rights, privileges, immunities, and protection aforesaid, and do oppose and obstruct the laws of the United States and their due execution, and impede and obstruct the due course of justice under the same; and whenever such combinations shall be organized and armed, and so numerous and powerful as to be able by violence either to overthrow or to set at defiance the constituted authorities of said State and of the United States within such State; and whenever, by reason of said causes, the conviction of such offenders and the preservation of the public peace shall become in such State or part of a State impracticable;

And whereas such unlawful combinations and conspiracies for the purposes aforesaid are declared by the act of Congress aforesaid to be rebellion against the Government of the United States;

And whereas by said act of Congress it is provided that before the President shall suspend the privileges of the writ of habeas corpus, he shall first have made proclamation commanding such insurgents to disperse;

And whereas on the twelfth day of the present month of October the President of the United States did issue his proclamation, reciting therein, among other things, that such combinations and conspiracies did then exist in the counties of Spartansburg, York, Marion, Chester, Laurens, Newberry, Fairfield, Lancaster, and Chesterfield, in the State of South Carolina, and commanding thereby all persons composing such unlawful combinations and conspiracies to disperse and retire peaceably to their homes within five days from the date thereof, and to deliver either to the marshal of the United States for the district of South Carolina, or to any of his deputies, or to any military officer of the United States within said counties, all arms, ammunition, uniforms, disguises, and other means and implements used, kept, possessed, or controlled by them for carrying out the unlawful purposes for which the said combinations and conspiracies are organized;

And whereas the insurgents engaged in such unlawful combinations and conspiracies within the counties aforesaid have not dispersed and retired peaceably to their respective homes, and have not delivered to the marshal of the United States, or to any of his deputies, or to any military officer of the United States within said counties, all arms, ammunition, uniforms, disguises, and other means and implements used, kept, possessed, or controlled by them for carrying out the unlawful purposes for which the combinations and conspiracies are organized, as commanded by said proclamation, but do still persist in the unlawful combinations and conspiracies aforesaid:

Now, therefore, I, Ulysses S. Grant, President of the United States of America, by virtue of the authority vested in me by the Constitution of the United States, and the act of Congress aforesaid, do hereby declare that, in my judgment, the public safety especially requires that the privileges of the writ of habeas corpus be suspended to the end that such rebellion may be overthrown, and do hereby suspend the privileges of the writ of habeas corpus within the counties of Spartansburg, York, Marion, Chester, Laurens, Newberry, Fairfield, Lancaster, and Chesterfield, in said State of South

Carolina, in respect to all persons arrested by the marshal of the United States for the said district of South Carolina, or by any of his deputies, or by any military officer of the United States, or by any soldier or citizen acting under the orders of said marshal, deputy, or such military officer within any one of said counties, charges with any violation of the act of Congress aforesaid during the continuance of such rebellion.

In witness whereof I have hereunto, set my hand, and caused the seal of the United States to be affixed.

Done at the city of Washington this seventeenth day of [Seal.] October, in the year of our Lord one thousand eight hundred and seventy-one, and of the Independence of the United States of America the ninety-sixth.

U.S. GRANT.

By the President:

J. C. Bancroft Davis, Acting Secretary of State.

A Proclamation by the President of the United States of America. No. 6. November 3, 1871.

Whereas in my proclamation of the twelfth day of October, in the year eighteen hundred and seventy-one, it was recited that certain unlawful combinations and conspiracies existed in certain counties in the State of South Carolina for the purpose of depriving certain portions and classes of the people of that State of the rights, privileges, and immunities and protection named in the Constitution of the United States and secured by the act of Congress, approved April the twentieth, one thousand eight hundred and seventy-one, entitled "An act to enforce the provisions of the fourteenth amendment to the Constitution of the United States," and the persons composing such combinations and conspiracies were commanded to disperse and to retire peaceably to their homes within five days from said date;

And whereas by my proclamation of the seventeenth day of October, in the year eighteen hundred and seventy-one, the privileges of the writ of habeas corpus were suspended in the counties named in said proclamation;

And whereas the county of Marion was named in said proclamations as one of the counties in which said unlawful combinations and conspiracies for the purposes aforesaid existed, and in which the privileges of the writ of habeas corpus were suspended;

And whereas it has been ascertained that in said county of Marion said combinations and conspiracies do not exist to the extent recited in said proclamations;

And whereas it has been ascertained that the unlawful combinations and conspiracies of the character and to the extent and for the purposes described in said proclamations do exist in the county of Union in said State:

Now, therefore, I, Ulysses S. Grant, President of the United States of America, do hereby revoke, as to the said county of Marion, the suspension of the privileges of the writ of habeas corpus directed in my said proclamation of the seventeenth day of October, eighteen hundred and seventy-one;

And I do hereby command all persons in the said county of Union composing the unlawful combinations and conspiracies aforesaid to disperse and to retire peaceably to their homes within five days of the date hereof, and to deliver either to the marshal of the United States for the district of South Carolina, or to any of his deputies, or to any military officer of the United States within said county, all arms, ammunitions, uniforms, disguises, and other means and implements used, kept, possessed, or controlled by them for carrying out the unlawful purposes for which the combinations and conspiracies are organized.

In witness whereof I have hereunto set my hand, and caused the seal of the United States to be affixed.

Done at the city of Washington this third day of [Seal.] November, in the year of our Lord one thousand eight hundred and seventy-one, and of the Independence of the United States of America the ninety-sixth.

U.S. GRANT.

By the President:
Hamilton Fish, Secretary of State.

A Proclamation by the President of the United States of America. No. 7. November 10, 1871.

Whereas by an act of Congress, entitled "An act to enforce the provisions of the fourteenth amendment to the Constitution of the United States, and for other purposes," approved the twentieth day of April, anno Domini one thousand eight hundred and seventy-one, power is given to the President of the United States, when, in his judgment, the public safety shall require it, to suspend the writ of habeas corpus in any State or part of a State, whenever combinations and conspiracies exist in such State or part of a State for the purpose of depriving any portion or class of the people of such State of the rights, privileges, immunities, and protection named in the Constitution of the United States, and secured by the act of Congress aforesaid; and whenever such combinations and conspiracies do so obstruct and hinder the execution of the laws of any such State, and of the United States, as to deprive the people aforesaid of the rights, privileges, immunities, and protection aforesaid, and do oppose and obstruct the laws of the United States and their due execution, and impede and obstruct the due course of justice under the same; and whenever such combinations shall be organized and armed, and so numerous and powerful as to be able by violence either to overthrow or to set at defiance the constituted authorities of said State and of the United States within such State; and whenever, by reason of said causes, the conviction of such offenders and the preservation of the public peace shall become in such State or part of a State impracticable:

And whereas such unlawful combinations and conspiracies for the purposes aforesaid are declared by the act of Congress aforesaid to be rebellion against the Government of the United States;

And whereas, by said act of Congress, it is provided that, before the President shall suspend the privileges of the writ of habeas corpus, he shall first have made proclamation commanding such insurgents to disperse;

And whereas on the third day of the present month of November the President of the United States did issue his proclamation, reciting therein, among other things, that such combinations and conspiracies did then exist in the county of Union, in the State of South Carolina, and commanding thereby all persons composing such unlawful combinations and conspiracies to disperse and retire peaceably to their homes within five days from the date thereof, and to deliver either to the marshal of the United States for the district of South Carolina, or to any of his deputies, or to any military officer of the United States within said county, all arms, ammunition, uniforms, disguises, and other means and implements used, kept, possessed, or controlled by them for carrying out the unlawful purposes for which the said combinations and conspiracies are organized;

And whereas the insurgents engaged in such unlawful combinations and conspiracies within the county aforesaid have not dispersed and retired peaceably to their respective homes, and have not delivered to the marshals of the United States, or to any of his deputies, or to any military officer of the United States within said county, all arms, ammunition, uniforms, disguises, and other means and implements used, kept, possessed, or controlled by them for carrying out the unlawful purposes for which the combinations and conspiracies are organized, as commanded by said proclamation, but do still persist in the unlawful combinations and conspiracies aforesaid:

Now, therefore, I, Ulysses S. Grant, President of the United States of America, by virtue of the authority vested in me by the Constitution of the United States and the act of Congress aforesaid, do hereby declare that, in my judgment, the public safety especially requires that the privileges of the writ of habeas corpus be suspended, to the end that such rebellion may be overthrown, and do hereby suspend the privileges of the writ of habeas corpus within the county of Union, in said State of South Carolina, in respect to all persons arrested by the marshal of the United States for the said district of South Carolina, or by any of his deputies, or by any military officer of the United States, or by any soldier or citizen acting under the orders of said marshal, deputy, or such military officer within said county, charged with any violation of the act of Congress aforesaid during the continuance of such rebellion.

In witness whereof I have hereunto set my hand, and caused the seal of the United States to be affixed.

Done at the city of Washington this tenth day of [Seal.] November, in the year of our Lord one thousand eight hundred and seventy-one, and of the Independence of the United States of America the ninety-sixth.

U.S. GRANT.

By the President:
Hamilton Fish, Secretary of State.

An Act to protect all citizens in their civil and legal rights. March 1, 1875.

Whereas, it is essential to just government we recognize the equality of all men before the law, and hold that it is the duty of government in its dealings with the people to mete out equal and exact justice to all, of whatever nativity, race, color, or persuasion, religious or political; and it being the appropriate object of legislation to enact great fundamental principles into law: Therefore,

Be it enacted by the Senate and House of Representatives of the United States of America in Congress assembled, That all persons within the jurisdiction of the United States shall be entitled to the full and equal enjoyment of the accommodations, advantages, facilities, and privileges of inns, public conveyances on land or water, theaters, and other places of public amusement; subject only to the conditions and limitations established by law, and applicable alike to citizens of every race and color, regardless of any previous condition of servitude.

Sec. 2. That any person who shall violate the foregoing section by denying to any citizen, except for reasons by law applicable to citizens of every race and color, and regardless of any previous condition of servitude, the full enjoyment of any of the accommodations, advantages, facilities, or privileges in said section enumerated, or by aiding or inciting such denial, shall, for every such offense, forfeit and pay the sum of five hundred dollars to the person aggrieved thereby, to be recovered in an action of debt, with full costs; and shall also, for every such offense, be deemed guilty of a misdemeanor, and, upon conviction thereof, shall be fined not less than five hundred nor more than one thousand dollars, or shall be imprisoned not less than thirty days nor more than one year: Provided, That all persons may elect to sue for the penalty aforesaid or to proceed under their rights at common law and by State statutes; and having so elected to proceed in the one mode or the other, their right to proceed in the other jurisdiction shall be barred. But this proviso shall not apply to criminal proceedings, either under this act or the criminal law of any State: And provided further, That a judgment for the penalty in favor of the party aggrieved, or a judgment upon an indictment, shall be a bar to either prosecution respectively.

Sec. 3. That the district and circuit courts of the United States shall have, exclusively of the courts of the several States, cognizance of all crimes and offenses against, and violations of, the provisions of this act; and actions for the penalty given by the preceding section may be prosecuted in the territorial, district, or circuit courts of the United States wherever the defendant may be found, without regard to the other party; and the district attorneys, marshals, and deputy marshals of the United States, and commissioners appointed by the circuit and territorial courts of the United States, with powers of arresting and imprisoning or bailing offenders against the laws of the United States, are hereby specially authorized and required to institute proceedings against every person who shall violate the provisions of this act, and cause him to be arrested and imprisoned or bailed, as the case may be, for trial before such court of the United States, or territorial court, as by law has cognizance of the offense, except in respect of the right of action accruing to the person aggrieved; and such district attorneys shall cause such proceedings to be prosecuted to their termination as in other cases: Provided, That nothing contained in this section shall be construed to deny or defeat any right of civil action accruing to any person, whether by reason of this act or otherwise; and any district attorney who shall willfully fail to institute and prosecute the proceedings herein required, shall, for every such offense, forfeit and pay the sum of five hundred dollars to the person aggrieved thereby, to be recovered by an action of debt, with full costs, and shall, on conviction thereof, be deemed guilty of a misdemeanor, and be fined not less than one thousand nor more than five thousand dollars: And provided further, That a judgment for the penalty in favor of the party aggrieved against any such district attorney, or a judgment upon an indictment against any such district attorney, shall be a bar to either prosecution respectively.

Sec. 4. That no citizen possessing all other qualifications which are or may be prescribed by law shall be disqualified for service as grand or petit juror in any court of the United States, or of any State, on account of race, color, or previous condition of servitude; and any officer or other person charged with any duty in the selection or summoning of jurors who shall exclude or fail to summon any citizen for the cause aforesaid shall, on conviction thereof, be deemed guilty of a misdemeanor, and be fined not more than five thousand dollars.

Sec. 5. That all cases arising under the provisions of this act in the courts of the United States shall be reviewable by the Supreme Court of the United States, without regard to the sum in controversy, under the same provisions and regulations as are now provided by the law for the review of other causes in said court.

Approved, March 1, 1875.

Appendix A: Laws Providing for a Republican Form of Government for the Rebel States*

EXECUTIVE ORDER, EXECUTIVE CHAMBER, WASHINGTON CITY. NO. 4. MAY 9, 1865

Ordered:

First. That all acts and proceedings of the political, military, and civil organizations which have been in a state of insurrection and rebellion, within the State of Virginia, against the authority and laws of the United States and of which Jefferson Davis, John Letcher, and William Smith, were late and respective chiefs, are declared null and void. All persons who shall exercise, claim, pretend, or attempt to exercise any political, military, or civil power, authority, or right, by, through or under Jefferson Davis, late of the city of Richmond, and his confederates, or under John Letcher, or William Smith, and their confederates, or under any pretended political, military, or civil commission or authority issued by them, or either of them, since the 17th day of April 1861, shall be deemed and taken as in rebellion against the United States, and shall be dealt with accordingly.

Second. That the Secretary of State proceed to put in force all laws of the United States, the administration whereof belongs to the Department of State, applicable to the geographical limits aforesaid.

Third. That the Secretary of the Treasury proceed, without delay, to nominate for appointment, assessors of taxes and collectors of customs and internal revenue, and such other officers of the Treasury Department as are authorized by law, and shall put in execution the revenue laws of the United

*See also the proclamation of July 8, 1864, in the main body of this book.

States within the geographical limits aforesaid. In making appointments the preference shall be given to qualified loyal persons residing within the districts where their respective duties are to be performed. But if suitable persons shall not be found, residents of the districts, then persons residing in other states or districts shall be appointed.

Fourth. That the Postmaster-General shall proceed to establish post-offices and post-routes, and put into execution the postal laws of the United States within the said state, giving to loyal residents the preference of appointment; but if suitable persons are not found, then to appoint agents, &c., from other states.

Fifth. That the district judge of said district proceed to hold courts within said state, in accordance with the provisions of the act of congress. The Attorney-General will instruct the proper officers to libel, and bring judgment, confiscation, and sale, property subject to confiscation, and enforce the administration of justice with said state, in all matters civil and criminal within the cognizance and jurisdiction of the federal courts.

Sixth. That the Secretary of War assign such assistant provost-marshal general and such provost-marshals in each district of said state as he may deem necessary.

Seventh. The Secretary of the Navy will take possession of all public property belonging to the Navy Department within said geographical limits, and put in operation all acts of congress in relation to naval affairs having application to the said state.

Eight. The Secretary of the Interior will also put in force the laws relating to the Department of the Interior.

Ninth. That to carry into effect the guarantee by the federal constitution of a republican form of state government, and afford the advantage and security of domestic laws, as well as to complete the reestablishment of the authority and laws of the United States, and the full and complete restoration of peace within the limits aforesaid, Francis H. Pierpont, governor of the State of Virginia, will be aided by the federal government, so far as may be necessary, in the lawful measures which he may take for the extension and administration of the state government throughout the geographical limits of said state.

In testimony whereof, I have hereunto set my hand, and [L.S.] caused the seal of the United States to be affixed.

ANDREW JOHNSON.

By the President:

W. Hunter, Acting Secretary of State.

A Proclamation by the President of the United States of America. No. 38. May 29, 1865

Whereas the fourth section of the fourth article of the Constitution of the United States declares that the United States shall guarantee to every state in the Union a republican form of government, and shall protect each of them against invasion and domestic violence; and whereas the President of the United States is, by the constitution, made commander-in-chief of the army and navy, as well as chief executive officer of the United States, and is bound by solemn oath faithfully to execute the office of the President of the United States, and to take care that the laws be faithfully executed; and whereas the rebellion, which has been waged by a portion of the people of the United States against the properly constituted authorities of the government thereof, in the most violent and revolting form, but whose organized and armed forces have now been almost entirely overcome, has, in its revolutionary progress deprived the people of the State of North Carolina and all civil government; as whereas it becomes necessary and proper to carry out and enforce the obligations of the United States to the people of North Carolina, in securing them in the enjoyment of a republican form of government:

Now, therefore, in obedience to the high and solemn duties imposed upon me by the Constitution of the United States, and for the purpose of enabling the loyal people of said state to organize a state government, whereby justice may be established, domestic tranquility insured, and loyal citizens protected in all their rights of life, liberty, and property, I, Andrew Johnson, President of the United States, and commander-in-chief of the army and navy of the United States, do hereby appoint William W. Holden provisional governor of the State of North Carolina, whose duty it shall be, at the earliest practicable period, to prescribe such rules and regulations as may be necessary and proper for convening a convention, composed of delegates to be chosen by that portion of the people of said state who are loyal to the United States, and no others, for the purpose of altering or amending the constitution thereof; and with authority to exercise, within the limits of said state, all the powers necessary and proper to enable such loyal people of the State of North Carolina to restore said state to its constitutional relations to the federal government, and to present such a republican form of state government as will entitle the state to the guarantee of the United States therefor, and its people to protection by the United States against invasion, insurrection, and domestic violence; Provided that, in any election that may be hereafter held for choosing delegates to any state convention as aforesaid, no person shall be qualified as an elector, or shall be eligible as a member of such convention, unless he shall have previously taken and subscribed the oath of amnesty, as set forth in the President's Proclamation of May 29, A.D. 1865, and is a voter qualified as prescribed by the constitution and laws of the State of North Carolina in force immediately before the 20th day of May, A.D. 1861, the date of the so-called ordinance of secession; and the said convention, when convened, or the legislature that may be thereafter assembled, will prescribe the qualification of electors, and the eligibility of persons to hold office under the constitution and laws of the state, — a power the people of the several states composing the Federal Union have rightfully exercised from the origin of the government to the present time.

And I do hereby direct —

First. That the military commander of the department, and all officers and persons in the military and naval service, aid and assist the said provisional governor in carrying into effect this Proclamation, and they are enjoined to abstain from, in any way, hindering, impeding, or discouraging the loyal people from organization of a state government as herein authorized.

Second. That the Secretary of State proceed to put in force all laws of the United States, the administration whereof belongs to the State Department, applicable to the geographical limits aforesaid.

Third. That the Secretary of the Treasury proceed to nominate for appointment assessors of taxes, and collectors of customs and internal revenue, and such other officers of the Treasury Department as are authorized by law, and put in execution the revenue laws of the United States within the geographical limits aforesaid. In making appointments, the preference shall be given to qualified loyal persons residing within the districts where their respective duties are to be performed. But if suitable residents of the districts shall not be found, then persons residing in other states or districts shall be appointed.

Fourth. That the Postmaster-General proceed to establish post-offices and post-routes, and put into execution the postal laws of the United States within the said state, giving to loyal residents the preference of appointment; but if suitable residents are not found, then to appoint agents, &c., from other states.

Fifth. That the district judge for the judicial district in which North Carolina is included proceed to hold courts within said state, in accordance with the provisions of the act of congress. The Attorney-General will instruct the proper officers to libel, and bring to judgment, confiscation, and sale, property subject to confiscation, and enforce the administration of justice within said state in all matters within the cognizance and jurisdiction of the federal courts.

Sixth. That the Secretary of the Navy take possession of all public property belonging to the Navy Department within said geographical limits, and put in operation all acts of congress in relation to naval affairs having application to the said state.

Seventh. That the Secretary of the Interior put in force the laws relating to the Interior Department applicable to the geographical limits aforesaid.

In testimony whereof, I have hereunto set my hand, and caused the seal of the United States to be affixed.

Done at the city of Washington, this twenty-ninth [L. S.] day of May, in the year of our Lord one thousand eight hundred and sixty-five, and of the Independence of the United States the eighty-ninth.

ANDREW JOHNSON.

By the President:

William H. Seward, Secretary of State.

A Proclamation by the President of the United States of America. No. 39. June 13, 1865

Whereas the fourth section of the fourth article of the Constitution of the United States declares that the United States shall guarantee to every state in the Union a republican form of government, and shall protect each of them against invasion and domestic violence; and whereas the President of the United States is, by the constitution, made commander-in-chief of the army and navy, as well as chief executive officer of the United States, and is bound by solemn oath faithfully to execute the office of President of the United States, and to take care that the laws be faithfully executed; and whereas the rebellion, which has been waged by a portion of the people of the United States against the properly constituted authorities of the government thereof, in the most violent and revolting form, but whose organized and armed forces have now been almost entirely overcome, has, in its revolutionary progress, deprived the people of the State of Mississippi of all civil government; and whereas it becomes necessary and proper to carry out and enforce the obligations of the United States to the people of Mississippi, in securing them in the enjoyment of a republican form of government:

Now, therefore, in obedience to the high and solemn duties imposed upon me by the Constitution of the United States, and for the purpose of enabling the loyal people of said state to organize a state government, whereby justice may be established, domestic tranquility insured, and loyal citizens protected in all their rights of life, liberty, and property, I, Andrew Johnson,

President of the United States, and commander-in-chief of the army and navy of the United States do hereby appoint William L. Sharkey, of Mississippi, provisional governor of the State of Mississippi, whose duty it shall be, at the earliest practicable period, to prescribe such rules and regulations as may be necessary and proper for convening a convention, composed of delegates to be chosen by that portion of the people of said state who are loyal to the United States, and no others, for the purpose of altering or amending the constitution thereof; and with authority to exercise, within the limits of said state, all the powers necessary and proper to enable such loyal people of the State of Mississippi to restore said state to its constitutional relations to the federal government, and to present such a republican form of state government as will entitle the state to the guarantee of the United States therefor, and its people to protection by the United States against invasion, insurrection, and domestic violence; Provided that, in any election that may be hereafter held for choosing delegates to any state convention as aforesaid, no person shall be qualified as an elector, or shall be eligible as a member of such convention, unless he shall have previously taken and subscribed the oath of amnesty, as set forth in the President's Proclamation of May 29, A.D. 1865, and is a voter qualified as prescribed by the constitution and laws of the State of Mississippi in force immediately before the ninth (9th) of January, A.D. 1861, the date of the so-called ordinance of secession; and the said convention, when convened, or the legislature that may be thereafter assembled, will prescribe the qualification of electors, and the eligibility of persons to hold office under the constitution and laws of the state, —a power the people of the several states composing the Federal Union have rightfully exercised from the origin of the government to the present time.

And I do hereby direct—

First. That the military commander of the department, and all officers and persons in the military and naval service, aid and assist the said provisional governor in carrying into effect this proclamation, and they are enjoined to abstain from, in any way, hindering, impeding, or discouraging the loyal people from the organization of a state government as herein authorized.

Second. That the Secretary of State proceed to put in force all laws of the United States, the administration whereof belongs to the State Department, applicable to the geographical limits aforesaid.

Third. That the Secretary of the Treasury proceed to nominate for appointment assessors of taxes, and collectors of customs and internal revenue, and such other officers of the Treasury Department as are authorized by law, and put in execution the revenue laws of the United States within the geographical limits aforesaid. In making appointments, the preference shall be given to qualified loyal persons residing within the districts where their respective duties are to be performed. But if suitable residents of the district shall not be found, then persons residing in other states or districts shall be appointed.

Fourth. That the Postmaster-General proceed to establish post-offices and post-routes, and put into execution the postal laws of the United States within the said state, giving to loyal residents the preference of appointment; but if suitable residents are not found, then to appoint agents, &c., from other states.

Fifth. That the district judge for the judicial district in which Mississippi is included proceed to hold courts within said state, in accordance with the provisions of the act of Congress. The Attorney-General will instruct the proper officers to libel, and bring to judgment, confiscation, and sale, property subject to confiscation, and enforce the administration of justice within said state in all matters within the cognizance and jurisdiction of the federal courts.

Sixth. That the Secretary of the Navy take possession of all public property belonging to the Navy Department within said geographical limits, and put in operation all acts of Congress in relation to naval affairs having application to the said state.

Seventh. That the Secretary of the Interior put in force the laws relating to the Interior Department applicable to the geographical limits aforesaid.

In testimony whereof, I have hereunto set my hand, and caused the seal of the United States to be affixed.

Done at the city of Washington this thirteenth day [L.S.] of June, in the year of our Lord one thousand eight hundred and sixty-five, and of the Independence of the United States the eighty-ninth.

ANDREW JOHNSON.

By the President:

William H. Seward, Secretary of State.

A Proclamation by the President of the United States of America. No. 40. June 13, 1865

Whereas, by my Proclamation [Executive order] of the twenty-ninth of April, one thousand eight hundred and sixty-five, all restrictions upon internal, domestic, and commercial intercourse, with certain exceptions therein specified and set forth, were removed "in such parts of the States of Tennessee, Virginia, North Carolina, South Carolina, Georgia, Florida, Alabama, Mississippi, and so much of Louisiana as lies east of the Mississippi River, as shall be embraced within the lines of national military occupation";

And whereas, by my Proclamation of the twenty-second of May, one thousand eight hundred and sixty-five, for reasons therein given, it was declared that certain ports of the United States which had been previously closed against foreign commerce should, with certain specified exceptions, be reopened to such commerce on and after the first day of July next, subject to the laws of the United States, and in pursuance of such regulations as might be prescribed by the Secretary of the Treasury;

And whereas I am satisfactorily informed that dangerous combinations against the laws of the United States no longer exist within the State of Tennessee; that the insurrection heretofore existing within said state has been suppressed; that within the boundaries thereof the authority of the United States is undisputed, and that such officers of the United States as have been duly commissioned are in the undisturbed exercise of their official functions:

Now, therefore, be it known, that I, Andrew Johnson, President of the United States, do hereby declare that all restrictions upon the internal, domestic, and coastwise intercourse and trade, and upon the removal of products of states heretofore declared in insurrection, reserving and excepting only those relating to contraband of war, as hereinafter recited, and also those which relate to the reservation of the rights of the United States to property purchased in the territory of an enemy, heretofore imposed in the territory of the United States east of the Mississippi River, are annulled, and I do hereby direct that they be forthwith removed; and that, on and after the first day of July next, all restrictions upon foreign commerce with said ports, with the exception and reservation aforesaid, be likewise removed; and that the commerce of said states shall be conducted under the supervision of the regularly appointed officers of the customs provided by law; and such officers of the customs shall receive any captured and abandoned property that may be turned over to them, under the law, by the military or naval forces of the United States, and dispose of such property as shall be directed by the Secretary of the Treasury. The following articles of contraband of war are excepted from the effect of this Proclamation: arms, ammunition, all articles from which ammunition is made, and gray uniforms and cloth.

And I hereby also proclaim and declare that the insurrection, so far as it relates to and within the State of Tennessee, and the inhabitants of the said State of Tennessee as reorganized and constituted under their recently adopted constitution, and accepted by them is suppressed; and therefore, also, that all the disabilities and disqualifications attaching to said state and the inhabitants thereof consequent upon any proclamation issued by virtue of the fifth section of the act entitled "An act further to provide for the collection of duties on imports, and for other purposes," approved the thirteenth day of July, one thousand eight hundred and sixty-one, are removed.

But nothing herein contained shall be considered or construed as in any wise changing or impairing any of the penalties and forfeitures for treason heretofore incurred under the laws of the United States, or any of the provisions, restrictions, or disabilities set forth in my Proclamation bearing date the twenty-ninth day of May, one thousand eight hundred and sixty-five, or as impairing existing regulations for the suspension of the habeas corpus, and the exercise of military law in cases where it shall be necessary for the general public safety and welfare during the existing insurrection; nor shall this Proclamation affect, or in any way impair, any laws heretofore passed by congress, and duly approved by the President, or any proclamations or orders issued by him during the aforesaid insurrection, abolishing slavery, or in any way affecting the relations of slavery, whether of persons or [of] property; but, on the contrary, all such laws and proclamations heretofore made or issued are expressly saved and declared to be in full force and virtue.

In testimony whereof, I have hereunto set my hand, and caused the seal of the United States to be affixed.

Done at the city of Washington, this thirteenth [L. S.] day of June, in the year of our Lord one thousand eight hundred and sixty-five, and of the Independence of the United States of America the eighty-ninth.

ANDREW JOHNSON.

By the President:

William H. Seward, Secretary of State.

A Proclamation by the President of the United States of America. No. 41. June 17, 1865

Whereas the fourth section of the fourth article of the Constitution of the United States declares that the United States shall guarantee to every state in the Union a republican form of government, and shall protect each of them against invasion and domestic violence; and whereas the President of the United States is, by the constitution, made commander-in-chief of the army and navy, as well as chief civil executive officer of the United States, and is bound by solemn oath faithfully to execute the office of President of the United States, and to take care that the laws be faithfully executed; and whereas the rebellion, which has been waged by a portion of the people of the United States against the properly constituted authorities of the government thereof, in the most violent and revolting form, but whose organized and armed forces have now been almost entirely overcome, has, in its revolutionary progress, deprived the people of the State of Georgia of all civil government; and whereas it becomes necessary and proper to carry out and enforce the obligations of the United States to the people of Georgia, in securing them in the enjoyment of a republican form of government;

Now, therefore, in obedience to the high and solemn duties imposed upon me by the Constitution of the United States, and for the purpose of enabling the loyal people of said state to organize a state government, whereby justice may be established, domestic tranquility insured, and loyal citizens protected in all their rights of life, liberty, and property, I, Andrew Johnson, President of the United States, and commander-in-chief of the army and navy of the United States, do hereby appoint James Johnson, of Georgia, provisional governor of the State of Georgia, whose duty it shall be, at the earliest practicable period, to prescribe such rules and regulations as may be necessary and proper for convening a convention, composed of delegates to be chosen by that portion of the people of said state who are loyal to the United States, and no others, for the purpose of altering or amending the constitution thereof; and with authority to exercise, within the limits of said state, all the powers necessary and proper to enable such loyal people of the State of Georgia to restore said state to its constitutional relations to the federal government, and to present such a republican form of state government as will entitle the state to the guarantee of the United States therefor, and its people to protection by the United States against invasion, insurrection, and domestic violence; Provided that, in any election that may be hereafter held for choosing delegates to any state convention as aforesaid, no person shall be qualified as an elector, or shall be eligible as a member of such convention, unless he shall have previously taken and subscribed the oath of amnesty, as set forth in the President's Proclamation of May 29, A.D. 1865, and is a voter qualified as prescribed by the constitution and laws of the State of Georgia in force immediately before the nineteenth (19th) of January, A.D. 1861, the date of the so-called ordinance of secession; and the said convention, when convened, or the legislature that may be thereafter assembled, will prescribe the qualification of electors, and the eligibility of persons to hold office under the constitution and laws of the state, — a power the people of the several states composing the Federal Union have rightfully exercised from the origin of the government to the present time.

And I do hereby direct —

First. That the military commander of the department, and all officers and persons in the military and naval service, aid and assist the said provisional governor in carrying into effect this Proclamation, and they are enjoined to abstain from, in any way, hindering, impeding, or discouraging the loyal people from the organization of a state government as herein authorized.

Second. That the Secretary of State proceed to put in force all laws of the United States, the administration whereof belongs to the State Department, applicable to the geographical limits aforesaid.

Third. That the Secretary of the Treasury proceed to nominate for appointment assessors of taxes, and collectors of customs and internal revenue, and such other officers of the Treasury Department as are authorized by law, and put in execution the revenue laws of the United States within the geographical limits aforesaid. In making appointments, the preference shall be given to qualified loyal persons residing within the districts where their respective duties are to be performed. But if suitable residents of the districts shall not be found, then persons residing in other states or districts shall be appointed.

Fourth. That the Postmaster-General proceed to establish post-offices and post-routes, and put into execution the postal laws of the United States within the said state, giving to loyal residents the preference of appointment; but if suitable residents are not found, then to appoint agents, &c., from other states.

Fifth. That the district judge for the judicial district in which Georgia is included proceed to hold courts within said state, in accordance with the provisions of the act of congress. The Attorney-General will instruct the proper officers to libel, and bring to judgment, confiscation, and sale, property subject to confiscation, and enforce the administration of justice within said state in all matters within the cognizance and jurisdiction of the federal courts.

Sixth. That the Secretary of the Navy take possession of all public property belonging to the Navy Department within said geographical limits, and put in operation all acts of congress in relation to naval affairs having application to the said state.

Seventh. That the Secretary of the Interior put in force the laws relating to the Interior Department applicable to the geographical limits aforesaid.

In testimony whereof, I have hereunto set my hand, and caused the seal of the United States to be affixed.

Done at the city of Washington, this seventeenth [L.S.] day of June, in the year of our Lord one thousand eight hundred and sixty-five, and of the Independence of the United States the eighty-ninth.

ANDREW JOHNSON.

By the President:

William H. Seward, Secretary of State.

A Proclamation by the President of the United States of America. No. 42. June 17, 1865

Whereas the fourth section of the fourth article of the Constitution of the United States declares that the United States shall guarantee to every state in the Union a republican form of government, and shall protect each of them against invasion and domestic violence; and whereas the President of the United States is, by the constitution, made commander-in-chief of the army and navy, as well as chief civil executive officer of the United States, and is bound by solemn oath faithfully to execute the office of President of the United States, and to take care that the laws be faithfully executed; and whereas the rebellion, which has been waged by a portion of the people of the United States against the properly constituted authorities of the government thereof, in the most violent and revolting form, but whose organized and armed forces have now been almost entirely overcome, has, in its revolutionary progress, deprived the people of the State of Texas of all civil government; and whereas it becomes necessary and proper to carry out and enforce the obligations of the United States to the people of the State of Texas, in securing them in the enjoyment of a republican form of government:

Now, therefore, in obedience to the high and solemn duties imposed upon me by the Constitution of the United States, and for the purpose of enabling the loyal people of said state to organize a state government, whereby justice may be established, domestic tranquility insured, and loyal citizens protected in all their rights of life, liberty, and property, I, Andrew Johnson, President of the United States, and commander-in-chief of the army and navy of the United States, do hereby appoint Andrew J. Hamilton, of Texas, provisional governor of the State of Texas, whose duty it shall be, at the earliest practicable period, to prescribe such rules and regulations as may be necessary and proper for convening a convention, composed of delegates to be chosen by that portion of the people of said state who are loyal to the United States, and no others, for the purpose of altering or amending the constitution thereof; and with authority to exercise, within the limits of said state, all the powers necessary and proper to enable such loyal people of the State of Texas to restore said state to its constitutional relations to the federal government, and to present such a republican form of state government as will entitle the state to the guarantee of the United States therefor, and its people to protection by the United States against invasion, insurrection, and domestic violence; Provided that, in any election that may be hereafter held for choosing delegates to any state convention as aforesaid, no person shall be qualified as an elector, or shall be eligible as a member of such convention, unless he shall have previously taken and subscribed the oath of amnesty, as set forth in the President's Proclamation of May 29, A.D. 1865, and is a voter qualified as prescribed by the constitution and laws of the State of Texas in force immediately before the first [1st] day of February, A.D. 1861, the date of the so called ordinance of secession; and the said convention, when convened, or the legislature that may be thereafter assembled, will prescribe the qualification of electors, and the eligibility of persons to hold office under the constitution and laws of the state, — a power the people of the several states composing the Federal Union have rightfully exercised from the origin of the government to the present time.

And I do hereby direct,—

First. That the military commander of the department, and all officers and persons in the military and naval service, aid and assist the said provisional governor in carrying into effect this Proclamation, and they are enjoined to abstain from, in any way, hindering, impeding, or discouraging the loyal people from the organization of a state government as herein authorized.

Second. That the Secretary of State proceed to put in force all laws of the United States, the administration whereof belongs to the State Department, applicable to the geographical limits aforesaid.

Third. That the Secretary of the Treasury proceed to nominate for appointment assessors of taxes, and collectors of customs and internal revenue, and such other officers of the Treasury Department as are authorized by law, and put in execution the revenue laws of the United States within the geographical limits aforesaid. In making appointments, the preference shall be given to qualified loyal persons residing within the districts where their respective duties are to be performed. But if suitable residents of the districts shall not be found, then persons residing in other states or districts shall be appointed.

Fourth. That the Postmaster-General proceed to establish post-offices and post-routes, and put into execution the postal laws of the United States within the said state, giving to loyal residents the preference of appointment; but if suitable residents are not found, then to appoint agents, &c., from other states.

Fifth. That the district judge for the judicial district in which Texas is included proceed to hold courts within said state, in accordance with the provisions of the act of congress. The Attorney-General will instruct the proper officers to libel, and bring to judgment, confiscation, and sale, property subject to confiscation, and enforce the administration of justice within said state in all matters within the cognizance and jurisdiction of the federal courts.

Sixth. That the Secretary of the Navy take possession of all public property belonging to the Navy Department within said geographical limits, and put in operation all acts of congress in relation to naval affairs having application to the said state.

Seventh. That the Secretary of the Interior put in force the laws relating to the Interior Department applicable to the geographical limits aforesaid.

In testimony whereof, I have hereunto set my hand, and caused the seal of the United States to be affixed.

Done at the city of Washington this seventeenth day of [L.S.] June, in the year of our Lord one thousand eight hundred and sixty-five, and of the Independence of the United States the eighty-ninth.

ANDREW JOHNSON.

By the President:

William H. Seward, Secretary of State.

A Proclamation by the President of the United States of America. No. 43. June 21, 1865

Whereas the fourth section of the fourth article of the Constitution of the United States declares that the United States shall guarantee to every state in the Union a republican form of government, and shall protect each of them against invasion and domestic violence; and whereas the President of the United States is, by the constitution, made commander-in-chief of the army and navy as well as chief executive officer of the United States, and is bound by solemn oath faithfully to execute the office of President of the United States, and to take care that the laws be faithfully executed; and whereas the rebellion, which has been waged by a portion of the people of the United States against the properly constituted authorities of the government thereof, in the most violent and revolting form, but whose organized and armed forces have now been almost entirely overcome, has, in its revolutionary progress, deprived the people of the State of Alabama of all civil government; and whereas it becomes necessary and proper to carry out and enforce the obligations of the United States to the people of Alabama, in securing them in the enjoyment of a republican form of government:

Now, therefore, in obedience to the high and solemn duties imposed upon me by the Constitution of the United States, and for the purpose of enabling the loyal people of said state to organize a state government, whereby justice may be established, domestic tranquility insured, and loyal citizens protected in all their rights of life, liberty, and property, I, Andrew Johnson,

President of the United States, and commander-in-chief of the army and navy of the United States, do hereby appoint Lewis E. Parsons, of Alabama, provisional governor of the State of Alabama, whose duty it shall be, at the earliest practicable period, to prescribe such rules and regulations as may be necessary and proper for convening a convention, composed of delegates to be chosen by that portion of the people of said state who are loyal to the United States, and no others, for the purpose of altering or amending the constitution thereof; and with authority to exercise, within the limits of said state, all the powers necessary and proper to enable such loyal people of the State of Alabama to restore said state to its constitutional relations to the federal government, and to present such a republican form of state government as will entitle the state to the guarantee of the United States therefor, and its people to protection by the United States against invasion, insurrection, and domestic violence; Provided that, in any election that may be hereafter held for choosing delegates to any state convention as aforesaid, no person shall be qualified as an elector, or shall be eligible as a member of such convention, unless he shall have previously taken and subscribed the oath of amnesty, as set forth in the President's Proclamation of May 29, A.D. 1865, and is voter qualified as prescribed by the constitution and laws of the State of Alabama in force immediately before the eleventh day of January, A.D. 1861, the date of the so-called ordinance of secession; and the said convention, when convened, or the legislature that may be thereafter assembled, will prescribe the qualification of electors, and the eligibility of persons to hold office under the constitution and laws of the state, — a power the people of the several states composing the Federal Union have rightfully exercised from the origin of the government to the present time.

And I do hereby direct,—

First. That the military commander of the department, and all officers, and persons in the military and naval service, aid and assist the said provisional governor in carrying into effect the Proclamation, and they are enjoined to abstain from, in any way, hindering, impeding, or discouraging the loyal people from the organization of a state government as herein authorized.

Second. That the Secretary of State proceed to put in force all laws of the United States, the administration whereof belongs to the State Department, applicable to the geographical limits aforesaid.

Third. That the Secretary of the Treasury proceed to nominate for appointment assessors of taxes, and collectors of customs and internal revenue, and such officers of the Treasury Department as are authorized by law, and put in execution the revenue laws of the United States with the geographical limits aforesaid. In making appointments, the preference shall be given to qualified loyal persons residing within the districts where their respective duties are to be performed. But if suitable residents of the districts shall not be found, then persons residing in other states or districts shall be appointed.

Fourth. That the Postmaster-General proceed to establish post-offices and post-routes, and put into execution the postal laws of the United States within the said state, giving to loyal residents the preference of appointment; but if suitable residents are not found, then to appoint agents, &c., from other states.

Fifth. That the district judge for the judicial district in which Alabama is included proceed to hold courts within said state, in accordance with the provisions of the act of Congress. The Attorney-General will instruct the proper officers to libel, and bring to judgment, confiscation, and sale, property subject to confiscation, and enforce the administration of justice within said state in all matters within the cognizance and jurisdiction of the federal courts.

Sixth. That the Secretary of the Navy take possession of all public property belonging to the Navy Department within said geographical limits, and put in operation all acts of Congress in relation to naval affairs having application to the said state.

Seventh. That the Secretary of the Interior put in force the laws relating to the Interior Department applicable to the geographical limits aforesaid.

In testimony whereof, I have hereunto set my hand, and caused the seal of the United States to be affixed.

Done at the city of Washington, this twenty-first [L.S.] day of June, in the year of our Lord one thousand eight hundred and sixty-five, and of the Independence of the United States the eighty-ninth.

ANDREW JOHNSON.

By the President:

William H. Seward, Secretary of State.

A Proclamation by the President of the United States of America. No. 46. June 30, 1865

Whereas the fourth section of the fourth article of the Constitution of the United States declares that the United States shall guarantee to every state in the Union a republican form of government, and shall protect each of them against invasion and domestic violence; and whereas the President of the

United States is, by the constitution, made commander-in-chief of the army and navy, as well as chief civil executive officer of the United States, and is bound by solemn oath faithfully to execute the office of President of the United States, and to take care that the laws be faithfully executed; and whereas the rebellion, which has been waged by a portion of the people of the United States against the properly constituted authorities of the government thereof, in the most violent and revolting form, but whose organized and armed forces have now been almost entirely overcome, has, in its revolutionary progress, deprived the people of the State of South Carolina of all civil government; and whereas it becomes necessary and proper to carry out and enforce the obligations of the United States to the people of South Carolina, in securing them in the enjoyment of a republican form of government:

Now, therefore, in obedience to the high and solemn duties imposed upon me by the Constitution of the United States, and for the purpose of enabling the loyal people of said state to organize a state government, whereby justice may be established, domestic tranquility insured, and loyal citizens protected in all their rights of life, liberty, and property, I, Andrew Johnson, President of the United States, and commander-in-chief of the army and navy of the United States, do hereby appoint Benjamin F. Perry, of South Carolina, provisional governor of the State of South Carolina, whose duty it shall be, at the earliest practicable period, to prescribe such rules and regulations as may be necessary and proper for convening a convention, composed of delegates to be chosen by that portion of the people of said state who are loyal to the United States, and no others, for the purpose of altering or amending the constitution thereof; and with authority to exercise, within the limits of said state, all the powers necessary and proper to enable such loyal people of the State of South Carolina to restore said state to its constitutional relations to the federal government, and to present such a republican form of state government as will entitle the state to the guarantee of the United States therefor, and its people to protection by the United States against invasion, insurrection, and domestic violence; Provided that, in any election that may be hereafter held for choosing delegates to any state convention as aforesaid, no person shall be qualified as an elector, or shall be eligible as a member of such convention, unless he shall have previously taken and subscribed the oath of amnesty, as set forth in the President's Proclamation of May 29, A.D., 1865, and is a voter qualified and prescribed by the constitution and laws of the State of South Carolina in force immediately before the seventeenth (17th) day of November, A.D. 1860, the date of the so-called ordinance of secession; and the said convention, when convened, or the legislature that may be thereafter assembled, will prescribe the qualifications of electors, and the eligibility of persons to hold office under the constitution and laws of the state, — a power the people of the several states composing the Federal Union have rightly exercised from the origin of the government to the present time.

And I do hereby direct—

First. That the military commander of the department, and all officers and persons in the military and naval service, aid and assist the said provisional governor in carrying into effect this Proclamation, and they are enjoined to abstain from, in any way, hindering, impeding, or discouraging the loyal people from the organization of a state government as herein authorized.

Second. That the Secretary of State proceed to put in force all laws of the United States, the administration whereof belongs to the State Department, applicable to the geographical limits aforesaid.

Third. That the Secretary of the Treasury proceed to nominate for appointment assessors of taxes, and collectors of customs and internal revenue, and such other officers of the Treasury Department as are authorized by law, and put in execution the revenue laws of the United States within the geographical limits aforesaid. In making appointments, the preferences shall be given to qualified loyal persons residing within the districts where their respective duties are to be performed. But if suitable residents of the districts shall not be found, then persons residing in other states or districts shall be appointed.

Fourth. That the Postmaster-General proceed to establish post-offices and post-routes, and put into execution the postal laws of the United States within the said state, giving to loyal residents the preference of appointment; but if suitable residents are not found, then to appoint agents, &c., from other states.

Fifth. That the district judge for the judicial district in which South Carolina is included proceed to hold courts within said state, in accordance with the provisions of the act of congress. The Attorney-General will instruct the proper officers to libel, and bring to judgment, confiscation, and sale, property subject to confiscation, and enforce the administration of justice within said state in all matters within the cognizance and jurisdiction of the federal courts.

Sixth. That the Secretary of the Navy take possession of all public property belonging to the Navy Department within said geographical limits, and put in operation all acts of congress in relation to naval affairs having application to the said state.

Seventh. That the Secretary of the Interior put in force the laws relating to the Interior Department applicable to the geographical limits aforesaid.

In testimony whereof, I have hereunto set my hand, and caused the seal of the United States to be affixed.

Done at the city of Washington this thirtieth day [L.S.] of June, in the year of our Lord one thousand eight hundred and sixty-five, and of the Independence of the United States the eighty-ninth.

ANDREW JOHNSON.

By the President:

William H. Seward, Secretary of State.

A Proclamation by the President of the United States of America. No. 47. July 13, 1865

Whereas the fourth section of the fourth article of the Constitution of the United States declares that the United States shall guarantee to every state in the Union a republican form of government, and shall protect each of them against invasion and domestic violence; and whereas the President of the United States is, by the constitution, made commander-in-chief of the army and navy, as well as chief civil executive officer of the United States, and is bound by solemn oath faithfully to execute the office of President of the United States, and to take care that the laws be faithfully executed; and whereas the rebellion, which has been waged by a portion of the people of the United States against the properly constituted authorities of the government thereof, in the most violent and revolting form, but whose organized and armed forces have now been almost entirely overcome, has, in its revolutionary progress, deprived the people of the State of Florida of all civil government; and whereas it becomes necessary and proper to carry out and enforce the obligations of the United States to the people of Florida, in securing them in the enjoyment of a republican form of government:

Now, therefore, in obedience to the high and solemn duties imposed upon me by the Constitution of the United States, and for the purpose of enabling the loyal people of said state to organize a state government, whereby justice may be established, domestic tranquility insured, and loyal citizens protected in all their rights of life, liberty, and property, I, Andrew Johnson, President of the United States, and commander-in-chief of the army and navy of the United States, do hereby appoint William Marvin provisional governor of the State of Florida, whose duty it shall be, at the earliest practicable period, to prescribe such rules and regulations as may be necessary and proper for convening a convention, composed of delegates to be chosen by that portion of the people of said state who are loyal to the United States, and no others, for the purpose of altering or amending the constitution thereof; and with authority to exercise, within the limits of said state, all the powers necessary and proper to enable such loyal people of the State of Florida to restore said state to its constitutional relations to the federal government, and to present such a republican form of state government as will entitle the state to the guarantee of the United States therefor, and its people to protection by the United States against invasion, insurrection, and domestic violence; Provided that, in any election that may be hereafter held for choosing delegates to any state convention as aforesaid, no person shall be qualified as an elector, or shall be eligible as a member of such convention, unless he shall have previously taken and subscribed the oath of amnesty, as set forth in the President's Proclamation of May 29, A.D. 1865, and is a voter qualified as prescribed by the constitution and laws of the State of Florida in force immediately before the 10th day of January, A.D. 1861, the date of the so-called ordinance of secession; and the said convention, when convened, or the legislature that may be thereafter assembled, will prescribe the qualification of electors, and the eligibility of persons to hold office under the constitution and laws of the state, — a power the people of the several states composing the Federal Union have rightfully exercised from the origin of the government to the present time.

And I do hereby direct —

First. That the military commander of the department, and all officers and persons in the military and naval service, aid and assist the said provisional governor in carrying into effect this Proclamation, and they are enjoined to abstain from, in any way, hindering, impeding, or discouraging the loyal people from the organization of a state government as herein authorized.

Second. That the Secretary of State proceed to put in force all laws of the United States, the administration whereof belongs to the State Department, applicable to the geographical limits aforesaid.

Third. That the Secretary of the Treasury proceed to nominate for appointment assessors of taxes, and collectors of customs and internal revenue, and such other officers of the Treasury Department as are authorized by law, and put in execution the revenue laws of the United States within the geographical limits aforesaid. In making appointments, the preference shall be given to qualified loyal persons residing within the districts where their respective duties are to be performed. But if suitable residents of the districts shall not be found, then persons residing in other states or districts shall be appointed.

Fourth. That the Postmaster-General proceed to establish post-offices and post-routes, and put into execution the postal laws of the United States within the said state, giving to loyal residents the preference of appointment; but if suitable residents are not found, then to appoint agents, &c., from other states.

Fifth. That the district judge for the judicial district in which Florida is included proceed to hold courts within said state, in accordance with the provisions of the act of congress. The Attorney-General will instruct the proper officers to libel, and bring to judgment, confiscation, and sale, property subject to confiscation, and enforce the administration of justice within said state in all matters within the cognizance and jurisdiction of the federal courts.

Sixth. That the Secretary of the Navy take possession of all public property belonging to the Navy Department within said geographical limits, and put in operation all acts of congress in relation to naval affairs having application to the said State.

Seventh. That the Secretary of the Interior put in force the laws relating to the Interior Department applicable to the geographical limits aforesaid.

In testimony whereof, I have hereunto set my hand, and caused the seal of the United States to be affixed.

Done at the city of Washington, this thirteenth [L.S.] day of July, in the year of our Lord one thousand eight hundred and sixty-five, and of the Independence of the United States the ninetieth.

ANDREW JOHNSON.

By the President:

William H. Seward, Secretary of State.

Appendix B: Laws Providing for the Readmission of the Rebel States to the Union

JOINT RESOLUTION RESTORING TENNESSEE TO HER RELATIONS TO THE UNION. NO. 73. JULY 24, 1866

Whereas, in the year eighteen hundred and sixty-one, the government of the State of Tennessee was seized upon and taken possession of by persons in hostility to the United States, and the inhabitants of said State in pursuance of an act of Congress were declared to be in a state of insurrection against the United States; and whereas said State government can only be restored to its former political relations in the Union by the consent of the law-making power of the United States; and whereas the people of said State did, on the twenty-second day of February, eighteen hundred and sixty-five, by a large popular vote, adopt and ratify a constitution of government whereby slavery was abolished, and all ordinances and laws of secession and debts contracted under the same were declared void; and whereas a State government has been organized under said constitution which has ratified the amendment to the Constitution of the United States abolishing slavery, also the amendment proposed by the thirty-ninth Congress, and has done other acts proclaiming and denoting loyalty: Therefore,

Be it resolved by the Senate and House of Representatives of the United States of America in Congress assembled, That the State of Tennessee is hereby restored to her former proper, practical relations to the Union, and is again entitled to be represented by senators and representatives in Congress.

Approved, July 24, 1866.

An Act to Admit the State of Arkansas to Representation in Congress. June 22, 1868

Whereas the people of Arkansas, in pursuance of the provisions of an act entitled "An act for the more efficient government of the rebel States," passed March second, eighteen hundred and sixty-seven, and the acts supplementary thereto, have framed and adopted a constitution of State government, which is republican, and the legislature of said State has duly ratified the amendment to the Constitution of the United States proposed by the Thirty-ninth Congress, and known as article fourteen: Therefore,

Be it enacted by the Senate and House of Representatives of the United States of America in Congress assembled, That the State of Arkansas is entitled and admitted to representation in Congress as one of the States of the Union upon the following fundamental condition: That the constitution of Arkansas shall never be so amended or changed as to deprive any citizen or class of citizens of the United States of the right to vote who are entitled to vote by the constitution herein recognized, except as a punishment for such crimes as are now felonies at common law, whereof they shall have been duly convicted, under laws equally applicable to all the inhabitants of said State: Provided, That any alteration of said constitution prospective in its effect may be made in regard to the time and place of residence voters.

SCHUYLER COLFAX.
Speaker of the House of Representatives.
B. F. WADE.
President of the Senate pro tempore.

In the House of Representatives U.S.,}
June 20, 1868. }

The President of the United States having returned to the House of Representatives, in which it originated, the bill entitled, "An act to admit the State of Arkansas to representation in Congress," with his objections thereto, the House of Representatives proceeded, in pursuance of the Constitution, to reconsider the same; and

Resolved, That the said bill do pass, two thirds of the House of Representatives agreeing to pass the same.

Attest: EDWD. McPHERSON,
Clerk H.R.U.S.

In Senate of the United States,}
June 22, 1868. }

The Senate having proceeded, in pursuance of the Constitution, to reconsider the bill entitled "An act to admit the State of Arkansas to representation in Congress," returned to the House of Representatives by the President of the United States, with his objections, and sent by the House of Representatives to the Senate, with the message of the President returning the bill:

Resolved, That the bill do pass, two thirds of the Senate agreeing to pass the same.

Attest: GEO. C. GORHAM,
Secretary of the Senate.

A Proclamation by the President of the United States of America. No. 7. July 11, 1868

Whereas by an Act of Congress, entitled "An act to admit the States of North Carolina, South Carolina, Louisiana, Georgia, Alabama, and Florida, to representation in Congress," passed on the twenty-fifth day of June, one thousand eight hundred and sixty-eight, it is declared that it is made the duty of the President, within ten days after receiving official information of the ratification by the legislature of either of said States of a proposed amendment to the Constitution known as article fourteen, to issue a proclamation announcing that fact;

And whereas the said act seems to be prospective;

And whereas a paper purporting to be a resolution of the legislature of Florida, adopting the amendment of the thirteenth and fourteenth articles of the Constitution of the United States, was received at the Department of State on the sixteenth of June, one thousand eight hundred and sixty-eight, prior to the passage of the act of Congress referred to, which paper is attested by the names of Horatio Jenkins, Jr., as President pro tem. of the Senate, and W. W. Moore, as Speaker of the Assembly, and of William L. Apthoop, as Secretary of the Senate, and William Forsyth Bynum, as clerk of the Assembly, and which paper was transmitted to the Secretary of State in letter dated Executive Office, Tallahassee, Florida, June tenth, one thousand eight hundred and sixty-eight, from Harrison Reed, who therein signs himself governor;

And whereas on the sixth day of July one thousand eight hundred and sixty-eight, a paper was received by the President, which paper being addressed to the President bears date of the fourth of July, one thousand eight hundred and sixty-eight, and was transmitted by and under the name of W. W. Holden, who therein writes himself Governor of the State of North Carolina, which paper certifies that the said proposed amendment, known as article fourteen, did pass the Senate and House of Representatives of the General Assembly of North Carolina, on the second day of July instant, and is attested by the names of John H. Boner, or Bower, as Secretary of the House of Representatives, and T. A. Byrnes, as Secretary of the Senate; and its ratification on the fourth of July, one thousand eight hundred and sixty-eight, is attested by Tod R. Caldwell, as Lieutenant-Governor, President of Senate, and Jo. W. Holden as Speaker House of Representatives;

Now, therefore, be it known that I, Andrew Johnson, President of the United States of America, in compliance with and execution of the act of Congress aforesaid, do issue this proclamation announcing the fact of the ratification of the said amendment by the legislature of the State of North Carolina, in the manner hereinbefore set forth.

In testimony whereof I have signed these presents with my hand, and have caused the seal of the United States to be hereto affixed.

Done at the city of Washington, this eleventh day of July, in the year of our Lord one thousand eight [L.S.] hundred and sixty-eight, and the Independence of the United States of America the ninety-third.

ANDREW JOHNSON.

By the President:

Wm. H. Seward, Secretary of State.

A Proclamation by the President of the United States of America. No. 8. July 18, 1868

Whereas by an act of Congress entitled "An act to admit the States of North Carolina, South Carolina, Louisiana, Georgia, Alabama, and Florida to representation in Congress," passed the twenty-fifth day of June, one thousand eight hundred and sixty-eight, it is declared that it is made the duty of the President, within ten days after receiving official information of the ratification by the legislature of either of said States of a proposed amendment to the Constitution, known as article fourteen, to issue a proclamation announcing that fact;

And whereas, on the eighteenth day of July, one thousand eight hundred and sixty-eight, a letter was received by the President, which letter being addressed to the President, bears date of July fifteen, one thousand eight hundred and sixty-eight, and was transmitted by and under the name of R. K. Scott, who therein writes himself Governor of South Carolina, in which letter was enclosed, and received at the same time by the President, a paper purporting to be a resolution of the Senate and House of Representatives of the General Assembly of the State of South Carolina, ratifying the said proposed amendment, and also purporting to have passed the two said Houses, respectively, on the seventh and ninth of July, one thousand eight hundred and sixty-eight, and to have been approved by the said R. K. Scott as Governor of said State on the fifteenth of July, one thousand eight hundred and sixty-eight, which circumstances are attested by the signatures of D. T. Corbin, as President pro tempore of the Senate, and of F. J. Moses, Jr. as Speaker of the House of Representatives of said State, and of the said R. K. Scott as Governor.

Now, therefore, be it known that I, Andrew Johnson, President of the United States of America, in compliance with the execution of the act of Congress aforesaid, do issue this, my proclamation, announcing the fact of the ratification of the said amendment by the legislature of the State of South Carolina in the manner hereinbefore set forth.

In testimony whereof I have signed these presents with my hand, and have caused the seal of the United States to be hereto affixed.

Done at the city of Washington, this eighteenth day of July, in the year of our Lord one thousand [L.S.] eight hundred and sixty-eight, and of the Independence of the United States of America the ninety-third.

ANDREW JOHNSON.

By the President:

Wm. H. Seward, Secretary of State.

A Proclamation by the President of the United States of America. No. 9. July 18, 1868

Whereas by an act of Congress entitled "An act to admit the States of North Carolina, South Carolina, Louisiana, Georgia, Alabama, and Florida to representation in Congress," passed on the twenty-fifth day of June, one thousand eight hundred and sixty-eight, it is declared that it is made the duty of the President, within ten days after receiving official information of ratification by the legislature of either of said States of a proposed amendment to the Constitution, known as article fourteen, to issue a proclamation announcing that fact;

And whereas a paper was received at the Department of State on the seventeenth day of July, one thousand eight hundred and sixty-eight, which paper, bearing date of the ninth day of July, one thousand eight hundred and sixty-eight, purports to be a resolution of the Senate and House of Representatives of the State of Louisiana in General Assembly convened, ratifying the aforesaid amendment, and is attested by the signature of George E. Bovee, as Secretary of State, under a seal purporting to be the seal of the State of Louisiana;

Now, therefore, be it known that I, Andrew Johnson, President of the United States of America, in compliance with the execution of the act of Congress before mentioned, do issue this, my proclamation, announcing the fact of the ratification of the said amendment by the legislature of the State of Louisiana in the manner hereinbefore set forth.

In testimony whereof I have signed these presents with my hand, and have caused the seal of the United States to be hereto affixed.

Done at the city of Washington, this eighteenth day of July, in the year of our Lord one thousand [Seal.] eight hundred and sixty-eight, and of the Independence of the United States of America the ninety-third.

ANDREW JOHNSON.

By the President:

Wm. H. Seward Secretary of State.

A Proclamation by the President of the United States of America. No. 10. July 20, 1868

Whereas by an act of Congress entitled "An act to admit the States of North Carolina, South Carolina, Louisiana, Georgia, Alabama, and Florida to representation in Congress," passed the twenty-fifth day of June, one thousand eight hundred and sixty-eight, it is declared that it is made the duty of the President, within ten days after receiving official information of the ratification by the legislature of either of said states of a proposed amendment to the Constitution, known as article fourteen, to issue a proclamation announcing that fact;

And whereas a letter was received this day by the President, which letter, being addressed to the President, bears date of July sixteen, one thousand eight hundred and sixty-eight, and was transmitted by and under the name of William H. Smith, who therein writes himself Governor of Alabama, in which letter was enclosed and received at the same time by the President, a paper purporting to be a resolution of the Senate and House of Representatives of the General Assembly of the State of Alabama, ratifying the said proposed amendment, which paper is attested by the signature of Chas. A. Miller, as Secretary of State, under a seal purporting to be the seal of the State of Alabama, and bears the date of approval of July thirteen, one thousand eight hundred and sixty-eight, by William H. Smith, as Governor of said State.

Now, therefore, be it known that I, Andrew Johnson, President of the United States of America, in compliance with an execution of the act of Congress before mentioned, do issue this my proclamation, announcing the fact of the ratification of the said amendment by the legislature of the State of Alabama, in the manner hereinbefore set forth.

In testimony whereof I have signed these presents with my hand, and have caused the seal of the United States to be hereto affixed.

Done at the city of Washington, this twentieth day of July, in the year of our Lord one thousand [Seal.] eight hundred and sixty-eight, and of the Independence of the United States of America the ninety-third.

ANDREW JOHNSON.

By the President:

Wm. H. Seward, Secretary of State.

An Act to admit the State of Virginia to representation in the Congress of the United States. January 26, 1870.

Whereas the people of Virginia have framed and adopted a constitution of State government which is republican; and whereas the legislature of Virginia elected under said constitution have ratified the fourteenth and fifteenth amendments to the Constitution of the United States; and whereas the performance of these several acts in good faith was a condition precedent to the representation of the State in Congress:

Therefore,

Be it enacted by the Senate and House of Representatives of the United States of America in Congress assembled, That the said State of Virginia is entitled to representation in the Congress of the United States: Provided, That before any member of the legislature of said State shall take or resume his seat, or any officer of said State shall enter upon the duties of his office, he shall take, and subscribe, and file in the office of the secretary of state of Virginia, for permanent preservation, an oath in the form following: "I,__________,do solemnly swear that I have never taken an oath as a member of Congress, or as an officer of the United States, or as a member of any State legislature, or as an executive or judicial officer of any State, to support the Constitution of the United States, and afterward engaged in insurrection or rebellion against the same, or given aid or comfort to the enemies thereof, so help me God"; or such person shall in like manner take, subscribe, and file the following oath: "I,_____ _____, do solemnly swear that I have, by act of Congress of the United States, been relieved from the disabilities imposed upon me by the fourteenth amendment of the Constitution of the United States, so help me God"; which oaths shall be taken before and certified by any officer lawfully authorized to administer oaths. And any person who shall knowingly swear falsely in taking either of such oaths shall be deemed guilty of perjury, and shall be punished therefor by imprisonment not less than one year, and not more than ten years, and shall be fined not less than one thousand dollars, and not more than ten thousand dollars. And in all trials for any violation of this act the certificate of taking of either of said oaths, with proof of the signature of the party accused, shall be taken and held as conclusive evidence that such oath was regularly and lawfully administered by competent authority: And provided further, That every such person who shall neglect for the period of thirty days next after the passage of this act to take, subscribe, and file such oath as aforesaid, shall be deemed and taken, to all intents and purposes, to have vacated his office: And provided further, That the State of Virginia is admitted to representation in Congress as one of the States of the Union upon the following fundamental conditions: First, That the Constitution of Virginia shall never be so amended or changed as to deprive any citizen or class of citizens of the United States of the right to vote who are entitled to vote by the Constitution herein recognized, except as a punishment for such crimes as are now felonies at common law, whereof they shall have been duly convicted under laws equally applicable to all the inhabitants of said State: Provided, That any alteration of said Constitution, prospective in its effects, may be made in regard to the time and place of residence of voters. Second, That it shall never be lawful for the said State to deprive any citizen of the United States, on account of his race, color, or previous condition of servitude, of the right to hold office under the constitution and laws of said State, or upon any such ground to require of him any other qualifications for office than such as are required of all citizens. Third, That the constitution of Virginia shall never be amended or changed as to deprive any citizen or class of citizens of the United States of the school rights and privileges secured by the constitution of said State.

Approved, January 26, 1870.

An Act to amend an Act entitled "An Act to admit the State of Virginia to representation in the Congress of the United States." February 1, 1870

Be it enacted by the Senate and House of Representatives of the United States of America in Congress assembled, That whenever the word "oath" is used in the act entitled "An act to admit the State of Virginia to representation in the Congress of the United States," it shall be construed to include an affirmation; and every person required by said act to take either of the oaths therein prescribed, who has religious or conscientious scruples against taking an oath, may make and file an affirmation to the same purport and effect: Provided, That all the pains and penalties of perjury prescribed by said act shall apply also to any false affirmation taken hereunder.

Approved, February 1, 1870.

An Act to admit the State of Mississippi to representation in the Congress of the United States. February 23, 1870.

Whereas the people of Mississippi have framed and adopted a constitution of State government which is republican; and whereas the legislature of Mississippi elected under said constitution has ratified the fourteenth and fifteenth amendments to the Constitution of the United States; and whereas the performance of these several acts in good faith is a condition precedent to the representation of the State in Congress: therefore,

Be it enacted by the Senate and House of Representatives of the United States of America in Congress assembled, That the said State of Mississippi is entitled to representation in the Congress of the United States: Provided, That before any member of the legislature of said State shall take or resume his seat, or any officer of said State shall enter upon the duties of his office, he shall take and subscribe, and file in the office of the secretary of state of Mississippi, for permanent preservation, and oath or affirmation in the form following: "I, ____ ____, do solemnly swear (or affirm) that I have never taken an oath as a member of Congress, or as an officer of the United States, or as a member of any State legislature, or as an executive or judicial officer of any State, to support the Constitution of the United States, and afterward engaged in insurrection or rebellion against the same, or given aid or comfort to the enemies thereof, so help me God"; or under the pains and penalties of perjury, (as the case may be;) or such person shall in like manner take, subscribe, and file the following oath or affirmation: "I,____ ____, do solemnly swear (or affirm) that I have, by act of Congress of the United States, been relieved from the disabilities imposed upon me by the fourteenth amendment of the Constitution of the United States, so help me God"; or under the pains and penalties of perjury, (as the case may be;) which oaths or affirmations shall be taken before and certified by any officer lawfully authorized to administer oaths. And any person who shall knowingly swear or affirm falsely in taking either of such oaths or affirmations shall be deemed guilty of perjury, and shall be punished therefor by imprisonment not less than one year, and not more than ten years, and shall be fined not less than one thousand dollars, and not more than ten thousand dollars. And in all trials for any violation of this act, the certificate of the taking of either of said oaths or affirmations, with proof of the signature of the party accused, shall be taken and held as conclusive evidence that such oath or affirmation was regularly and lawfully administered by competent authority: And provided further, That every such person who shall neglect for the period of thirty days next after the passage of this act to take, subscribe, and file such oath or affirmation as aforesaid, shall be deemed and taken, to all intents and purposes, to have vacated his office: And provided further, That the State of Mississippi is admitted to representation in Congress as one of the States of the Union, upon the following fundamental conditions: First, That the constitution of Mississippi shall never be so amended or changed as to deprive any citizen or class of citizens of the United States of the right to vote who are entitled to vote by the constitution herein recognized, except as a punishment for such crimes as are now felonies at common law, whereof they shall have been duly convicted under laws equally applicable to all the inhabitants of said State: Provided, That any alteration of said constitution, prospective in its effects, may be made in regard to the time and place of residence of voters. Second, That it shall never be lawful for the said State to deprive any citizen of the United States, on account of his race, color, or previous condition of servitude, of the right to hold office under the constitution and laws of said State, or upon any such ground to require of him any other qualifications for office than such as are required of all other citizens. Third, That the constitution of Mississippi shall never be so amended or changed as to deprive any citizen or class of citizens of the United States of the school rights and privileges secured by the constitution of said State.

Approved, February 23, 1870.

An Act to admit the State of Texas to representation in the Congress of the United States. March 30, 1870.

Whereas the people of Texas have framed and adopted a constitution of State government which is republican; and whereas the legislature of Texas elected under said constitution has ratified the fourteenth and fifteenth amendments to the Constitution of the United States; and whereas the performance of these several acts in good faith is a condition precedent to the representation of the State in Congress: Therefore,

Be it enacted by the Senate and House of Representatives of the United States of America in Congress assembled, That the said State of Texas is entitled to representation in the Congress of the United States: Provided, That before any member of the legislature of said State shall take or resume his seat, or any officer of said State shall enter upon the duties of his office he shall take and subscribe and file in the office of the secretary of State of Texas, for permanent preservation, and oath of affirmation in the form following: "I____ ____, do solemnly swear (or affirm) that I have never taken an oath as a member of Congress, or as an officer of the United States, or as a member of any State legislature, or as an executive or judicial officer of any State, to support the Constitution of the United States, and afterward engaged in insurrection or rebellion against the same, or given aid or comfort to the enemies thereof, so help me God"; or under the pains and penalties of perjury (as the case may be); or such person shall, in like manner, take, subscribe, and file the following oath or affirmation: "I,_____ ____, do solemnly swear (or affirm) that I have, by act of Congress of the United States, been relieved from the disabilities imposed upon me by the fourteenth amendment of the Constitution of the United States, so help me God"; or under the pains and penalties of perjury (as the case may be); which oaths or affirmations shall be taken before, and certified by, any officer lawfully authorized to administer oaths. And any person who shall knowingly swear or affirm falsely in taking either of such oaths or affirmations, shall be deemed guilty of perjury, and shall be punished therefor by imprisonment not less than one year, and not more than ten years, and shall be fined not less than one thousand dollars, and not more than ten thousand dollars. And in all trials for any violation of this act, the certificate of the taking of either of said oaths or affirmations, with proof of signature of the party accused shall be taken and held as conclusive evidence that such oath or affirmation was regularly and lawfully administered by competent authority: And provided further, That such person who shall neglect for the period of thirty days next after the passage of this act to take, subscribe, and file such oath or affirmation as aforesaid, shall be deemed and taken to all intents and purposes to have vacated his office: And provided further, That the State of Texas is admitted to representation in Congress as one of the States of the Union, upon the following fundamental conditions: First. That the constitution of Texas shall never be so amended or changed as to deprive any citizen or class of citizens of the United States of the right to vote who are entitled to vote by the constitution herein recognized, except as a punishment for such crimes as are now felonies at common law, whereof they shall have been duly convicted under laws equally applicable to all the inhabitants of said State: Provided, That any alteration of said constitution, prospective in its effects, may be made in regard to the time and place of residence of voters. Second. That it shall never be lawful for the said State to deprive any citizen of the United States on account of his race, color, or previous condition of servitude, of the right to hold office under the constitution and laws of said State, or upon any such ground to require of him any other qualifications for office than such as are required of all other citizens. Third. That the constitution of Texas shall never be so amended or changed as to deprive any citizen or class of citizens of the United States of the school rights and privileges secured by the constitution of said State.

Approved, March 30, 1870.

An Act relating to the State of Georgia. July 15, 1870

Be it enacted by the Senate and House of Representatives of the United States of America in Congress assembled, That the State of Georgia having complied with the reconstruction acts, and the fourteenth and fifteenth articles of amendments to the Constitution of the United States having been ratified in good faith by a legal legislature of said State, is hereby declared that the State of Georgia is entitled to representation in the Congress of the United States. But nothing in this act contained shall be construed to deprive the people of Georgia of the right to an election for member of the general assembly of said State, as provided for in the Constitution thereof; and nothing in this or any other act of Congress shall be construed to affect the term to which any officer has been appointed or any member of the general assembly elected as prescribed by the Constitution of the State of Georgia.

Sec. 2. And be it further enacted, That so much of the act entitled "An act making appropriations for the support of the army for the year ending June thirty, eighteen hundred and sixty-eight, and for other purposes," approved March two, eighteen hundred and sixty-seven, as prohibits the organization, arming, or calling into service of the militia forces in the States of Georgia, Mississippi, Texas, and Virginia, be, and the same is hereby, repealed.

Approved, July 15, 1870.

Appendix C: Principal Laws (1861–1863) for the Identification of Those States in Rebellion and for the Suspension of Habeas Corpus

A Proclamation by the President of the United States of America. No. 3. April 15, 1861

Whereas the laws of the United States have been, for some time past, and now are opposed, and execution thereof obstructed, in the States of South Carolina, Georgia, Alabama, Florida, Mississippi, Louisiana, and Texas, by combinations too powerful to be suppressed by the ordinary course of judicial proceedings, or by the powers vested in the marshals by law:

Now, therefore, I, ABRAHAM LINCOLN, President of the United States, in virtue of the power in me vested by the Constitution and laws, have thought fit to call forth, and hereby do call forth, the militia of the several States of the Union, to the aggregate number of seventy-five thousand, in order to suppress said combinations, and to cause the laws to be duly executed.

The details for this object will be immediately communicated to the State authorities through the War Department.

I appeal to all loyal citizens to favor, facilitate, and aid this effort to maintain the honor, the integrity, and the existence of our National Union, and the perpetuity of poplar government; and to redress wrongs already long enough endured.

I deem it proper to say that the first service assigned to the forces hereby called forth will probably be to repossess the forts, places, and property which have been seized from the Union; and in every event, the utmost care will be observed, consistently with the objects aforesaid, to avoid any devastation, any destruction of, or interference with, property, or any disturbance of peaceful citizens in any part of the country.

And I hereby command the persons composing the combinations aforesaid to disperse, and retire peaceably to their respective abodes within twenty days from this date.

Deeming that the present condition of public affairs presents an extraordinary occasion, I do hereby, in virtue of the power in me vested by the Constitution, convene both Houses of Congress. Senators and Representatives are therefore summoned to assemble at their respective chambers, at twelve o'clock, noon on Thursday, the fourth day of July next, then and there to consider and determine such measures as, in their wisdom, the public safety and interest may seem to demand.

In witness whereof, I have hereunto set my hand, and caused the seal of the United States to be affixed.

Done at the City of Washington, this fifteenth day of April, in the year of our Lord one thousand [L.S.] eight hundred and sixty-one, and of the Independence of the United States the eighty-fifth.

ABRAHAM LINCOLN.

By the President:

William H. Seward, Secretary of State.

A Proclamation by the President of the United States of America. No. 9. August 16, 1861

Whereas, on the fifteenth day of April, eighteen hundred and sixty-one, the President of the United States, in view of an insurrection against the Laws, Constitution, and Government of the United States, which had broken out within the States of South Carolina, Georgia, Alabama, Florida, Mississippi, Louisiana, and Texas, in pursuance of the provisions of the act entitled "An Act to provide for calling forth the militia to execute the laws of the Union, suppress insurrections, and repel invasions, and to repeal the act now in force for that purpose," approved February twenty-eight, seventeen hundred and ninety-five, did call forth the militia to suppress said insurrection, and to cause the laws of the Union to be duly executed, and insurgents have failed to disperse by the time directed by the President; and whereas, such insurrection has since broken out, and yet exists, within the States of Virginia, North Carolina, Tennessee, and Arkansas; and, whereas, the insurgents in all the said States claim to act under the authority thereof, and such claim is not disclaimed or repudiated by the persons exercising the functions of government in such State or States, or in the part or parts thereof in which such combinations exist, nor has such insurrection been suppressed by said States:

Now, therefore, I, ABRAHAM LINCOLN, President of the United States, in pursuance of an act of Congress, approved July thirteen, eighteen hundred and sixty-one, do hereby declare that the inhabitants of the said States of Georgia, South Carolina, Virginia, North Carolina, Tennessee, Alabama, Louisiana, Texas, Arkansas, Mississippi, and Florida (except the inhabitants of that part of the State of Virginia lying west of the Allegheny mountains, and of such other parts of the State and the other States hereinbefore named as may maintain a loyal adhesion to the Union and the Constitution, or may be, from time to time, occupied and controlled by forces of the United States engaged in the dispersion of said insurgents) are in a state of insurrection against the United States, and that all commercial intercourse between the same and the inhabitants thereof, with the exceptions aforesaid, and the citizens of other States and other parts of the United States is unlawful, and will remain unlawful until such insurrection shall cease or has been suppressed; that all goods and chattels, wares and merchandise, coming from any of said States, with the exceptions aforesaid, into other parts of the United States, without the special license and permission of the President, through the Secretary of the Treasury, or proceeding to any of said States, with the exceptions aforesaid, by land or water, together with the vessel or vehicle conveying the same, or conveying persons to or from said States, with said exceptions, will be forfeited to the United States; and that from and after fifteen days from the issuing of this proclamation, all ships and vessels belonging in whole or in part to any citizen or inhabitant of any of said States, with said exceptions, found at sea, or in any port of the United States, will be forfeited to the United States; and I hereby enjoin upon all district attorneys, marshals, and officers of the revenue and of the military and naval forces of the United States to be vigilant in the execution of said act, and in the enforcement of the penalties and forfeitures imposed or declared by it; leaving any party who may think of himself aggrieved thereby to his application to the Secretary of the Treasury for the remission of any penalty or forfeiture, which the said Secretary is authorized by law to grant if, in his judgment, the special circumstances of any case shall require such remission.

In witness whereof, I have hereunto set my hand, and caused the seal of the United States to be affixed.

Done at the City of Washington, this sixteenth day [L.S.] of

August, in the year of our Lord eighteen hundred and sixty-one, and of the Independence of the United States of America the eighty-sixth.

ABRAHAM LINCOLN.

By the President:

William H. Seward, Secretary of State.

A Proclamation by the President of the United States of America. No. 1. September 24, 1862

Whereas, it has become necessary to call into service not only volunteers but also portions of the militia of the states by draft in order to suppress the insurrection existing in the United States, and disloyal persons are not adequately restrained by the ordinary processes of law from hindering this measure and from giving aid and comfort in various ways to the insurrection:

Now, therefore, be it ordered, First.—That during the existing insurrection and as a necessary measure for suppressing the same, all rebels and insurgents, their aiders and abettors within the United States, and all persons discouraging volunteer enlistments, resisting militia drafts, or guilty of any disloyal practice, affording aid and comfort to the rebels against the authority of the United States, shall be subject to martial law and liable to trial and punishment by courts-martial or military commissions:

Second.—That the writ of habeas corpus is suspended in respect to all persons arrested, or who are now, or hereafter during the rebellion shall be, imprisoned in any fort, camp, arsenal, military prison, or other place of confinement by any military authority or by the sentence of any court-martial or military commission.

In witness whereof, I have hereunto set my hand, and caused the seal of the United States to be affixed.

Done at the city of Washington, this twenty-fourth [L.S.] day of September, in the year of our Lord one thousand eight hundred and sixty-two, and of the Independence of the United States the eighty-seventh.

ABRAHAM LINCOLN.

By the President:

William H. Seward, Secretary of State.

An Act Relating to Habeas Corpus, and Regulating Judicial Proceedings in Certain Cases. March 3, 1863

Be it enacted by the Senate and House of Representatives of the United States of America in Congress assembled, That, during the present rebellion, the President of the United States, whenever, in his judgment, the public safety may require it, is authorized to suspend the privilege of the writ of habeas corpus in any case throughout the United States, or any part thereof. And whenever and wherever the said privilege shall be suspended, as aforesaid, no military or other officer shall be compelled, in answer to any writ of habeas corpus, to return the body of any person or persons detained by him by authority of the President; but upon the certificate, under oath, of the officer having charge of any one so detained that such person is detained by him as a prisoner under authority of the President, further proceedings under the writ of habeas corpus shall be suspended by the judge or court having issued the said writ, so long as said suspension by the President shall remain in force, and said rebellion continue.

Sec. 2. And be it further enacted, That the Secretary of State and the Secretary of War be, and they are hereby, directed, as soon as may be practicable, to furnish to the judges of the circuit and district courts of the United States and of the District of Columbia a list of names of all persons, citizens of states in which the administration of the laws has continued unimpaired in the said Federal courts, who are now, or may hereafter be, held as prisoners of the United States, by order or authority of the President of the United States or either of said Secretaries, in any fort, arsenal, or other place, as state or political prisoners, or otherwise than as prisoners of war; and said list to contain the names of all those who reside in the respective jurisdictions of said judges, or who may be deemed by the said Secretaries, or either of them, to have violated any law of the United States in any of said jurisdictions, and also the date of each arrest; the Secretary of State to furnish a list of such persons as are imprisoned by the order or authority of the President, acting through the State Department, and the Secretary of War a list of such as are imprisoned by the order or authority of the President, acting through the Department of War. And in all cases where a grand jury, having attended any of said courts having jurisdiction in the premises, after the passage of this act, and after the furnishing of said list, as aforesaid, has terminated its session without finding an indictment or presentment, or other proceeding against any such person, it shall be the duty of the judge of said court forthwith to make an order that any such prisoner desiring a discharge from said imprisonment be brought before him to be discharged; and every officer of the

United States having custody of such prisoner is hereby directed immediately to obey and execute said judge's order; and in case he shall delay or refuse so to do, he shall be subject to indictment for a misdemeanor, and be punished by a fine of not less than five hundred dollars and imprisonment in the common jail for a period not less than six months, in the discretion of the court: Provided, however, That no person shall be discharged by virtue of the provisions of this act until after he or she shall have taken an oath of allegiance to the Government of the United States, and to support the Constitution thereof; and that he or she will not hereafter in any way encourage or give aid and comfort to the present rebellion, or the supporters thereof: And provided, also, That the judge or court before whom such person may be brought, before discharging him or her from imprisonment, shall have power, on examination of the case, and, if the public safety shall require it, shall be required to cause him or her to enter into recognizance, with or without surety, in sum to be fixed by said judge or court, to keep the peace and be of good behavior towards the United States and its citizens, and from time to time, and at such times as such judge or court may direct, appear before said judge or court to be further dealt with, according to law, as the circumstances may require. And it shall be the duty of the district attorney of the United States to attend such examination before the judge.

Sec. 3. And be it further enacted, That in case any of such prisoners shall be under indictment or presentment for any offence against the laws of the United States, and by existing laws bail or a recognizance may be taken for the appearance for trial of such person, it shall be the duty of said judge at once to discharge such person upon bail or recognizance for trial as aforesaid. And in case the said Secretaries of State and War shall for any reason refuse or omit to furnish the said list of persons held as prisoners as aforesaid at the time of the passage of this act within twenty days thereafter, and of such persons as hereafter may be arrested within twenty days from the time of the arrest, any citizen may, after a grand jury shall have terminated its session without finding an indictment or presentment, as provided in the second section of this act, by a petition alleging the facts aforesaid touching any of the persons so as aforesaid imprisoned, supported by the oath of such petitioner or any other credible person, obtain and be entitled to have the said judge's order to discharge such prisoner on the same terms and conditions prescribed in the second section of this act: Provided, however, That the said judge shall be satisfied such allegations are true.

Sec. 4. And be it further enacted, That any order of the President, or under his authority, made at any time during the existence of the present rebellion, shall be a defense in all courts to any action or prosecution, civil or criminal, pending, or to be commenced, for any search, seizure, arrest, or imprisonment, made, done, or committed, or acts omitted to be done, under and by virtue of such order, or under color of any law of Congress, and such defense may be made by special plea, or under the general issue.

Sec. 5. And be it further enacted, That if any suit or prosecution, civil or criminal, has been or shall be commenced in any state court against any officer, civil or military, or against any other person, for any arrest or imprisonment made, or other trespasses or wrongs done or committed, or any act omitted to be done, at any time during the present rebellion, by virtue or under color of any authority derived from or exercised by or under the President of the United States, or any act of Congress, and the defendant shall, at the time of entering his appearance in such court, or if such appearance shall have been entered before the passage of this act, then at the next session of the court in which such suit or prosecution is pending, file a petition, stating the facts and verified by affidavit, for the removal of the cause for trial at the next circuit court of the United States, to be holden in the district where the suit is pending, and offer good and sufficient surety for his filing in such court, on the first day of its session, copies of such process and other proceedings against him, and also for his appearing in such court and entering special bail in the cause, if special bail was originally required therein. It shall be the duty of the state court to accept the surety and proceed no further in the cause or prosecution, and the bail that shall have been originally taken shall be discharged. And such copies being filed as aforesaid in such court of the United States, the cause shall proceed therein in the same manner as if it had been brought in said court by original process, whatever may be the amount in dispute or the damages claimed, or whatever the citizenship of the parties, any former law to the contrary not withstanding. And any attachment of the goods or estate of the defendant by the original process shall hold the goods or estate so attached to answer the final judgment in the same manner as by the laws of such state they would have been holden to answer final judgment had it been rendered in the court in which the suit or prosecution was commenced. And it shall be lawful in any such action or prosecution which may be now pending, or hereafter commenced, before any state court whatever, for any cause aforesaid, after final judgment, for either party to remove and transfer, by appeal, such case during the session or term of said court at which the same shall have taken place, from such court to the next circuit court of the United States to be held in the district in which such appeal shall be taken, in manner aforesaid. And it shall be the duty of the person taking such appeal to produce and file in the said circuit court attested copies of the process, proceedings, and judgments in such cause; and it shall also be competent for either party, within six months after the rendition of a judgment in any such cause, by writ of error or other process, to remove the same to the circuit court of the United States of that district in which such judgment shall have been rendered; and the said circuit court shall thereupon proceed to try and determine the facts and the law in such action, in the same manner as if the same had been there originally commenced, the judgment in such case notwithstanding. And any bail which may have been taken, or property attached, shall be holden on the final judgment of the said circuit court in such action, in the same manner as if no such removal and transfer had been made, as aforesaid. And the state court, from which any such action, civil or criminal, may be removed and transferred as aforesaid, upon the parties giving good and sufficient security for the prosecution thereof, shall allow the same to be removed and transferred, and proceed no further in the case: Provided, however, That if the party aforesaid shall fail duly to enter the removal and transfer, as aforesaid, in the circuit court of the United States, agreeably to this act, the state court, by which judgment shall have been rendered, and from which the transfer and removal shall have been made, as aforesaid, shall be authorized, on motion for that purpose, to issue execution, and to carry into effect any such judgment, the same as if no such removal and transfer had been made. And provided also, That no such appeal or writ of error shall be allowed in any criminal action or prosecution where final judgment shall have been rendered in favor of the defendant or respondent by the state court. And if in any suit hereafter commenced the plaintiff is non-suited or judgment pass against him, the defendant shall recover double cost.

Sec. 6. And be it further enacted, That any suit or prosecution described in this act, in which final judgment may be rendered in the circuit court, may be carried by writ of error to the supreme court, whatever may be the amount of said judgment.

Sec. 7. And be it further enacted, That no suit or prosecution, civil or criminal, shall be maintained for any arrest or imprisonment made, or other trespasses or wrongs done or committed, or act omitted to be done, at any time during the present rebellion, by virtue or under color of any authority derived from or exercised by or under the President of the United States, or by or under any act of Congress, unless the same shall have been commenced within two years next after such arrest, imprisonment, trespass, or wrong may have been done or committed or act may have been omitted to be done: Provided, That in no case shall the limitation herein provided commence to run until the passage of this act, so that no party shall, by virtue of this act, be debarred of his remedy by suit or prosecution until two years from and after the passage of this act.

Approved, March 3, 1863.

A Proclamation by the President of the United States of America. No. 7. September 15, 1863

Whereas, the Constitution of the United States has ordained that the privilege of the writ of habeas corpus shall not be suspended unless when in cases of rebellion or invasion the public safety may require it; and whereas, a rebellion was existing on the third day of March, 1863, which rebellion is still existing; and whereas, by a statute which was approved on that day, it was enacted by the Senate and House of Representatives of the United States, in congress assembled, that during the present insurrection, the President of the United States, whenever in his judgment the public safety may require it, is authorized to suspend the privilege of the writ of habeas corpus in any case throughout the United States, or any part thereof; and whereas, in the judgment of the President, the public safety does require that the privilege of the said writ shall now be suspended throughout the United States in the cases where, by the authority of the President of the United States, military, naval, and civil officers of the United States, or any of them, hold persons under their command or in their custody, either as prisoners of war, spies, or aiders or abettors of the enemy, or officers, soldiers, or seamen enrolled or drafted or mustered or enlisted in, or belonging to, the land or naval forces of the United States, or as deserters therefrom, otherwise amenable to military law, or the rules and articles of war, or the rules or regulations prescribed for the military or naval services by authority of the President of the United States, or for resisting a draft, or for any other offence against the military or naval service:

Now, therefore, I, Abraham Lincoln, President of the United States, do hereby proclaim and make known to all whom it may concern, that the privilege of the writ of habeas corpus is suspended throughout the United States in the several cases before mentioned, and that this suspension will continue throughout the duration of the said rebellion, or until this proclamation shall, by a subsequent one to be issued by the President of the United States, be modified or revoked. And I do hereby require all magistrates, attorneys, and other civil officers within the United States, and all officers and others in the military and naval services of the United States, to take distinct notice of this suspension, and to give it full effect, and all citizens of the United States to conduct and govern themselves accordingly, and in conformity with the constitution of the United States and the laws of congress in such case made and provided.

In testimony whereof, I have hereunto set my hand, [L.S.] and caused the seal of the United States to be affixed, this fifteenth day of September, in the year of our Lord one thousand eight hundred and sixty-three, and of the Independence of the United States of America the eighty-eighth.

ABRAHAM LINCOLN.

By the President:

William H. Seward, Secretary of State.

Appendix D: Several Regulations and a Speech That Are Relevant to the Reconstruction

Special Field Order No. 15, by Order of Major General W. T. Sherman. January 16, 1865

I. The islands from Charleston, south, the abandoned rice fields along the rivers for thirty miles back from the sea, and the country bordering the St. Johns river, Florida, are reserved and set apart for the settlement of the negroes now made free by acts of war and the proclamation of the President of the United States.

II. At Beaufort, Hilton Head, Savannah, Fernandina, St. Augustine and Jacksonville, the blacks may remain in their chosen or accustomed vocations — but on the islands, and in the settlements hereafter to be established, no white person whatever, unless military officer and soldiers detailed for duty, will be permitted to reside; and the sole and exclusive management of affairs will be left to the freed people themselves, subject only to the United States military authority and the acts of Congress. By the laws of war, and orders of the President of the United States, the negro is free and must be dealt with as such. He cannot be subjected to conscription or forced military service, save by the written orders of the highest military authority of the Department, under such regulations as the President or Congress may prescribe. Domestic servants, blacksmiths, carpenters and other mechanics, will be free to select their own work and residence, but the young and able-bodied negroes must be encouraged to enlist as soldiers in the service of the United States, to contribute their share towards maintaining their own freedom, and securing their rights as citizens of the United States.

Negroes so enlisted will be organized into companies, battalions and regiments, under the orders of the United States military authorities, and will be paid, fed and clothed according to law. The bounties paid on enlistment may, with the consent of the recruit, go to assist his family and settlement in procuring agricultural implements, seed, tools, boots, clothing, and other articles necessary for their livelihood.

III. Whenever three respectable negroes, heads of families, shall desire to settle on land, and shall have selected for that purpose an island or a locality clearly defined, within the limits above designated, the Inspector of Settlements and Plantations will himself, or by such subordinate officer as he may appoint, give them a license to settle such island or district, and afford them such assistance as he can to enable them to establish a peaceable agricultural settlement. The three parties named will subdivide the land, under the supervision of the Inspector, among themselves and such others as may choose to settle near them, so that each family shall have a plot of not more than (40) forty acres of tillable ground, and when it borders on some water channel, with not more than 800 feet water front, in the possession of which land the military authorities will afford them protection, until such time as they can protect themselves, or until Congress shall regulate their title. The Quartermaster may, on the requisition of the Inspector of Settlements and Plantations, place at the disposal of the Inspector, one or more of the captured steamers, to ply between the settlements and one or more of the commercial points heretofore named in orders, to afford the settlers the opportunity to supply their necessary wants, and to sell the products of their land and labor.

IV. Whenever a negro has enlisted in the military service of the United States, he may locate his family in any one of the settlements at pleasure, and acquire a homestead, and all other rights and privileges of a settler, as though present in person. In like manner, negroes may settle their families and engage on board the gunboats, or in fishing, or in the navigation of the inland waters without loosing any claim to land or other advantages derived from this system. But no one, unless an actual settler as above defined, or unless absent on Government service, will be entitled to claim any right to land or property in any settlement by virtue of these orders.

V. In order to carry out this system of settlement, a general officer will be detailed as Inspector of Settlements and Plantations, whose duty it shall be to visit the settlements, to regulate their police and general management, and who will furnish personally to each head of a family, subject to the approval of the President of the United States, a possessory title in writing, giving as near as possible the description of boundaries; and who shall adjust all claims or conflicts that may arise under the same, subject to the like approval, treating such titles altogether as possessory. The same general officer will also be charged with the enlistment and organization of the negro recruits, and protecting their interests while absent from their settlements; and will be governed by the rules and regulations prescribed by the War Department for such purposes.

VI. Brigadier General R. SAXTON is hereby appointed Inspector of Settlements and Plantations, and will at once enter on the performance of his duties. No change is intended or desired in the settlement now on Beaufort [Port Royal] Island, nor will any rights to property heretofore acquired be affected thereby.

BY ORDER OF MAJOR GENERAL W. T. SHERMAN:

President Lincoln's Second Inaugural Address. March 4, 1865

Fellow-countrymen: At this second appearing to take the oath of the Presidential office, there is less occasion for an extended address than there was at the first. Then, a statement, somewhat in detail, of a course to be pursued, seemed fitting and proper. Now, at the expiration of four years, during which public declarations have been constantly called forth on every point and phase of the great contest which still absorbs the attention and engrosses the energies of the nation, little that is new could be presented. The Progress of our arms, upon which all else chiefly depends, is as well known to the public as to myself; and it is, I trust, reasonably satisfactory and encouraging to all. With high hope for the future, no prediction in regard to it is ventured.

On the occasion corresponding to this four years ago, all thoughts were anxiously directed to an impending civil war. All dreaded it—all sought to avert it. While the inaugural address was being delivered from this place, devoted altogether to saving the Union without war, insurgent agents were in the city seeking to destroy it without war—seeking to dissolve the Union, and divide effects, by negotiation. Both parties deprecated war; but one of them would make war rather than let the nation survive; and the other would accept war rather than let it perish. And the war came.

One-eighth of the whole population were colored slaves, not distributed generally over the Union, but localized in the Southern part of it. These slaves constituted a peculiar and powerful interest. All knew that his interest was, somehow, the cause of the war. To strengthen, perpetuate, and extend this interest was the object for which the insurgents would rend the Union, even by war; while the government claimed no right to do more than to restrict the territorial enlargement of it. Neither party expected for the war the magnitude or the duration which it has already attained. Neither anticipated that the cause of the conflict might cease with, or even before, the conflict itself should cease. Each looked for an easier triumph, and a result less fundamental and astounding. Both read the same Bible, and pray to the same God; and each invokes his aid against the other. It may seem strange that any men should dare to ask a just God's assistance in wringing their bread from the sweat of other men's faces; but let us judge not, that we be not judged. The prayers of both could not be answered — that of neither has been answered fully. The Almighty has his own purpose. "Woe unto the world because of offenses! for it must needs be that offenses come; but woe to that man by whom the offense cometh." If we shall suppose that American slavery is one of those offenses which, in the providence of God, must needs come, but which, having continued through his appointed time, he now wills to remove, and that he gives both North and South this terrible war, as the woe due to those by whom the offense came, shall we discern therein any departure from those divine attributes which the believers in a living God always ascribe to him? Fondly do we hope — fervently do we pray — that this mighty scourge of war may speedily pass away. Yet, if God wills that it continue until all the wealth piled by the bondsman's two hundred and fifty years of unrequited toil shall be sunk, and until every drop of blood drawn with the lash shall be paid by another drawn with the sword, as was said three thousand years ago, so still it must be said: "The judgments of the Lord are true and righteous altogether."

With malice toward none; with charity for all; with firmness in the right, as God gives us to see the right, let us strive on to finish the work we are in; to bind up the nation's wounds; to care for him who shall have borne the battle, and for his widow, and his orphan — to do all which may achieve and cherish a just and lasting peace among ourselves, and with all nations.

Circular #13 of the War Department, Bureau of Refugees, Freedmen, and Abandoned Lands, issued by O. O. Howard, Major General. July 28, 1865

In order to establish a definite and uniform policy relative to confiscated and Abandoned Lands, and other confiscated and abandoned property which are now or that may hereafter come under the control of this Bureau by virtue of the Act approved March 3, 1865, establishing the Bureau, and other acts and sections of Acts and orders of the president relative to captured, confiscated and Abandoned property, to wit: SEC 2 Act approved July 21, 1864, and General Orders No. 110, War Dept June 7, 1865, the following rules and regulations are established.

I. All confiscated and abandoned land, and other confiscated and abandoned property, that now and or that may hereafter come under the control of the Bureau of Refugees, Freedmen & Abandoned Lands, by virtue of said acts and Sections of Acts and order of the President, are and shall be set apart for the use of loyal refugees and freedmen and as much as be necessary, assigned to them as provided in Sect. 4. of the act establishing the Bureau viz: "to every male citizen, whether refugee or freedman, as aforesaid, there shall be assigned not more than forty acres of such land, and the person to whom it was so assigned shall be protected in the use and enjoyment of the land for the term of three years at an annual rent not exceeding six per centum upon the value of such land, as it was appraised by the state authorities in the year eighteen hundred and sixty, for the purpose of taxation, and in case no such appraisal can be found, then the rental shall be based upon the estimated value of the land in said year, to be ascertained in such manner as the commissioner may by regulation prescribe. At the end of said term, or at any time during said term, the occupants of any parcels so assigned may purchase the land and receive such title thereto as the United States can convey, upon paying therefor the value of the land, as ascertained and fixed for the purpose of determining the annual rent aforesaid."

II. All lands, or other property, within the several insurrectionary States, viz: Virginia, North Carolina, South Carolina, Georgia, Florida, Alabama, Mississippi, Kentucky, Tennessee, Missouri, Arkansas, Louisiana, & Texas, to which the US have or shall have acquired title by confiscation, or sale, or otherwise during the late rebellion, and all abandoned lands, or other abandoned property in those states, have become so by the construction of Sec 2 of act approved July 21, 1864, viz: "Property, real or personal, shall be regarded as abandoned when the lawful owner thereof shall be voluntarily absent therefrom and engaged either in arms or otherwise, in aiding or encouraging the rebellion, and which remains unsold or otherwise disposed of are, and shall be considered as under the control of the Commissioner of the Bureau of Refugees, Freedmen & Abandoned Lands, for the purposes herein before set forth, and for this time authorized by the Act establishing the Bureau; and no part or parcel of said confiscated or Abandoned property shall be surrendered and or restored to the former owner thereof, or other claimants thereby, except such surrender or restoration be authorized by said Commissioner.

III. Whenever any abandoned lands or other abandoned property that shall have come into the possession of the Bureau does not fall under the definition of "Abandoned," as set forth in Sec. 2 of the Act approved July 2, 1864, it will be formally surrendered by the Commissioner or Asst Commissioners of the Bureau, upon clear proof that the claimant did not abandon the property in the sense defined in said Section and Act.

IV. In the surrender or restoration of any property the requirements of Circular No. 3 current [?] from this Bureau will be carefully observed.

V. Asst Commissioners will as rapidly as possible, cause accurate description of all confiscated and abandoned lands and other confiscated and abandoned property that are now or that may here after come under their control, to be made, and besides keeping a record of such themselves, will forward monthly to the Commissioner of the Bureau, copies of such descriptions in the manner prescribed by Circular No 10 of July 11, 1865 from this Bureau. They will, with as little delay as possible, select and set apart such confiscated and abandoned lands and property as may be deemed necessary for the immediate use of Refugees and Freedmen, the specific division of which into lots, and the rental or sale thereof according to the law establishing the Bureau, will be completed as soon as practicable and reported to the Commissioner. In the selection and setting apart of such lands and property, care will be used to take that about which there is the least doubt as to the proper custody and control of the Bureau.

VI. The pardon of the President will not be understood to extend to the surrender of abandoned or confiscated property which by law has been "set apart for Refugees and Freedmen" or "in use for the employment and general welfare of all persons within the lines of National Military occupation within said insurrectionary States formerly held as slaves who are or shall become free."

(See Act of Mar 3, 1865 and Act of July 21, 1864. Secs 1, Chapter 225)

O. O. Howard
Major General, Commissioner,
Bureau of Refugees, Freedmen,
and Abandoned Lands

Not promulgated
Rescinded by Circular No. 15 of date Sep 12, 1865.

Circular #15 of the War Department, Bureau of Refugees, Freedmen, and Abandoned Lands, Issued by O. O. Howard, Major General. September 12, 1865

I. Circular No 13 of July 28, 1865, from this Bureau, and all portions of Circulars from this Bureau conflicting with the provisions of this Circular are hereby rescinded.

II.This Bureau has charge of such tracts of lands within the insurrectionary states as shall have acquired title by confiscation or sale, or otherwise, and no such lands now in its possession shall be surrendered to any claimant except as having after provided.

III. Abandoned lands are defined in Sec 2 of the Act of Congress, approved July 2, 1864, as lands, the lawful owner whereof shall be voluntarily absent, therefrom, and engaged either in arms or otherwise in aiding or encouraging the rebellion.

IV. Land will not be regarded as confiscated until it has been condemned, and sold by decree of the U.S. Court for the District in which the property may be found, and the title thereto thus vested in the United States.

V. Upon its appearing satisfactorily to any Assistant Commissioner that any property under his control is not abandoned as above defined, and that the U.S. has acquired no title to it, by confiscation, sale, or otherwise, he will formally surrender it to the authorized claimant or claimants promptly reporting his action to the Commissioner.

VI. Asst Commissioners will prepare accurate descriptions of all confiscated and abandoned lands under their control, keeping a record thereof themselves, and forwarding monthly, to the Commissioner, copies of these descriptions in the manner prescribed in Circular No. 10 of July 11, 1865, from this Bureau.

They will set apart as much of said lands as is necessary for the immediate use of loyal Refugees and Freedmen, being careful to select for this purpose those lands which most clearly fall under the control of this Bureau, which selection must be submitted to the Commissioner for his approval.

The specific division of lands so set apart, into lots and the rental of sale thereof, according to Sec. 4 of the law establishing the Bureau, will be completed as soon as practicable and reported to the Commissioner.

VII.Abandoned Lands held by this Bureau may be restored to owners pardoned by the President, by the Asst Commissioners to whom applications for such restoration should be forwarded, so far as practicable through the Supts of the Districts in which the lands are situated.

Each application must be accompanied by—

1st Evidence of especial pardon by the President, or a copy of the oath of amnesty prescribed in the President's Proclamation of May 29, 1865, when the applicants is not included in any of the classes therein exempted from the benefits of said oath.

2nd Proof of title.

Officers of the Bureau through whom this application passes will endorse thereon such facts as may assist the Asst Commissioner in his decision, stating especially the use made by the Bureau of the Land.

VIII. No lands under cultivation by loyal Refugees or Freedmen, will be restored under this Circular, until the crops now growing shall be secured for the benefit of the cultivators unless full and just compensation be made for their labor and its products, and for their expenditures.

O. O. Howard
Major Genl. Commissioner

Approved
Andrew Johnson.
President of the United States

Appendix E: Laws Authorizing a Response to Rebellion or Insurrection

An Act to provide for calling forth the militia to execute the laws of the Union, suppress insurrection, and repel invasions; and to repeal the act now in force for those purposes. February 28, 1795.

Section 1. Be it enacted by the Senate and House of Representatives of the United States of America in Congress assembled, That whenever the United States shall be invaded, or be in imminent danger of invasion from any foreign nation or Indian tribe, it shall be lawful for the President of the United States to call forth such number of the militia of the state, or states, most convenient to the place of danger, or scene of action, as he may judge necessary to repel such invasion, and to issue his orders for that purpose, to such officer or officers of the militia, as he shall think proper. And in case of an insurrection in any state against the government thereof, it shall be lawful for the President of the United States, on application of the legislature of such state, or of the executive, (when the legislature cannot be convened,) to call forth such number of the militia of any other state or states, as may be applied for, as he may judge sufficient to suppress such insurrection.

Sec. 2. And be it further enacted, That whenever the laws of the United States shall be opposed, or the execution thereof obstructed, in any state, by combinations too powerful to be suppressed by the ordinary course of judicial proceedings, or by the powers vested in the marshals by this act, it shall be lawful for the President of the United States, to call forth the militia of such state, or of any other state or states, as may be necessary to suppress such combinations, and to cause the laws to be duly executed; and the use of militia so to be called forth may be continued, if necessary, until the expiration of thirty days after the commencement of the then next session of Congress.

Sec. 3. Provided always, and be it further enacted, That whenever it may be necessary, in the judgment of the President, to use the military force hereby directed to be called forth, the President shall forthwith, by proclamation, command such insurgents to disperse, and retire peaceably to their respective abodes, within a limited time.

Sec. 4. And be it further enacted, That the militia employed in the service of the United States, shall be subject to the same rules and articles of war, as the troops of the United States: And that no officer, non-commissioned officer, or private of the militia shall be compelled to serve more than three months, after his arrival at the place of rendezvous, in any one year, nor more than in due rotation with every other able-bodied man of the same rank in the battalion to which he belongs.

Sec. 5. And be it further enacted, That every officer, non-commissioned officer, or private of the militia, who shall fail to obey the orders of the President of the United States, in any of the cases before recited, shall forfeit a sum not exceeding one year's pay, and not less than one month's pay, to be determined and adjudged by a court martial; and such officer shall, moreover, be liable to be cashiered by sentence of a court martial, and be incapacitated from holding a commission in the militia, for a term of not exceeding twelve months, at the discretion of the said court: And such non-commissioned officers and privates shall be liable to be imprisoned, by a like sentence, on failure of payment of the fines adjudged against them, for one calendar month, for every five dollars of such fine.

Sec. 6. And be it further enacted, That courts martial for the trial of militia shall be composed of militia officers only.

Sec. 7. And be it further enacted, That all fines to be assessed, as aforesaid, shall be certified by the presiding officer of the court martial, before whom the same shall be assessed, to the marshal of the district, in which the delinquent shall reside, or to one of his deputies, and also to the supervisor of the revenue of the same district, who shall record the said certificate in a book to be kept for that purpose. The said marshal or his deputy shall forthwith proceed to levy the said fines with costs, by distress and sale of the goods and chattels of the delinquent; which costs and manner of proceeding, with respect to the sale of the goods distrained, shall be agreeable to the laws of the state, in which the same shall be, in other cases of distress. And where any non-commissioned officer or private shall be adjudged to suffer imprisonment, there being no goods or chattels to be found, whereof to levy the said fines, the marshal of the district, or his deputy, may commit such delinquent to gaol, during the term, for which he shall be adjudged to imprisonment, or until the fine shall be paid, in the same manner, as other persons condemned to fine and imprisonment at the suit of the United States may be committed.

Sec. 8. And be it further enacted, That the marshals and their deputies shall pay all such fines by them levied, to the supervisor of the revenue in the district in which they are collected, within two months after they shall have received the same, deducting therefrom five per centum, as a compensation for their trouble; and in case of failure, the same shall be recoverable by action of debt or information, in any court of the United States, of the district in which such fines shall be levied, having cognizance thereof, to be sued for, prosecuted, and recovered, in the name of the supervisor of the district, with interest and costs.

Sec. 9. And be it further enacted, That the marshals of the several districts, and their deputies, shall have the same powers in executing the laws of the United States, as sheriffs and their deputies, in the several states, have by law, in executing the laws of the respective states.

Sec. 10. And be it further enacted, That the act, intitled "An act to provide for calling forth the militia, to execute the laws of the Union, suppress insurrections, and repel invasions, passed the second day of May one thousand seven hundred and ninety-two, shall be, and the same is hereby repealed.

Approved, February 28, 1795.

An Act further to provide for the collection of duties on imports, and for other purposes. July 13, 1861

Be it enacted by the Senate and House of Representatives of the United States of America in Congress assembled, That whenever it shall in the judgment of the President, by reason of unlawful combinations of persons in opposition to the laws of the United States, become impracticable to execute the revenue laws and collect the duties on imports by the ordinary means, in the ordinary way, at any port of entry in any collection district, he is authorized to cause such duties to be collected at any port of delivery in said district until such obstruction shall cease; and in such case the surveyors at said port of delivery shall be clothed with all the powers, and be subject to all the obligations of collectors at ports of entry; and the Secretary of the Treasury, with the approbation of the President, shall appoint such number of weighers, gaugers, measurers, inspectors, appraisers, and clerks as may be necessary, in his judgment, for the faithful execution of the revenue laws at said ports of delivery, and shall fix and establish the limits within which such ports of delivery are constituted ports of entry, as aforesaid; and all the provisions of law regulating the issue of marine papers, the coasting trade, the warehousing of imports, and collection of duties, shall apply to the ports of entry so constituted, in the same manner as they do to ports of entry established by the law now in force.

Sec. 2. And be it further enacted, That if, from the cause mentioned in the foregoing section, in the judgment of the President, the revenue from duties on imports cannot be effectually collected at any port of entry in any collection district, in the ordinary way, and by the ordinary means, or by the course provided in the foregoing section, then and in that case he may direct that the custom-house for the district be established in any secure place within said district, either on land or on board any vessel in said district or at sea near the coast; and in such case the collector shall reside at such place, or on shipboard, as the case may be, and there detain all vessels and cargoes arriving within or approaching said district, until the duties imposed by law on said vessels and their cargoes are paid in cash: Provided, That if the owner or consignee of the cargo on board any vessel detained as aforesaid, or the master of said vessel shall desire to enter a port of entry in any other district in the United States where no obstructions to the executions of the laws exist, the master of such vessel may be permitted so to change the destination of the vessel and cargo in his manifest, whereupon the collector shall deliver him a written permit to proceed to the port so designated: And, provided further, That the Secretary of the Treasury shall, with the approbation of the President, make proper regulations for the enforcement on shipboard of such provisions of the laws regulating the assessment and collection of duties as in his judgment may be necessary and practicable.

Sec. 3. And be it further enacted, That it shall be unlawful to take any vessel or cargo detained as aforesaid from the custody of the proper officers of the customs, unless by process of some court of the United States; and in case of any attempt otherwise to take such vessel or cargo by any force, or combination, or assemblage of persons, too great to be overcome by the officers of the customs, it shall and may be lawful for the President, or such person or persons as he shall have empowered for that purpose, to employ such part of the army or navy or militia of the United States, or such force of citizen volunteers as may be deemed necessary for the purpose of preventing the removal of such vessel or cargo, and protecting the officers of the customs in retaining the custody thereof.

Sec. 4. And be it further enacted, That if, in the judgment of the President, from the cause mentioned in the first section of this act, the duties upon imports in any collection district cannot be effectually collected by ordinary means and in the ordinary way, or in the mode and manner provided in the foregoing sections of this act, then and in that case the President is hereby empowered to close the port or ports of entry in said district, and in such case give notice thereof by proclamation; and thereupon all right of importation, warehousing, and other privileges incident to ports of entry shall cease and be discontinued at such port so closed, until opened by the order of the President on the cessation of such obstructions; and if, while said ports are so closed, any ship or vessel from beyond the United States, or having on board any articles subject to duties, shall enter or attempt to enter any such port, the same, together with its tackle, apparel, furniture, and cargo, shall be forfeited to the United States.

Sec. 5. And be it further enacted, That whenever the President, in pursuance of the provisions of the second section of the act entitled "An act to provide for the calling forth the militia to execute the laws of the Union, suppress insurrections, and repel invasions, and to repeal the act now in force for that purpose," approved February twenty-eight, seventeen hundred and ninety-five, shall have called forth the militia to suppress combinations against the laws of the United States, and to cause the laws to be duly executed, and the insurgents shall have failed to disperse by the time directed by the President, and when said insurgents claim to act under the authority of any State or States, and such claim is not disclaimed or repudiated by the persons exercising the functions of government in such State or States, or in the part or parts thereof in which said combinations exists, nor such insurrection suppressed by said State or States, then and in such case it may and shall be lawful for the President, by proclamation, to declare that the inhabitants of such State, or any section or part thereof, where such insurrection exists, are in a state of insurrection against the United States; and thereupon all commercial intercourse by and between the same and the citizens thereof and the citizens of the rest of the United States shall cease and be unlawful so long as such condition of hostility shall continue; and all goods and chattels, wares and merchandise, coming from said State or section into the other parts of the United States, and all proceeding to such State or section, by land or water, shall, together with the vessel or vehicle conveying the same, or conveying persons to or from such State or section, be forfeited to the United States: Provided, however, That the President may, in his discretion, license and permit commercial intercourse with any such part of said State or section, the inhabitants of which are so declared in a state of insurrection, in such articles, and for such time, and by such persons, as he, in his discretion, may think most conducive to the public interest; and such intercourse, so far as by him licensed, shall be conducted and carried on only in pursuance of rules and regulations prescribed by the Secretary of the Treasury. And the Secretary of the Treasury may appoint such officers at places where officers of the customs are not now authorized by law as may be needed to carry into effect such licenses, rules and regulations; and officers of the customs and other officers shall receive for services under this section, and under said rules and regulations, such fees and compensation as are now allowed for similar service under other provisions of law.

Sec. 6. And be it further enacted, That from and after fifteen days after issuing of said proclamation, as provided in the last foregoing section of this act, any ship or vessel belonging in whole or in part to any citizen or inhabitant of said State or part of a State whose inhabitants are so declared in a state of insurrection, found at sea, or in any port of rest of the United States, shall be forfeited to the United States.

Sec. 7. And be it further enacted, That in the execution of the provisions of this act, and of the other laws of the United States providing for the collection of duties on imports and tonnage, it may and shall be lawful for the President, in addition to the revenue cutters in service, to employ in aid thereof such other suitable vessels as may, in his judgment, be required.

Sec. 8. And be it further enacted, That the forfeitures and penalties incurred by virtue of this act may be mitigated or remitted in pursuance of the authority vested in the Secretary of the Treasury by the act entitled "An act providing for mitigating or remitting for forfeitures, penalties, and disabilities accruing in certain cases therein mentioned," approved March third, seventeen hundred and ninety-seven, or in cases where special circumstances may seem to require it, according to regulations to be prescribed by the Secretary of the Treasury.

Sec. 9. And be it further enacted, That proceedings on seizures for forfeitures under this act may be pursued in the courts of the United States in any district into which the property so seized may be taken and proceedings instituted; and such courts shall have and entertain as full jurisdiction over the same as if the seizure was made in that district.

Approved, July 13, 1861.

An Act to provide for the suppression of rebellion against and resistance to the laws of the United States, and to amend the act entitled "An Act to Provide for Calling Forth the Militia to Execute the Laws of the Union," &c., passed February twenty-eight, seventeen hundred and ninety-five. July 29, 1861.

Be it enacted by the Senate and House of Representatives of the United States of America in Congress assembled, That whenever, by reason of unlawful obstructions, combinations, or assemblages of persons, or rebellion against the authority of the Government of the United States, it shall become impracticable, in the judgment of the President of the United States, to enforce, by the ordinary course of judicial proceedings, the laws of the United States within any State or Territory of the United States, it shall be lawful for the President of the United States to call forth the militia of any or all the States of the Union, and to employ such parts of the land and naval forces of the United States as he may deem necessary to enforce the faithful execution of the laws of the United States, or to suppress such rebellion in whatever State or Territory thereof the laws of the United States may be forcibly opposed, or the execution thereof forcibly obstructed.

Sec. 2. And be it further enacted, That whenever, in the judgment of the President, it may be necessary to use the military force hereby directed to be employed and called forth by him, the President shall forthwith, by proclamation, command such insurgents to disperse and retire peaceably to their respective abodes, within a limited time.

Sec. 3. And be it further enacted, That the militia so called into the service of the United States shall be subject to the same rules and articles of war as the troops of the United States, and be continued in the service of the United States until discharged by proclamation of the President: Provided, That such continuance in service shall not extend beyond sixty days after the commencement of the next regular session of Congress, unless Congress shall expressly provide by law therefor: And provided further, That the militia so called into the service of the United States shall, during their time of service, be entitled to the same pay, rations, and allowances for clothing as are or may be established by law for the army of the United States.

Sec. 4. And be it further enacted, That every officer, non-commissioned officer, or private of the militia, who shall fail to obey the orders of the President of the United States in any of the cases before recited, shall forfeit a sum not exceeding one year's pay, and not less than one month's pay, to be determined and adjudged by a court-martial; and such officer shall be liable to be cashiered by a sentence of court-martial, and be incapacitated from holding a commission in the militia for a term not exceeding twelve months, at the discretion of the court; and such non-commissioned officer and private shall be liable to imprisonment, by a like sentence, on failure of payment of the fines adjudged against them, for one calendar month for every twenty-five dollars of such fine.

Sec. 5. And be it further enacted, That courts-martial for the trial of militia shall be composed of militia officers only.

Sec. 6. And be it further enacted, That all fines to be assessed as aforesaid shall be certified by the presiding officer of the court-martial, and shall be collected and paid over according to the provisions and in the manner prescribed by the seventh and eighth sections of the act of February twenty-eight, seventeen hundred and ninety-five, to which this is an amendment.

Sec. 7. And be it further enacted, That the marshals of the several districts of the United States, and their deputies, shall have the same powers in executing the laws of the United States as sheriffs and their deputies in the several States, have by law, in executing the laws of the respective States.

Sec. 8. And be it further enacted, That sections two, three, and four of the act entitled "An Act to provide for calling forth the militia to execute the laws of the Union, suppress insurrections, and repel invasions, and to repeal the act now in force for those purposes," approved February twenty-eight, seventeen hundred and ninety-five, and so much of the residue of said act and of all other acts as conflict with this act are hereby repealed.

Approved, July 29, 1861.

Appendix F: Miscellaneous Laws Relevant to Reconstruction

A Proclamation by the President of the United States of America. No. 4. April 19, 1861

Whereas an insurrection against the Government of the United States has broken out in the States of South Carolina, Georgia, Alabama, Florida, Mississippi, Louisiana, and Texas, and the laws of the United States for the collection of the revenue cannot be effectually executed therein conformably to that provision of the Constitution which requires duties to be uniform throughout the United States:

And whereas a combination of persons, engaged in such insurrection, have threatened to grant pretended letters of marque to authorize the bearers thereof to commit assaults on the lives, vessels, and property of good citizens of the country lawfully engaged in commerce on the high seas, and in waters of the United States:

And whereas an Executive Proclamation has been already issued, requiring the persons engaged in these disorderly proceedings to desist therefrom, calling out a militia force for the purpose of repressing the same, and convening Congress in extraordinary session to deliberate and determine thereon:

Now, therefor, I, ABRAHAM LINCOLN, President of the United States, with a view to the same purposes before mentioned, and to the protection of the public peace, and the lives and property of quiet and orderly citizens pursuing their lawful occupations, until Congress shall haveassembled and deliberated on the said unlawful proceedings, or until the same shall have ceased, have further deemed it advisable to set on foot a blockade of the ports within the States aforesaid, in pursuance of the laws of the United States and of the law of nations in such case provided. For this purpose a competent force will be posted so as to prevent entrance and exit of vessels from the ports aforesaid. If, therefore, with a view to violate such blockade, a vessel shall approach, or shall attempt to leave either of the said ports, she will be duly warned by the commander of one of the blockading vessels, who will indorse on her register the fact and date of such warning, and if the same vessel shall again attempt to enter or leave the blockaded port, she will be captured and sent to the nearest convenient port, for such proceedings against her and her cargo as prize, as may be deemed advisable.

And I hereby proclaim and declare that if any person, under the pretended authority of said States, or under any other pretence, shall molest a vessel of the United States, or the persons or cargo on board of her, such person will be held amenable to the laws of the United States for the prevention and punishment of piracy.

In witness whereof, I have hereunto set my hand, and caused the seal of the United States to be affixed.

Done at the city of Washington, this nineteenth [L.S.] day of April, in the year of our Lord one thousand eight hundred and sixty-one, and of the Independence of the United States eighty-fifth.

ABRAHAM LINCOLN.

By the President:

William H. Seward, Secretary of State.

A Proclamation by the President of the United States of America. No. 5. April 27, 1861

Whereas, for the reasons assigned in my Proclamation of the nineteenth, a blockade of the ports of the States of South Carolina, Georgia, Florida, Alabama, Louisiana, Mississippi, and Texas was ordered to be established:

And whereas, since that date, public property of the United States has been seized, the collection of the revenue obstructed, and duly commissioned officers of the United States, while engaged in executing the orders of their superiors, have been arrested and held in custody as prisoners, or have been impeded in the discharge of their official duties without due legal process, by persons claiming to act under authorities of the States of Virginia and North Carolina:

An efficient blockade of the ports of those States will also be established.

In witness whereof, I have hereunto set my hand, and caused the seal of the United States to be affixed.

Done at the city of Washington, this twenty-[L.S.]seventh day of April, in the year of our Lord one thousand eight hundred and sixty-one, and of the Independence of the United States the eighty-fifth.

ABRAHAM LINCOLN.

By the President:

William H. Seward, Secretary of State.

A Proclamation by the President of the United States of America. No. 29. April 11, 1865

Whereas, by my Proclamations of the nineteenth and twenty-seventh days of April, one thousand eight hundred and sixty-one, the ports of the United States in the States of Virginia, North Carolina, South Carolina, Georgia, Florida, Alabama, Mississippi, Louisiana, and Texas, were declared to be subject to blockade; but whereas the said blockade has, in consequence of actual military occupation by this government, since been conditionally set aside or relaxed in respect to the ports of Norfolk and Alexandria, in the State of Virginia; Beaufort, in the State of North Carolina; Port Royal, in the State of South Carolina; Pensacola and Fernandina, in the State of Florida; and New Orleans, in the State of Louisiana;

And whereas, by the fourth section of the act of congress, approved on the thirteenth of July, eighteen hundred and sixty-one, entitled "An act further to provide for the collection of duties on imports and for other purposes," the President, for the reasons therein set forth, is authorized to close certain ports of entry:

Now, therefore, be it known, that I, Abraham Lincoln, President of the United States, do hereby proclaim that the ports of Richmond, Tappahannock, Cherrystone, Yorktown, and Petersburg, in Virginia; of Camden, (Elizabeth City,) Edenton, Plymouth, Washington, Newbern, Ocracoke, and Wilmington, in North Carolina; of Charleston, Georgetown, and Beaufort, in South Carolina; of Savannah, St. Mary's, and Brunswick, (Darien,) in Georgia; of Mobile, in Alabama; of Pearl River, (Shieldsborough,) Natchez, and Vicksburg, in Mississippi; of St. Augustine, Key West, St. Mark's (Port Leon,) St. John's, (Jacksonville,) and Apalachicola, in Florida; of Teche, (Franklin,) in Louisiana; of Galveston, La Salle, Brazos de Santiago, (Point Isabel,) and Brownsville, in Texas, are hereby closed, and all right of importation, warehousing, and other privileges, shall, in respect to the ports aforesaid, cease until they shall have again been opened by order of the President; and if, while said ports are closed, any ship or vessel from beyond the United States, or having on board any articles subject to duties, shall attempt to enter any such port, the same, together with its tackle, apparel, furniture, and cargo, shall be forfeited to the United States.

In witness whereof, I have hereunto set my hand, and caused the seal of the United States to be affixed.

Done at the city of Washington, this eleventh [L.S.] day of April, in the year of our Lord one thousand eight hundred and sixty-five, and of the Independence of the United States of America the eighty-ninth.

ABRAHAM LINCOLN.

By the President:

William H. Seward, Secretary of State.

A Proclamation by the President of the United States of America. No. 30. April 11, 1865

Whereas, by my Proclamation of this date, the port of Key West, in the State of Florida, was inadvertently included among those which are not open to commerce:

Now, therefore, be it known, that I, Abraham Lincoln, President of the United States, do hereby declare and make known that the said port of Key West is and shall remain open to foreign and domestic commerce upon the same conditions by which that commerce has there hitherto been governed.

In testimony whereof, I have hereunto set my hand, and caused the seal of the United States to be affixed.

Done at the city of Washington, this eleventh [L.S.] day of April, in the year of our Lord one thousand eight hundred and sixty-five, and of the Independence of the United States of America the eighty-ninth.

ABRAHAM LINCOLN.

By the President:

William H. Seward, Secretary of State.

Executive Order. No. 3. April 29, 1865

Executive Chamber, Washington, April 29,1865.

Being desirous to relieve all loyal citizens and well-disposed persons residing in insurrectionary states from unnecessary commercial restrictions, and to encourage them to return to peaceful pursuits,—

It is hereby ordered—

I. That all restrictions upon internal, domestic, and coastwise commercial intercourse be discontinued in such part of the States of Tennessee, Virginia, North Carolina, South Carolina, Georgia, Florida, Alabama, Mississippi, and so much of Louisiana as lies east of the Mississippi River, as shall be embraced within the lines of national military occupation; excepting only such restrictions as are imposed by acts of congress and regulations in pursuance thereof, prescribed by the Secretary of the Treasury, and approved by the President; and excepting, also, from the effect of this order the following articles, contraband of war, to wit: Arms, ammunition, all articles from which ammunition is manufactured, gray uniforms and cloth, locomotives, cars, railroad iron, and machinery for operating railroads, telegraph wires, insulators, and instruments for operating telegraphic lines.

II. That all existing military and naval orders in any manner restricting internal, domestic, and coastwise commercial intercourse and trade, with or in the localities above named, be and the same are hereby, revoked; and that no military or naval officer, in any manner, interrupt or interfere with the same, or with any boats or other vessels engaged therein, under proper authority, pursuant to the regulations of the Secretary of the Treasury.

ANDREW JOHNSON.

A Proclamation by the President of the United States of America. No. 36. May 22, 1865

Whereas, by the Proclamation of the President of the eleventh day of April last, certain ports of the United States therein specified, which had previously been subject to blockade, were, for objects of public safety, declared, in conformity with previous special legislation of congress, to be closed against foreign commerce during the national will, to be thereafter expressed and made known by the President; and whereas events and circumstances have since occurred which, in my judgment, render it expedient to remove that restriction, except as to the ports of Galveston, La Salle, Brazos de Santiago, (Point Isabel,) and Brownsville, in the State of Texas:

Now, therefore, be it known, that I, Andrew Johnson, President of the United States, do hereby declare that the ports aforesaid, not excepted as above, shall be open to foreign commerce from and after the first day of July next; that commercial intercourse with the said ports may, from that time, be carried on, subject to the laws of the United States and in pursuance of such regulations as may be prescribed by the Secretary of the Treasury. If, however, any vessel from a foreign port shall enter any of the before-named excepted ports in the State of Texas, she will continue to be held liable to the penalties prescribed by the act of congress approved on the thirteenth day of July, eighteen hundred and sixty-one, and the persons on board of her to such penalties as may be incurred, pursuant to the laws of war, for trading or attempting to trade with the enemy.

And I, Andrew Johnson, President of the United States, do hereby declare and make known that the United States of America do, henceforth, disallow to all persons trading, or attending to trade, in any ports of the United States in violation of the laws thereof, all pretence of belligerent rights and privileges; and I give notice that from the date of this Proclamation, all such offenders will be held and dealt with as pirates.

It is also ordered that all restrictions upon trade heretofore imposed in the territory of the United States east of the Mississippi River, save those relating to contraband of war, to the reservation of the rights of the United States to property purchased in the territory of an enemy, and to the twenty-five per cent upon purchases of cotton, be removed. All provisions of the internal revenue law will be carried into effect under the proper officers.

In witness whereof, I have hereunto set my hand, and caused the seal of the United States to be affixed.

Done at the city of Washington this twenty-[L.S.]second day of May, in the year of our Lord one thousand eight hundred and sixty-five, and of the Independence of the United States of America the eighty-ninth.

ANDREW JOHNSON.

By the President:

W. Hunter, Acting Secretary of State.

A Proclamation by the President of the United States of America. No. 44. June 23, 1865

Whereas, by the proclamations of the President of the nineteenth and twenty-seventh of April, eighteen hundred and sixty-one, a blockade of certain ports of the United States was set on foot; but, whereas, the reasons for that measure have ceased to exist:

Now, therefore, be it known, that I, Andrew Johnson, President of the United States, do hereby declare and proclaim the blockade aforesaid to be rescinded as to all the ports aforesaid, including that of Galveston and other ports west of the Mississippi River, which ports will be open to foreign commerce on the first of July next, on the terms and conditions set forth in my Proclamation of the twenty-second of May last.

It is to be understood, however, that the blockade thus rescinded was an international measure for the purpose of protecting the sovereign rights of the United States. The greater or less subversion of civil authority in the region to which it applied, and the impracticability of at once restoring that in due efficiency, may, for a season, make it advisable to employ the army and navy of the United States towards carrying the laws into effect, wherever such employment may be necessary.

In testimony whereof, I have hereunto set my hand, and caused the seal of the United States to be affixed.

Done at the city of Washington, this twenty-third [L.S.] day of June, in the year of our Lord one thousand eight hundred and sixty-five, and of the Independence of the United States of America the eighty-ninth.

ANDREW JOHNSON.

By the President:

W. Hunter, Acting Secretary of State.

A Proclamation by the President of the United States of America. No. 45. June 24, 1865

Whereas it has been the desire of the general government of the United States to restore unrestricted commercial intercourse between and in the several states, as soon as the same could be safely done in view of resistance to the authority of the United States by combinations of armed insurgents;

And whereas that desire has been shown in my proclamations of the twenty-ninth of April, 1/ one thousand eight hundred and sixty-five, and the twenty-third of June, one thousand eight hundred and sixty-five;

And whereas it now seems expedient and proper to remove restrictions upon internal, domestic, and coastwise trade and commercial intercourse between and within the states and territories west of the Mississippi River:

Now, therefore, be it known, that I, Andrew Johnson, President of the United States, do hereby declare that all restrictions upon internal, domestic, and coastwise intercourse and trade, and upon the purchase and removal of products of states and parts of states and territories heretofore declared in insurrection, lying west of the Mississippi River (excepting only those relating to property heretofore purchased by the agents, or captured by or surrendered to the forces of the United States, and to the transportation thereto or therein, on private account, of arms, ammunition, all articles from which ammunition is made, gray uniforms and gray cloth), and annulled; and I do hereby direct that they be forthwith removed; and also that the commerce of such states, and parts of states shall be conducted under the supervision of the regularly appointed officers of the customs, [who] shall receive any captured and abandoned property that may be turned over to them, under the law, by the military or naval forces of the United States, and dispose of the same in accordance with instructions on the subject, issued by the Secretary of the Treasury.

In testimony whereof, I have hereunto set my hand, and caused the seal of the United States to be affixed.

Done at the city of Washington, this twenty-[L.S.]fourth day of June, in the year of our Lord one thousand eight hundred and sixty-five, and of the Independence of the United States of America the eighty-ninth.

ANDREW JOHNSON.

By the President:

W. Hunter, Acting Secretary of State.

1/ Executive order.

AN ACT MAKING APPROPRIATIONS FOR THE SUPPORT OF THE ARMY FOR THE YEAR ENDING JUNE THIRTIETH, EIGHTEEN HUNDRED AND SIXTY-EIGHT, AND FOR OTHER PURPOSES. MARCH 2, 1867

Be it enacted by the Senate and House of Representatives of the United States of America in Congress assembled, That the following sums be, and the same are hereby, appropriated, out of any money in the treasury not otherwise appropriated, for the support of the army for the year ending the thirtieth of June, eighteen hundred and sixty-eight:—

For expenses of recruiting, transportation of recruits, and compensation to citizen surgeons for medical attendance, three hundred thousand dollars.

For pay of the army, fourteen million seven hundred and fifty-seven thousand nine hundred and fifty-two dollars.

For commutation of officers' subsistence, two million two hundred and twenty-eight thousand nine hundred and eighty-two dollars.

For commutation of forage for officers' horses, one hundred and four thousand six hundred dollars.

For payments in lieu of clothing for officers' servants, two hundred and seventy-six thousand nine hundred and seventy-eight dollars.

For payments to discharged soldiers for clothing not drawn, two hundred thousand dollars.

For contingencies of the army, one hundred thousand dollars.

For artificial limbs for soldiers and seamen, seventy thousand dollars.

For army medical museum, ten thousand dollars.

For medical works for library of surgeon-general's office, ten thousand dollars.

For expenses of commanding-general's office, ten thousand dollars.

For Repairs and Improvements of Armories and Arsenals.—For arsenal and armory at Rock Island, Illinois, six hundred and eighty-six thousand five hundred dollars.

For the erection of a bridge at Rock Island, Illinois, as recommended by the chief of ordnance, two hundred thousand dollars: Provided, That the ownership of said bridge shall be and remain in the United States, and the Rock Island and Pacific Railroad Company shall have the right of way over said bridge for all purposes of transit across the island and river, upon the condition that the said company shall, before any money is expended by the government, agree to pay and shall secure to the United States, first, half the cost of said bridge; and, second, half the expenses of keeping said bridge in repair, and upon guaranteeing said conditions to the satisfaction of the Secretary of War, by contract or otherwise, the said company shall have the free use of said bridge for purposes of transit, but without any claim to ownership thereof.

For Watervliet arsenal, West Troy, New York, thirty-eight thousand two hundred dollars.

For current expenses of the ordnance service, three hundred thousand dollars.

For Allegheny arsenal, Pittsburgh, Pennsylvania, thirty-four thousand dollars.

For Champlain arsenal at Vergennes, Vermont, eight hundred dollars.

For Columbus arsenal, Columbus, Ohio, one hundred and thirty-nine thousand six hundred and twenty-five dollars.

For Fort Monroe arsenal, Old Point Comfort, Virginia, six thousand dollars.

For Fort Union arsenal, Fort Union, New Mexico, ten thousand dollars.

For Frankford arsenal, Bridesburg, Pennsylvania, thirty thousand dollars.

For Kennebec arsenal, Augusta, Maine, one thousand five hundred and twenty-five dollars.

For Indianapolis arsenal, Indianapolis, Indiana, one hundred and sixty-nine thousand six hundred and twenty-five dollars.

For Leavenworth arsenal, Leavenworth, Kansas, fifteen thousand dollars.

For New York arsenal, Governor's Island, New York, one thousand two hundred dollars.

For Pikesville arsenal, Pikesville, Maryland, eight hundred dollars.

For Saint Louis arsenal, Saint Louis, Missouri, sixty-five thousand dollars.

For Washington arsenal, Washington, District of Columbia, fifty thousand dollars.

For Watertown arsenal, Watertown, Massachusetts, twenty-one thousand six hundred and sixty-seven dollars.

For the purchase of the Willard Sears estate, adjoining the Watertown arsenal grounds, forty-nine thousand and seven hundred dollars, or so much thereof as may be necessary; and the Secretary of War is hereby authorized to sell at public auction a lot of land belonging to the United States situated in South Boston, if, in his opinion, the same is not needed for the public service, and pay the proceeds thereof into the treasury.

Bureau of Refugees, Freedmen, and Abandoned Lands.— For salaries of assistant commissioners, sub-assistant commissioners, and agents, one hundred and forty-seven thousand five hundred dollars.

For salaries of clerks, eighty-two thousand eight hundred dollars.

For stationary and printing, sixty-three thousand dollars.

For quarters and fuel, two hundred thousand dollars.

For commissary stores, one million five hundred thousand dollars.

For medical department, five hundred thousand dollars.

For transportation, eight hundred thousand dollars.

For school superintendents, twenty-five thousand dollars.

For buildings for schools and asylums, including construction, rental, and repairs, five hundred thousand dollars.

For telegraphing and postage, eighteen thousand dollars: Provided, That the commissioner be hereby authorized to apply any balance on hand, at this date, of the Refugees and Freedmen's Fund, accounted for in his last annual report, to aid educational institutions actually incorporated for loyal refugees and freedmen: And provided further, That no agent or clerk not heretofore authorized by law shall receive a monthly allowance exceeding the sum of two hundred dollars.

Sec. 2. And be it further enacted, That the head-quarters of the General of the army of the United States shall be at the city of Washington, and all orders and instructions relating to military operations issued by the President or Secretary of War shall be issued through the General of the army, and, in case of his inability, through the next in rank. The General of the army shall not be removed, suspended, or relieved from command, or assigned to duty elsewhere than at said headquarters, except at his own request, without the previous approval of the Senate; and any orders or instructions relating to military operations issued contrary to the requirements of this section shall be null and void; and any officer who shall issue orders or instructions contrary to the provisions of this section shall be deemed guilty of a misdemeanor in office; and any officer of the army who shall transmit, convey, or obey any orders or instructions so issued contrary to the provisions of this section, knowing that such orders were so issued, shall be liable to imprisonment for not less than two nor more than twenty years, upon conviction thereof in any court of competent jurisdiction.

Sec. 3. And be it further enacted, That section three of the joint resolution relative to appointments to the military academy, approved June sixteen, eighteen hundred and sixty-six, be, and the same is hereby repealed.

Sec. 4. And be it further enacted, That the sum of one hundred and fifty thousand dollars be, as the same is hereby, appropriated out of any moneys in the treasury not otherwise appropriated, to be disbursed by the Secretary of War, in the erection of fire-proof buildings at or near the city of Jeffersonville, in the State of Indiana, to be used as storehouses for government property.

Sec. 5. And be it further enacted, That it shall be the duty of the officers of the army and navy, and of the Freedmen's Bureau, to prohibit and prevent whipping or maiming of the person, as a punishment for any crime, misdemeanor, or offence, by any pretended civil or military authority in any State lately in rebellion until the civil government of such State shall have been restored, and shall have been recognized by the Congress of the United States.

Sec. 6. And be it further enacted, That all militia forces now organized or in service in either of the States of Virginia, North Carolina, South Carolina, Georgia, Florida, Alabama, Louisiana, Mississippi, and Texas, be forthwith disbanded, and that the further organization, arming, or calling into service of the said militia forces, or any part thereof, is hereby prohibited under any circumstances whatever, until the same shall be authorized by Congress.

Sec. 7. And be it further enacted, That the paymaster-general be authorized to pay under such regulations as the Secretary of War shall prescribe in addition to the amount received by them, for the travel[l]ing expenses of such California and Nevada volunteers as were discharged in New Mexico, Arizona, or Utah, and at points distant from the place or places of enlistment, such proportionate sum according to the distance travel[l]ed as have been paid to the troops of other States similarly situated; and such amount as shall be necessary to pay the same is hereby appropriated out of any moneys in the treasury not otherwise appropriated.

Approved, March 2, 1867.

Appendix G: Laws Related to Slave and Peonage Labor

An Act Respecting Fugitives from Justice, and Persons Escaping from the Service of Their Masters. February 12, 1793.

Section 1. Be it enacted by the Senate and House of Representatives of the United States of America in Congress assembled, That whenever the executive authority of any state in the Union, or of either of the territories northwest or south of the river Ohio, shall demand any person as a fugitive from justice, of the executive authority of any such state or territory to which such person shall have fled, and shall moreover produce the copy of an indictment found, or an affidavit made before a magistrate of any state or territory as aforesaid, charging the person so demanded, with having committed treason, felony or other crime, certified as authentic by the governor or chief magistrate of the state or territory from whence the person so charged fled, it shall be the duty of the executive authority of the state or territory to which such person shall have fled, to cause him or her to be arrested and secured, and notice of the arrest to be given to the executive authority making such demand, or to the agent of such authority appointed to receive the fugitive, and to cause the fugitive to be delivered to such agent when he shall appear: But if no such agent shall appear within six months from the time of arrest, the prisoner may be discharged. And all costs or expenses incurred in the apprehending, securing, and transmitting such fugitive to the state or territory making such demand, shall be paid by such state or territory.

Sec. 2. And be it further enacted, That any agent, appointed as aforesaid, who shall receive the fugitive into his custody, shall be empowered to transport him or her to the state or territory from which he or she shall have fled. And if any person or persons shall by force set at liberty, or rescue the fugitive from such agent while transporting, as aforesaid, the person or persons so offending shall, on conviction, be fined not exceeding five hundred dollars, and be imprisoned not exceeding one year.

Sec. 3. And be it also enacted, That when a person held to labour in any of the United States, or in either of the territories on the northwest or south of the river Ohio, under the laws thereof, shall escape into any other of the said states or territory, the person to whom such labour or service may be due, his agent or attorney, is hereby empowered to seize or arrest such fugitive from labour, and to take him or her before any judge of the circuit or district courts of the United States, residing or being within the state, or before any magistrate of a county, city, or town corporate, wherein such seizure or arrest shall be made, and upon proof to the satisfaction of such judge or magistrate, either by oral testimony or affidavit taken before and certified by a magistrate of any such state or territory, that the person so seized or arrested, doth, under the laws of the state or territory from which he or she fled, owe service or labour to the person claiming him or her, it shall be the duty of such judge or magistrate to give a certificate thereof to such claimant, his agent or attorney, which shall be sufficient warrant for removing the said fugitive from labour, to the state or territory from which he or she fled.

Sec. 4. And be it further enacted, That any person who shall knowingly and willingly obstruct or hinder such claimant, his agent or attorney in so seizing or arresting such fugitive from labour, or shall rescue such fugitive from such claimant, his agent or attorney when so arrested pursuant to the authority herein given or declared; or shall harbor or conceal such person after notice that he or she was a fugitive from labour, as aforesaid, shall for either of the said offences, forfeit and pay the sum of five hundred dollars. Which penalty may be recovered by and for the benefit of such claimant, by action of debt, in any court proper to try the same; saving moreover to the person claiming such labour or service, his right of action for or on account of the said injuries or either of them.

Approved, February 12, 1793.

Editor's note: Various and extensive litigation, court decisions, and legal precedents are cited in conjunction with this act, but have not been reproduced for this work.

An Act To amend, and supplementary to, the Act entitled "An act respecting fugitives from justice, and persons escaping from the service of their masters," approved February twelfth, one thousand seven hundred and ninety-three. September 18, 1850

Be it enacted by the Senate and House of Representatives of the United States of America in congress assembled, That the persons who have been, or may hereafter be, appointed commissioners, in virtue of any act of Congress, by the Circuit Courts of the United States, and who, in consequence of such appointment, are authorized to exercise the powers that any justice of the peace, or other magistrate of any of the United States, may exercise in respect to offenders for any crime or offence against the United States, by arresting, imprisoning, or bailing the same under and by virtue of the thirty-third section of the act of the twenty-fourth of September seventeen hundred and eighty-nine, entitled "An act to establish the judicial courts of the United States," shall be, and are hereby, authorized and required to exercise and discharge all the powers and duties conferred by this act.

Sec. 2. And be it further enacted, That the Superior Court of each organized Territory of the United States shall have the same power to appoint commissioners to take acknowledgements of bail and affidavits, and to take depositions of witnesses in civil causes, which is now possessed by the Circuit Court of the United States; and all commissioners who shall hereafter be appointed for such purposes by the Superior Court of any organized Territory of the United States, shall possess all the powers, and exercise all the duties, conferred by law upon the commissioners appointed by the Circuit Courts of the United States for similar purposes, and shall moreover exercise and discharge all the powers and duties conferred by this act.

Sec. 3. And be it further enacted, That the Circuit Courts of the United States, and the Superior Courts of each organized Territory of the United States, shall from time to time enlarge the number of commissioners, with a view to afford reasonable facilities to reclaim fugitives from labor, and to the prompt discharge of the duties imposed by this act.

Sec. 4. And be it further enacted, That the commissioners above named shall have concurrent jurisdiction with the judges of the Circuit and District Courts of the United States, in their respective circuits and districts within the several States, and the judges of the Superior Courts of the Territories, severally and collectively, in term-time and vacation; and shall grant certificates to such claimants, upon satisfactory proof being made, with authority to take and remove such fugitives from service or labor, under the restrictions herein contained, to the State or Territory from which such persons may have escaped or fled.

Sec. 5. And be it further enacted, That it shall be the duty of all marshals and deputy marshals to obey and execute all warrants and precepts issued under the provisions of this act, when to them directed; and should any marshal or deputy marshal refuse to receive such warrant, or other process, when tendered, or to use all proper means diligently to execute the same, he shall, on conviction thereof, be fined in the sum of one thousand dollars, to the use of such claimant, on the motion of such claimant, by the Circuit or District Court for the district of such marshal; and after arrest of such fugitive, by such marshal or his deputy, or whilst at any time in his custody under the provisions of this act, should such fugitive escape, whether with or without the assent of such marshal or his deputy, such marshal shall be liable, on his official bond, to be prosecuted for the benefit of such claimant, for the full value of the service or labor of said fugitive in the State, Territory, or District whence he escaped; and the better to enable the said commissioners, when thus appointed, to execute their duties faithfully and efficiently, in conformity with the requirements of the Constitution of the United States and of this act, they are hereby authorized and empowered, within their counties respectively, to appoint, in writing under their hands, any one or more suitable persons, from time to time, to execute all such warrants and other process as may be issued by them in the lawful performance of their respective duties; with authority to such commissioners, or the persons to be appointed by them, to execute process as aforesaid, to summon and call to their aid the bystanders, or posse comitatus of the proper county, when necessary to ensure a faithful observance of the clause of the Constitution referred to, in conformity with the provisions of this act; and all good citizens are hereby commanded to aid and assist in the prompt and efficient execution of this law, whenever their services may be required, as aforesaid, for that purpose; and said warrants shall run, and be executed by said officers, any where in the State within which they are issued.

Sec. 6. And be it further enacted, That when a person held to service or labor in any State or Territory of the United States, has heretofore or shall hereafter escape into another State or Territory of the United States, the person or persons to whom such service or labor may be due, or his, her, or their agent or attorney, duly authorized, by power of attorney, in writing, acknowledged and certified under the seal of some legal officer or court of the State or Territory in which the same may be executed, may pursue and reclaim such fugitive person, either by procuring a warrant from some one of the courts, judges, or commissioners aforesaid, of the proper circuit, district, or county, for the apprehension of such fugitive from service or labor, or by seizing and arresting such fugitive, where the same can be done without process, and by taking, causing such person to be taken, forthwith before such court, judge, or commissioner, whose duty it shall be to hear and determine the case of such claimant in a summary manner; and upon satisfactory proof being made, by deposition or affidavit, in writing, to be taken and certified by such court, judge, or commissioner, or by other satisfactory testimony, duly taken and certified by some court, magistrate, justice of the peace, or other legal officer authorized to administer an oath and take depositions under the laws of the State or Territory from which such person owing service or labor may have escaped, with a certificate of such magistracy or other authority, as aforesaid, with the seal of the proper court or officer thereto attached, which seal shall be sufficient to establish the competency of the proof, and with proof, also by affidavit, of the identity of the person whose service or labor is claimed to be due as aforesaid, that the person so arrested does in fact owe service or labor to the person or persons claiming him or her, in the State or Territory from which such fugitive may have escaped as aforesaid, and that said person escaped, to make out and deliver to such claimant, his or her agent or attorney, a certificate setting forth the substantial facts as to the service or labor due from such fugitive to the claimant, and of his or her escape from the State or Territory in which such service or labor was due, to the State or Territory in which he or she was arrested, with authority of such claimant, or his or her agent or attorney, to use such reasonable force and restraint as may be necessary, under the circumstances of the case, to take and remove such fugitive person back to the State or Territory whence he or she may have escaped as aforesaid. In no trial or hearing under this act shall the testimony of such alleged fugitive be admitted in evidence; and the certificates in this and the first [fourth] section mentioned, shall be conclusive of the right of the person or persons in whose favor granted, to remove such fugitive to the State or Territory from which he escaped, and shall prevent all molestation of such person or persons by any process issued by any court, judge, magistrate, or other person whomsoever.

Sec. 7. And be it further enacted, That any person who shall knowingly and willingly obstruct, hinder, or prevent such claimant, his agent or attorney, or any person or persons lawfully assisting him, her, or them from arresting such fugitive from service or labor, either with or without process aforesaid, or shall rescue, or attempt to rescue, such fugitive from service or labor, from the custody of such claimant, his or her agent or attorney, or other person or persons lawfully assisting as aforesaid, when so arrested, pursuant to the authority herein given and declared; or shall aid, abet, or assist such person so owing service or labor as aforesaid, directly or indirectly, to escape from such claimant, his agent or attorney, or other person or persons legally authorized as aforesaid; or shall harbor or conceal such fugitive, so as to prevent the discovery and arrest of such person, after notice or knowledge of the fact that such person was a fugitive from service or labor as aforesaid, shall, for either of said offences, be subject to a fine not exceeding one thousand dollars, and imprisonment not exceeding six months, by indictment and conviction before the District Court of the United States for the district in which such offence may have been committed, or before the proper court of criminal jurisdiction, if committed within any one of the organized Territories of the United States; and shall moreover forfeit and pay, by way of civil damages to the party injured by such illegal conduct, the sum of one thousand dollars, for each fugitive so lost as aforesaid, to be recovered by action of debt, in any of the District or Territorial Courts aforesaid, within whose jurisdiction the said offence may have been committed.

Sec. 8. And be it further enacted, That the marshals, their deputies, and the clerks of the said District and Territorial Courts, shall be paid, for their services, the like fees as may be allowed to them for similar services in other cases; and where such services are rendered exclusively in the arrest, custody, and delivery of the fugitive to the claimant, his or her agent or attorney, or where such supposed fugitive may be discharged out of custody for the want of sufficient proof as aforesaid, then such fees are to be paid in the whole by such claimant, his agent or attorney; and in all cases where the proceedings are before a commissioner, he shall be entitled to a fee of ten dollars in full for his services in each case, upon the delivery of the said certificate to the claimant, his or her agent or attorney; or a fee of five dollars in cases where the proof shall not, in the opinion of such commissioner, warrant such certificate and delivery, inclusive of all services incident to such arrest and examination, to be paid, in either case, by the claimant, his agent or her agent or attorney. The person or persons authorized to execute the process to be issued by such commissioners for the arrest and detention of fugitives from service or labor as aforesaid, shall also be entitled to a fee of five dollars each for each person he or they may arrest and take before any such commissioner as aforesaid, at the instance and request of such claimant, with such other fees as may be deemed reasonable by such commissioner for such other additional services as may be necessarily performed by him or them; such as attending at the examination, keeping the fugitive in custody, and providing him with food and lodging during his detention, and until the final determination of such commissioner; and, in general, for performing such other duties as may be required by such claimant, his or her attorney or agent, or commissioner in the premises, such fees to be made up in conformity with the fees usually charged by the officers of the courts of justice within the proper district or county, as near as may be practicable, and paid by such claimants, their agents or attorneys, whether such supposed fugitives from service or labor be ordered to be delivered to such claimants by the final determination of such commissioners or not.

Sec. 9. And be it further enacted, That upon affidavit made by the claimant of such fugitive, his agent or attorney, after such certificate has been issued, that he has reason to apprehend that such fugitive will be rescued by force from his or their possession before he can be taken beyond the limits of the State in which the arrest is made, it shall be the duty of the officer making the arrest to retain such fugitive in his custody, and to remove him to the State whence he fled, and there to deliver him to said claimant, his agent, or attorney. And to this end, the officer aforesaid is hereby authorized and required to employ so many persons as he may deem necessary to overcome such force, and to retain them in his service so long as circumstances may require. The said officer and his assistants, while so employed, to receive the same compensation, and to be allowed the same expenses, as are now allowed by law for transportation of criminals, to be certified by the judge of the district within which the arrest is made, and paid out of the treasury of the United States.

Sec. 10. And be it further enacted, That when any person held to service or labor in any State or Territory, or in the District of Columbia, shall escape therefrom, the party to whom such service or labor shall be due, his, her, or their agent or attorney, may apply to any court of record therein, or judge thereof in vacation, and make satisfactory proof to such court, or judge in vacation, of the escape aforesaid, and that the person escaping owed service or labor to such party. Whereupon the court shall cause a record to be made of the matters so proved, and also a general description of the person so escaping, with such convenient certainty as may be; and a transcript of such record, authenticated by the attestation of the clerk and of the seal of the said court, being produced in any other State, Territory, or district in which the person so escaping may be found, and being exhibited to any judge, commissioner, or other officer authorized by the law of the United States to cause persons escaping from service or labor to be delivered up, shall be held and taken to be full and conclusive evidence of the fact of escape, and that the service or labor of the person escaping is due to the party in such record mentioned. And upon the production by the said party of other and further evidence if necessary, either oral or affidavit, in addition to what is contained in the said record of the identity of the person escaping, he or she shall be delivered up to the claimant. And the said court, commissioner, judge, or other person authorized by this act to grant certificates to claimants of fugitives, shall, upon the production of the record and other evidences aforesaid, grant to such claimant a certificate of his right to take any such person identified and proved to be owing service or labor as aforesaid, which certificate shall authorize such claimant to seize or arrest and transport such person to the State or Territory from which he escaped: Provided, That nothing herein contained shall be construed as requiring the production of a transcript of such record as evidence as aforesaid. But in its absence the claim shall be heard and determined upon other satisfactory proofs, competent in law.

Approved, September 18, 1850.

An Act to abolish and forever prohibit the system of peonage in the Territory of New Mexico and other parts of the United States. March 2, 1867.

Be it enacted by the Senate and House of Representatives of the United States of America in Congress assembled, That the holding of any person to service or labor under the system known as peonage is hereby declared to be unlawful, and the same is hereby abolished and forever prohibited in the Territory of New Mexico, or in any other Territory or State of the United States; and all acts, laws, resolutions, orders, regulations, or usages of the Territory of New Mexico, or of any other Territory or State of the United States, which have heretofore established, maintained, or enforced, or by virtue of which any attempt shall hereafter be made to establish, maintain, or enforce, directly or indirectly, the voluntary or involuntary service or labor of any persons as peons, in liquidation of any debt or obligation, or otherwise, be, and the same are hereby, declared null and void; and any person or persons who shall hold, arrest, or return, or cause to be held, arrested, or returned, or in any manner aid in the arrest or return of any person or persons to a condition of peonage, shall, upon conviction, be punished by fine not less than one thousand nor more than five thousand dollars, or by imprisonment not less than one nor more than five years, or both, at the discretion of the court.

Sec. 2. And be it further enacted, That it shall be the duty of all persons in the military or civil service in the Territory of New Mexico to aid in the enforcement of the foregoing section of this act; and any person or persons who shall obstruct or attempt to obstruct, or in any way interfere with, or prevent the enforcement of this act, shall be liable to the pains and penalties hereby provided; and any officer or other person in the military service of the United States who shall so offend, directly or indirectly, shall, on conviction before a court-martial, be dishonorably dismissed the service of the United States, and shall thereafter be ineligible to reappointment to any office of trust, honor, or profit under the government.

Approved, March 2, 1867.

Bibliography

Bell, Howard Wilford, ed. *National Documents.* New York: Unit Book Publishing Co., 1906.

Brunn, Eric, and Jay Crosby, eds. *Our Nation's Archive: The History of the United States in Documents.* New York: Black Dog & Leventhal Publishers, Inc., 1999.

Commager, Henry Steele, and Eric Brunn, eds. *The Civil War in Documents.* New York: Black Dog & Levanthal Publishers, Inc., 2000.

Foley, June, Mark Hoffman, and Tom McGuire, eds. *The World Almanac, Commemorative Edition: The Complete 1868 Original.* New York: World Almanac, 1992.

Foner, Eric. *A Short History of Reconstruction, 1863–1877.* New York: Harper & Row, 1988.

Index

www.ingramcontent.com/pod-product-compliance
Ingram Content Group UK Ltd.
Pitfield, Milton Keynes, MK11 3LW, UK
UKHW041834100926
8556IPUK00018B/964